Math Links

**Teaching the NCTM 2000 Standards
Through Children's Literature**

Caroline W. Evans

Anne J. Leija

Trina R. Falkner

Illustrated by Cherie Blackmore

2001

Teacher Ideas Press

A Division of
Libraries Unlimited, Inc.
Englewood, Colorado

TEACHER IDEAS PRESS
A Division of
Libraries Unlimited, Inc.
P.O. Box 6633
Englewood, CO 80155-6633
1-800-237-6124
www.lu.com/tip

ISBN 1-56308-787-1

To my wonderful mother, who taught me to love books.
Caroline W. Evans

To my students who inspire me, to my family who supports me,
and to my husband who is my best friend.
Anne J. Leija

To my husband Steve,
who always gave me the encouragement and support I needed.
Trina R. Falkner

Contents

Foreword by Pat Hagerty xi
Foreword by Fredrick L. "Rick" Silverman xiii
Acknowledgments xv
Introduction xvii
   What This Book Is About xvii
   The Purpose of This Book xvii
   How We Have Arranged This Book xviii
   Who We Are xix
   How to Introduce a Book xix

1—NUMBER AND OPERATIONS 1
   Lesson 1: Count from One to Ten 2
      Ten Tiny Turtles, a Crazy Counting Book (Cherrill)
   Lesson 2: Count to Twelve and Back 8
      Frogs Jump: A Counting Book (Brooks)
   Lesson 3: Count and Add 13
      Quack and Count (Baker)
   Lesson 4: Count Back and Subtract 17
      One Less Fish (Toft and Sheather)
   Lesson 5: Find and Multiply Sets 22
      2x2 = BOO! A Set of Multiplication Stories (Leedy)
   Lesson 6: Divide Fare Shares 26
      One of Each (Hoberman)
   Lesson 7: Identify and Build Fraction Models 31
      Fraction Fun (Adler)

2—ALGEBRA 49
   Lesson 1: Discover and Repeat Patterns 50
      The Little Scarecrow Boy (Brown)
   Lesson 2: Create Symbols and Patterns 53
      The Talking Cloth (Mitchell)
   Lesson 3: Design and Build a Town 59
      The Teeny Tiny Teacher (Calmenson)
   Lesson 4: Classify and Sort Beads; Model and String Bead Necklaces . . . 64
      A String of Beads (Reid)

3—GEOMETRY 85

Lesson 1: Discover, Identify, and Label Two-Dimensional Shapes 86
When a Line Bends . . . A Shape Begins (Greene)
Lesson 2: Illustrate and Hide Two-Dimensional Shapes. 90
Bear in a Square (Blackstone)
Lesson 3: Arrange Shapes; Measure Sides and Space
(Perimeter and Area) 95
Spaghetti and Meatballs for All: A Mathematical Story (Burns)
Lesson 4: Identify and Model Three-Dimensional Shapes
and Sculptures 99
The Clay Ladies (Bedard)

4—MEASUREMENT 111

Lesson 1: Measure Length with Nonstandard and
Standard Measuring Tools. 112
*Twelve Snails to One Lizard, a Tale of Mischief and
Measurement* (Hightower)
Lesson 2: Measure Length, Weight, Volume, and Time 115
The Giant Carrot (Peck)
Lesson 3: Measure Time. 120
Ten Minutes Till Bedtime (Rathmann)
Lesson 4: Measure Capacity. 124
Cook-a-Doodle-Doo! (Stevens and Crummel)

5—DATA ANALYSIS AND PROBABILITY 141

Lesson 1: Build and Launch Boats; Learn about Probability. 142
Where Go the Boats? (Stevenson)
Lesson 2: Make a Flipbook and Determine Combinations 147
A Cheese and Tomato Spider (Sharratt)
Lesson 3: What Will Happen "If . . . "? Is the Future a Matter of
Chaos, Chance, or Probability? 153
If You Give a Pig a Pancake (Numeroff)
Lesson 4: Make Snowflakes, Then Collect, Record, and Analyze Data . . 160
Snowflake Bentley (Martin)

6—PROBLEM SOLVING 177

Lesson 1: Use a Calculator to Solve a Big Addition Problem. 178
My Little Sister Ate One Hare (Grossman)
Lesson 2: Discover Math Problems Everywhere 184
Math Curse (Scieszka and Smith)
Lesson 3: Solve Money Problems 189
Bunny Money (Wells)

7—REASONING AND PROOF 209

Lesson 1: Classify, Sort, and Skip Count by Fives 210
   Arctic Fives Arrive (Pinczes)
Lesson 2: Prove the Power of Doubling Numbers 215
   One Grain of Rice (Demi)
Lesson 3: Compare Fractions 221
   Fraction Action (Leedy)

8—COMMUNICATION 233

Lesson 1: Compare Sizes and Organize a Parade of Animals 234
   The Best Bug Parade (Murphy)
Lesson 2: Match Fractions with Fraction Symbols 239
   Tops and Bottoms (Stevens)

9—CONNECTIONS 249

Lesson 1: Discover Mathematics in Baseball 250
   The Baseball Counting Book (McGrath)
Lesson 2: Recognize That Everyday Objects Come in Sets 257
   7 Sector 7 (Wiesner)

10—REPRESENTATION 267

Lesson 1: Use Jelly Beans to Represent the Value of Coins 268
   Jelly Beans for Sale (McMillan)
Lesson 2: Draw Clocks and Create Timelines 274
   Clean Your Room, Harvey Moon (Cummings)
Lesson 3: Estimate, Record, and Count Clothing and Other Objects . . . 279
   The Girl Who Wore Too Much: A Folktale from Thailand (Read)

Author/Title Index 297
Subject Index 303
About the Authors 309

Foreword by Pat Hagerty

In this age of high stakes testing, many teachers struggle to find time to teach any subject that is not going to be tested. This is often true of math, science, and social studies. As a university professor, I often hear my students say that the classroom teachers they observe lament the fact that there is not enough time in the day to teach all subjects. They often don't teach as much math, science, and social studies as they would like. Because literacy is the first subject to get tested in most states and school districts, it seems to get the most instructional time.

Integration of curriculum is one of the answers to this dilemma. By integrating, teachers can teach more than one content area at a time. Numerous texts have been published that help teachers learn how to integrate reading and writing into various content areas. Often these books are designed for teachers at the middle school and high school levels. *Math Links: Teaching the NCTM 2000 Standards Through Children's Literature* is specifically written for teachers in the elementary grades by elementary grade teachers. Caroline, Anne, and Trina have created numerous, easy to teach, literature-based math lessons based on the NCTM 2000 Standards. Each lesson has been "classroom tested" by the authors and other teachers. The books suggested in the lessons are popular children's literature selections that should be available in any school or public library.

The beauty of this book is its comprehensiveness. Each lesson includes a suggested time frame, a list of materials, a lesson plan, ideas for assessment, and suggestions for adapting the lesson for children with special needs. Teachers will find the numerous reproducible charts an added bonus. Teachers are some of the busiest people on the planet. This book will be the kind you will reach for over and over again when looking for ways to integrate literacy and math.

Pat Hagerty
Associate Professor
Initial and Professional Teacher Education
School of Education
University of Colorado at Denver

*F*oreword *by F*redrick *L*. "*R*ick" *S*ilverman

Math Links: Teaching the NCTM 2000 Standards Through Children's Literature by Caroline W. Evans, Anne J. Leija, and Trina R. Falkner is a book that elementary school teachers will find genuinely useful and exciting. Reading this creative resource is likely to drive the eagerness of teachers into high gear to prepare for leading mathematics lessons that use children's literature. The authors present thirty-six lessons for mathematics using children's literature. Chapters contain lesson plans, lists of needed materials, masters to reproduce, extensions, related children's books, software, and other useful items, such as a model letter to send to parents for helping their children collect items for building a miniature model town as part of a lesson that uses *The Teeny Tiny Teacher* by Stephanie Calmenson. In an accountability-conscious era, documents to assist teachers with assessment are a real help, and *Math Links* includes instruments to evaluate performance for number and shape recognition, patterns, fractions, and ways to make change for a quarter, to name a few. The authors have also been especially attentive to offer adaptations for students with special needs.

The professional teacher will certainly appreciate that this book's chapters correspond to the ten standards that appear in the *Principles and Standards for School Mathematics (PSSN),* published in April 2000 by the National Council of Teachers of Mathematics. *PSSN* is a successor to the Council's highly influential 1989 *Curriculum and Evaluation Standards for School Mathematics,* which the authors also reference for their lessons. The authors describe each of the standards in *PSSN* and invite readers who want to delve more deeply into them to consult a copy of this visionary and very practical publication. It is available for purchase through the Council, and a comprehensive version is accessible at the Council's Web site through the following link: http://www.nctm.org. Each chapter of *Math Links* features lessons using children's literature that students will enjoy, that will pique their curiosity, and that teachers will find effective for developing mathematical concepts and skills in context, particularly integrated with literacy.

It is important for children to know from an early age that mathematics is relevant in all of our lives, and children's books offer an excellent springboard to accomplish that. *Math Links* includes the works of familiar, popular authors such as Jon Scieszka and Lane Smith, who brought us *Math Curse,* Marilyn Burns, who wrote *Spaghetti and Meatballs for All,* and Loreen Leedy, who penned *2x2 = BOO!* and *Fraction Action.* Evans, Leija, and Falkner's *Math Links* offers the added benefit of lessons that help teachers to implement the most up-to-date standards for teaching and learning mathematics and that have been effective for promoting children's learning of mathematics. I am, indeed, delighted that this fine, new resource will help bring mathematics in context through children's literature into elementary school classrooms and into the hands of inservice and preservice teachers. I will use it with my own students in teacher education.

Fredrick L. "Rick" Silverman, Ed.D.
Professor of Education
School for the Study of Teaching and Teacher Education
College of Education
University of Northern Colorado
Greeley, Colorado

Acknowledgments

We gratefully acknowledge support and assistance from Fredrick L. "Rick" Silverman, Ed.D., of the University of Northern Colorado, who encouraged us with this project from its conception, and to Pat Hagerty, University of Colorado at Denver, for modeling sure-fire, fail-safe lesson presentation. Thanks to Terry Leija for his support, patience, and ideas; to the Estes Park Public Library and especially to Kerry Aiken, Children's Librarian; and to Charlotte Baxter. Special thanks to principal John Wahler and the entire staff of Estes Park Elementary School, particularly to librarian Kathy Schaps and those who tested lessons, including Kris Axtell, Jenny Blackmore, Estelle Boles, Toni Hurr, Sara Huth, Sarah Kastendieck, Judy Portman, Pat Reed, Lesley Switzer, Ruth Wallman, and Keri Vik. Thanks to Tana Sholly from The Community School, Naples, Florida. Thanks to Norman H. Wakeman for inspiration. In addition, thanks to advisors and coaches Joe Evans, Russell Evans, Austin Powers, Barb Steele, Julie Poole, Kathy Littlejohn, Gene and Julie Jackson, Jack and Nick Jackson, Obi Wan, Holly Daley, Stephen Falkner, Terry and Marcella Swanson, Zang Ho Chi, Poncho, Bunji, and Bogey. Thanks to Libby Evans for artwork and assistance, to Celeste Magnuson and Hattie Schetzsle for typing chapters, and to Webmeister Laurie Annya Linfoot. Many thanks to the Libraries Unlimited acquisitions, production, design, editing, and marketing staff, including Jan Adam, Debbie Cottin, Barb Ittner, Debby Mattil, and Kay Minnis. Special thanks to Carmel Huestis for her guidance and to Sharon DeJohn, editor extraordinaire.

Introduction

What This Book Is About

Dear Math Teacher,

We have included in this book a series of math lessons organized to correspond to the ten mathematics standards presented by the National Council of the Teachers of Mathematics (NCTM) *Principles and Standards for School Mathematics* (2000). Each lesson is inspired by books you can find in your school or public library. We use a postcard or letter format to introduce each new chapter. Postcards also highlight special notes to you, the teacher. Use the "address" space for notes. To use the math lessons in this book, 1) determine which standard you wish to use, 2) scan the lessons provided to meet that standard, 3) locate the sources in your library, and 4) have at it!

Best regards,

Caroline, Anne, and Trina

The Purpose of This Book

Dear Math Teacher,

Just like you, we teach students in grades K–3 with diverse gifts and needs. This book provides lessons designed to meet the needs of your many different children. The lessons 1) *engage* students through literature, 2) *introduce* new skills and concepts, 3) *connect* literature with new learning, 4) provide time to *apply and practice* new skills and concepts, and 5) give students the opportunity *to reflect upon and communicate* about what they have learned.

Best regards,

Caroline, Anne, and Trina

How We Have Arranged This Book

Dear Math Teacher,

We have divided this book into chapters corresponding to the mathematics standards presented by the National Council of Teachers of Mathematics (NCTM). Chapters 1 through 5 include lessons that pertain to the first five standards: number sense, algebra, geometry, measurement, and data analysis and probability.

Chapters 6 through 10 refer to the process standards: problem solving, reasoning and proof, communication, connections, and representation. Each of these last five standards represents ways students think about and express mathematical ideas. Please note that although the lessons included in Chapters 6 through 10 pertain to the last five standards, each of these standards and corresponding lessons directly relates to one or more of the content standards in Chapters 1 through 5.

You will find this book packed with lessons based on literature that complements the standard for each chapter. Each math lesson includes the following elements, in this order:

(continued)

1. book title and summary
2. time frame allotted
3. materials needed
4. story and mini-lesson
5. group lesson
6. discovery activity
7. reflection activity
8. suggestions for assessment
9. adaptations for children with special needs
10. lesson extensions
11. bibliography of resources, software, and related literature (All Web sites listed were accessed in February 2001 and were active at that time.)
12. list of related standards

We designed the lessons in this sequence so you will be able to quickly scan the lessons and determine how each one meets your needs.

We recommend you refer to NCTM, *Principles and Standards for School Mathematics* (2000) for a thorough explanation of the standards and mathematics teaching philosophy.

Sincerely,

Caroline, Anne, and Trina

Who We Are

Dear Math Teacher,

Just like you, we work in elementary schools, doing what we love to do best. We teach ordinary children who are math wizards but cannot see, who can think but cannot walk, who are washed and unwashed, who are savants and slow to process information, who are small in body but big in energy and eagerness to learn. We teach children, and we are taught by all of our students. In this book we have identified the best, most recent literature to use as a vehicle to help students understand and practice math skills and concepts. The empathy students feel toward story characters, and the vicarious adventure they enjoy through plot, both provide a strong connection between literature and children's understanding of new concepts. This book has become our own best math resource. We hope it will become yours too. We'll look for you at the next NCTM or International Reading Association (IRA) convention.

We'll be there,

Caroline, Anne, and Trina

How to Introduce a Book

Dear Math Teacher,

We like to use the Preview, Predict, Read, Retell, and Connect (PPRRC) method to introduce books. This is the best way we know to engage students in the beauty of the illustrations and content of the story. This process will also help you and your students notice connections between the literature selected and mathematics. Students will become adept at discovering math in the books you introduce in the classroom, and later they will apply connections to math from the world around them.

Read on to find out how we do this,

Caroline, Anne, Trina

Gather Your Students

Dear Teacher,

Here we go! Gather your students on a rug or in a cozy space you have set up for read-aloud time. I call my special space for group read-alouds and class gatherings, "The Community Center," Anne calls hers "The Magic Carpet," and Trina calls hers the "Reading Corner." Whatever you call this place, require the same behavior each time you visit it: faces and eyes forward, ears attentive, hands and feet to oneself, and bodies sitting tall for good oxygen supply and smart thinking. Maintain and model the same posture in yourself that you expect in your students.

Now, you're ready to begin,

Caroline

Preview the Book

Dear Teacher,

First, Preview the book. Hold the book so your students see the book jacket. Ask students some of the following questions: "What do you notice about the cover? What is the title of the book? Why do you think I chose this book to introduce a math lesson? What math do you think we'll find in this book?"

Then, slowly flip through the pages of the book so students see the pictures. Say, "As I turn the pages, raise your hands and I'll call on you to tell me what you notice." Call on five or so students to describe or tell about what they see. Encourage and support all responses.

Keep going,

Caroline

Predict What Will Happen

Dear Teacher,

Now is the time to Predict. Close the book and show the cover again. Call on students to share their predictions. Say, "Now, after you've had a preview, what do you think the book is about?" Welcome all predictions. Draw out predictions by saying, "Tell me more," or, "Explain that."

The best part is yet to come,

Anne

Read the Story

Dear Reader,

Now comes the best step of all: Reading the book. Before you begin, check to make sure students are attentive. Straighten yourself up to model good listening and learning posture. Be sure all students are in a place where they can see the illustrations and hear your voice. Begin.

Your students will hear the rhythm and patterns of the language, see the bright and colorful illustrations, and become a part of the story themselves as the tale unfolds. Allow yourself to become involved in the story just as your students become involved. Laugh. Enjoy the book along with your students. Encourage them to chime in if the story uses repeated phrases or predictable patterns. When you finish reading the book, close it reverently.

You are now ready for the final part of introducing a book.

Anne

Retell and Connect

Dear Reader and Teacher,

Encourage students to Retell the story. Ask questions such as, "What was this story about? Tell me what you thought of this story. Did your predictions hold up? Tell me how. What surprised you? What did you wonder about?"

Draw connections between the story and the upcoming math lesson. Say, "Tell me about what math you noticed in the story." A student might respond, "I noticed that on every page there was a new animal to add." Encourage all responses. Help focus seemingly irrelevant responses such as, "I lost my tooth today," by responding, "Wonderful! Then you *subtracted* a tooth today, and you'll *add* a new tooth later."

Students may notice some things that we have not. Listen to children just as you expect them to listen to you. You and your students will make math and literature connections together.

In the following math lessons we have included examples of how to connect math lessons and stories.

Now, begin the math lessons.

Caroline

Chapter 1

Number and Operations

Dear Math Teacher,

We have gathered an assortment of children's literature and compiled lessons to help students become familiar, comfortable, and fluent with numbers and number operations. The literature and lessons in this chapter encourage students to count, add, subtract, skip count, multiply, divide numbers, and identify fractions. Included here are lessons for your students to demonstrate one to one correspondence between numbers and concrete models and to manipulate and arrange models to represent number operations. Throughout these lessons you and your students will use children's literature as a gateway to understand, connect, and apply mathematics to everyday life.

These are lessons you can count on,
Caroline

LESSON 1

Count from One to Ten

Cherrill, Paul. *Ten Tiny Turtles, a Crazy Counting Book.* New York: Houghton Mifflin, 1995.

One playful dog, two dancing rabbits, and three baking pies begin this counting book of crazy characters from one to ten. While you read aloud this jolly book, children's attention will stay focused on numbers as they count along with you and mimic the actions described in the story. The bold and simple illustrations provide pictures that are easy for young children to count. You and your students will enjoy reading this book over and over again.

If you cannot find *Ten Tiny Turtles, a Crazy Counting Book*, you may adapt the lesson and substitute the following books:

Demi. *Demi's Count the Animals 1 2 3*. New York: Grosset & Dunlap, 1986.

Edwards, Pamela Duncan. *Roar! A Noisy Counting Book*. New York: HarperCollins, 2000.

Grossman, Virginia, and Sylvia Long. *Ten Little Rabbits*. San Francisco: Chronicle Books, 1991.

Kirk, David. *Miss Spider's Tea Party*. New York: Scholastic, 1994.

Lobel, Anita. *One Lighthouse One Moon*. New York: HarperCollins, 2000.

Saul, Carol P. *Barn Cat, a Counting Book*. Boston: Little, Brown, 1998.

Tudor, Tasha. *1 Is One*. New York: Simon & Schuster, 1956.

Time Frame

50 minutes

Materials

> *Dear Math Teacher,*
>
> Prior to the lesson, set up a center in your room with several containers, each filled with manipulatives or concrete objects for students to count. One container could be filled with cubes; another with tiles; and others with sets of beans, erasers, pencils, crayons, paper clips, pennies, or plastic animals. Provide each student with a plastic bowl for collecting objects.
>
> *Caroline*

_____

_____

_____

_____

_____

For the teacher:

Four or more containers, each filled with a set of manipulatives (see mini-postcard)

Figure 1.1.1. *Ten Tiny Turtles Number Play,* transferred onto chart paper or the chalkboard

Figure 1.1.2. *Number Recognition, Matching, and Writing Assessment*

Figure 1.1.3. *Sample—Anecdotal Record*

Figure 1.1.4. *Anecdotal Record*

For each student:

One plastic bowl or small container with which to scoop manipulatives (see above)

Story and Mini-Lesson

1. In a comfortable gathering place or classroom community center, preview *Ten Tiny Turtles* with your students. Share the book jacket and title page. Leaf through the book from cover to cover. Invite students to respond to the numbers, words, and pictures. Students might exclaim, "I see numbers!" or "Look at the cool worms in sunglasses."

2. Ask your students to predict what kind of book this is. You might begin by asking, "Do you think this is going to be an alphabet book?" Students will respond with a resounding, "No!" Continue by asking, "Well then, what kind of a book is it?" Your class will respond, "It's a counting book!"

3. **R**ead the book aloud to students. Encourage them to count and repeat the words along with you. You may want to re-read the story with your students several times, each time encouraging them to join you in the read-aloud and counting.

4. **C**onnect the book with the lesson by saying, "Today we'll use our imaginations to act out the actions of the characters in the story. We'll call this the *Ten Tiny Turtles* Number Play."

Group Lesson

1. Discuss with the students what actions one might do if one were a playful dog, a rabbit dancing about, or a pie that is baking.

2. Set ground rules. Tell students you will have a signal to begin and a signal to stop. Practice this. Have students stand up and disperse throughout the classroom so each child has a personal space in which to move. When you say, "Begin!" students mime the actions of "One playful dog." Challenge students to stop the moment you give the "Stop!" signal.

3. Tell students that throughout the *Ten Tiny Turtles* Number Play they must listen carefully and follow directions. You will give them signals and directions as you read the book. Direct their attention to the chalkboard or chart paper list from **Figure 1.1.1. *Ten Tiny Turtles Number Play*.** Tell students to follow along as you read.

4. Continue by reading, "Two rabbits dancing, how about that." Direct students to join a partner and boogie together. If you have an odd number of students, have the lone student act out, "One playful dog," as the other students dance, or you may boogie with the single student.

5. Now read, "Three pies baked by the rat dressed for dinner." Pairs of partners must find a third member, then they must crouch motionless and pretend to be a baking pie. Students who are not in groups of three may act out, "Two rabbits dancing," or "One dog playing."

> Observe how students move about and how they join up with other children. If some students appear to be left out, gently direct them to groups that need more members.

6. Continue to read *Ten Tiny Turtles* aloud. With each consecutive number, students must join a group to make up the number read. Students who are "left over" and cannot find partners to form the correct group number may join together to do other actions, as in item 5.

7. When you have finished reading the *Ten Tiny Turtles* Number Play, stop, then start over again. Repeat the play as long as students remain interested and attentive.

Discovery

Gather students again in the community center. Discuss how one might arrange manipulatives or concrete models in groups that correspond to the numbers from one to ten. Then ask students to give you directions for arranging a set of manipulatives, such as the cubes, in groups in consecutive order from one to ten. After you have successfully followed the children's directions, tell students that it is their turn to examine and explore the manipulatives. Allow five to ten minutes for students to gather, examine, and explore sets of objects. Then have students arrange the manipulatives in groups, in order, from one to ten.

Reflection

After ten or fifteen minutes, give the signal to stop. Direct students to walk slowly in a clockwise circle around the room to look at the object arrangements other students have made. Encourage students to share comments about what they observe, such as, "I like the way Maria put her groups of tiles in rows. Each row of tiles got bigger." Another student might say, "Look at Latisha's blocks. The group of three looks like a triangle and the group of four looks like a square."

Provide closure to the lesson by adding your own observations, such as, "Look at the many ways you have grouped objects from one to ten. Throughout the rest of today, I'd like you to look for ways we group objects from one to ten. I'll check with you at the end of the day to see what you have noticed."

Assessment

- Use **Figure 1.1.2. *Number Recognition, Matching, and Writing Assessment*,** to pre- and post-assess students' ability to do the following: recognize numbers, match numbers and concrete models with one-to-one correspondence, and write numerals.

- Use **Figure 1.1.3. *Sample—Anecdotal Record*,** as a model for writing anecdotal records. Keep a clipboard or indexed notebook with copies of **Figure 1.1.4. *Anecdotal Record*** to make notes of each student's progress. You might consider the following questions as you record notes:

  ✓ During the Group Lesson, did some students have difficulty determining which group of students to join?

  ✓ During the Discovery activity, did students correctly group objects into groups from one to ten?

  ✓ Did students arrange objects in sequential order from one to ten?

Special Needs Adaptations

Auditory disability: An interpreter should sign the lesson. Students with auditory disabilities can participate with the class in all the activities.

Motor disability: Student partners or volunteers could assist these students in moving about the room during the Group Lesson. During the Discovery activity, partners could assist these students with collecting, carrying, and arranging manipulatives. Students with motor disabilities could take leadership roles by directing other students on how to arrange and sequence manipulatives.

Visual disability: Provide these students with assistance from a peer or adult partner. During the *Ten Tiny Turtles* Number Play, partners could lead these students to join others in groups. During the Discovery activity, partners could assist in collecting, identifying, counting, and grouping the concrete objects.

English Language Learners: Partner these students with a bilingual classmate or teacher. Have English Language Learners teach the numbers from one to ten in their native languages to the rest of the class. When you read *Ten Tiny Turtles*, say the number words in students' native languages.

Extensions

Provide plenty of opportunity for students to gain strength in number sense by doing these lesson extensions.

- Draw a hopscotch grid of ten numbers. Encourage students to recite number rhymes, such as *Ten Little Rabbits* by Virginia Grossman and Sylvia Long, as students jump from one hopscotch square to the next.

- Demonstrate how to play jacks.

- Ask students to sing and say jump rope number rhymes.

- Create a bulletin board with number words, symbols, and pictures of objects to correspond with the numbers.

- Have the students create number mobiles to hang from the ceiling. For example, for the number one, they can hang a symbol of the number 1, with one whale attached underneath.

- Go on a scavenger hunt around the school to look for groups or sets of objects from one to ten. As students become adept at this, have them look for groups in numbers from ten to fifteen, and so on.

- Encourage students to notice the arrangements of groups of things, such as different ways in which four chairs are placed. Are they grouped in a square shape, a row, or a diamond shape? Practice *subitizing*, that is, help children recognize different arrangements for groups of six items or fewer.

- Introduce *Ten Black Dots* by Donald Crews to model a lesson for students to make "dot" pictures. Use a dye-cut tool to make dots, or students may use a hole punch to make their own dots for the project.

- Have students count the steps they take to go out the door, down the hall, and to the playground.

- Ask students to take daily attendance and lunch count. Begin a 100s chart to count the days of school. (See **Figure 7.1.1. *100s Chart*** for an example.) Check off one number on the chart each day until you reach 100. Then celebrate 100 days of school.

Bibliography

Anno, Mitsumasa. *Anno's Counting Book.* New York: Harper, 1986.

Baker, Keith. *Big Fat Hen.* New York: Voyager Books. 1999.

Crews, Donald. *Ten Black Dots*. New York: Mulberry Books, 1995.

Cuyler, Margery. *100th Day Worries*. New York: Simon & Schuster Books for Young Readers, 2000.

Geisel, Theodor (Dr. Seuss). *One Fish Two Fish, Red Fish Blue Fish*. New York: Random House, 1988.

Geisert, Arthur. *Roman Numerals I to MM*. Boston: Houghton Mifflin, 1996.

Grossman, Virginia, and Sylvia Long. *Ten Little Rabbits*. San Francisco: Chronicle Books, 1991.

Kitchen, Bert. *Animal Numbers*. New York: Penguin, 1992.

McGrath, Barbara Barbieri. *The Cheerios Counting Book*. New York: Scholastic, 1998.

———. *The M & M's Chocolate Candies Counting Book*. Watertown, MA: Charlesbridge, 1994.

Micklethwait, Lucy. *I Spy Two Eyes, Numbers in Art*. New York: Mulberry Books, 1998.

Pallotta, Jerry. *Reese's Pieces Count by Fives*. New York: Scholastic, 2000.

Slate, Joseph. *Miss Bindergarten Celebrates the 100th Day of Kindergarten*. New York: Dutton Children's Books, 1998

Sloat, Teri. *From One to One Hundred*. New York: Puffin Books, 1995.

Stickland, Paul. *Ten Terrible Dinosaurs*. New York: Puffin Books, 2000.

Tafuri, Nancy. *Who's Counting*. New York: Greenwillow, 1986.

Wells, Rosemary. *Emily's First 100 Days of School*. New York: Hyperion Books for Children, 1999.

Related Standards 2000

Standard 2: Algebra

Standard 8: Communication

Standard 9: Connections

Standard 10: Representation

Related Standards 1989

Standard 1: Mathematics as Problem Solving

Standard 2: Mathematics as Communication

Standard 3: Mathematics as Reasoning

Standard 4: Mathematical Connections

Standard 6: Number Sense and Numeration

Standard 13: Patterns and Relationships

LESSON 2

Count to Twelve and Back

Brooks, Alan. *Frogs Jump: A Counting Book.* New York: Scholastic, 1996.

One frog jumps, two ducks dive, and three elephants trumpet, followed by a series of other animals who run, honk, swing, spin, and slide. Alan Brooks's jaunty text and Steven Kellogg's energetic illustrations keep children's attention as they chime in by repeating the sequence of numbers from one to twelve and back down again. This counting book gives children practice in matching number symbols to equivalent numbers of animals, as well as providing practice in adding and subtracting the number 1.

Students who thrive on more difficult problems will enjoy determining the sum total of animals when one is added to two, two is added to three, and so forth, all the way up to twelve. So, what's the answer? There are many ways to figure out this problem. Have students write in their personal math journals at least two ways to determine that our answer, 78, is correct.

_____

_____

_____

_____

_____

Time Frame

Day One: 50 minutes
Read the story and begin the mural.

Day Two: 50 minutes
Complete the mural, review the lesson, and celebrate children's learning.

If you cannot find *Frogs Jump: A Counting Book,* you may adapt the lesson and substitute the following book:

Sendak, Maurice. One Was Johnny: A Counting Book. New York: Harper Trophy, 1991.

_____

_____

_____

_____

Materials

➢ **Day One**

For the teacher:

Number line and/or 100s chart (posted; see **Figure 7.1.1. 100s Chart**)

List of numbers and animals from **Figure 1.2.1. List of Numbers, Animals, and Group Assignments,** transferred onto chart paper or the chalkboard

Four long sheets of chart paper (each sheet approximately 5 feet long)

Four large areas where students can spread out the chart paper and draw

Figure 1.1.4. Anecdotal Record

Assign students to the groups listed in **Figure 1.2.1. List of Numbers, Animals, and Group Assignments.**

For each student:

Pencils and crayons

Markers (optional)

Materials

➢ **Day Two**

For the teacher:

Chart paper or chalkboard showing the list from **Figure 1.2.1. List of Numbers, Animals, and Group Assignments**

Chalk or pen

Mural sections from Day One

Group assignments from Day One

Three or four sets of 3-by-5-inch cards, each card labeled with a numeral and its corresponding number word from one to twelve

Two to four counting and sorting centers, with manipulatives such as crayons, tiles, paper clips, plastic figures, erasers, cubes, and rods for students to count

In conspicuous places about the room, place sets of objects such as one teddy bear, two erasers, three pencils, four apples, five books, six pieces of chalk, and so on up to twelve. When students have completed their mural sections (see Group Lesson), have them go on a treasure hunt to find these sets of objects.

For each student:

Pencils and crayons

Markers (optional)

Story and Mini-Lesson: Day One

1. **P**review the story by showing the book cover, reading the book title, and slowly flipping through the pages of *Frogs Jump: A Counting Book*. Ask students to tell you what they notice about the book. Many children will answer by describing the animals and their antics.

2. Encourage students to make **p**redictions about the story. Some students will notice the book is about counting consecutive numbers up to twelve and then counting back down to one. Support all answers.

3. **R**ead the story aloud. Encourage students to chime in with each consecutive number as they catch on to the story pattern. Pause for emphasis after you reach the number twelve and read, "Twelve whales blow bubbles." Then exclaim, as in the book, "What? Whales don't blow soap bubbles." As you continue to read, "Pigs don't squeal on motorcycles," and "Snakes don't slide on water slides," students will realize that the story pattern has changed and now they are counting down as well as contradicting the antics of each animal group.

4. When you have finished reading the story, **r**eview the numbers by counting numbers up to twelve and back down to one. Direct attention to the posted number line or 100s chart; call on a child to point to the numbers with a ruler or yardstick as you count the numbers together.

5. **C**onnect the book to the following Group Lesson by telling students they will now make a number mural by drawing the animal groups from one to twelve.

Group Lesson: Day One

1. Tell students that they will work in groups. Each group will have the job of completing a part of the whole mural. Explain that students must draw the correct number of animals for the numbers they are assigned; that is, if they had the number one, they would draw one frog. For the number two, they would draw two ducks, and so forth.

2. Use **Figure 1.2.1. *List of Numbers, Animals, and Group Assignments*** to divide students into four groups and to assign numbers and animals to those groups.

3. Provide each group with chart paper, pencils, and crayons. Begin the mural.

Reflection: Day One

After your students have rolled up the mural sections and cleaned up materials for this day's lesson, ask them to line up in one line. Together, count from the first student to the last and then count back to one again. This ends the lesson for Day One.

Story and Mini-Lesson: Day Two

1. **R**eread the story and count the numbers from one to twelve and back down again.

2. Discuss and problem solve progress on the mural sections. For example, if one group is nearly done but another needs help, enlist helpers to assist other groups.

3. Have groups complete the mural sections.

Discovery: Day Two

As groups complete their sections of the mural, invite them on a treasure hunt to find sets of objects you have distributed about the room (*see mini-postcard, p. 9*). As students discover sets of objects, they must match the 3-by-5-inch number cards to corresponding sets of objects. That is, when students discover a set of four apples, they must place a number card labeled with the numeral 4 and the word "four" next to the apples. They must proceed throughout the room until they have discovered and labeled twelve sets of objects. Next, direct students to the sorting and counting centers where they can sort, stack, arrange, and group manipulatives.

Reflection: Day Two

When the mural sections are complete, have children arrange the sections in sequential order and tape the sections together. Post the completed mural in a conspicuous place. Encourage students to share, describe, and celebrate their drawings.

Assessment

- Use **Figure 1.1.4. *Anecdotal Record*** to record notes.
- Use **Figure 1.1.5. *Sample—Anecdotal Record*** as a model for your notes.

Special Needs Adaptations

Auditory disability: An interpreter should sign the lesson. These students and the interpreter should be encouraged to share and teach the signs for the numbers one through twelve to other students.

Motor disability: Provide access and a comfortable location for these students to work on their mural sections.

Visual disability: Assign a peer partner for these students. Provide stuffed animals or plastic models of the characters in the story for these students to explore with their hands. As other students work on mural sections, these students could work with clay to make beads or simple animal figures to represent one-to-one correspondence for the numbers one through twelve.

English Language Learners: At a listening center, provide a cassette recording of the story along with a copy of the book in English, so these students hear the story and connect the illustrations to the text with repeated story readings. Ask these children to share the numbers from one to twelve in their native languages with other students.

Extensions

- Have students create puppets and act out the story by drawing and cutting out pictures of the animals in the story and taping them onto Popsicle sticks. Gather together to sequence puppets by numerical order.

- Decorate a bulletin board. Have the students draw or cut out animals, fruit, or toys in quantities from one to twelve and post those cutouts on a class bulletin board next to the corresponding number symbols.

- Have the students write and illustrate theme-counting books. For example, if your class is studying amphibians, have students illustrate and label an amphibian counting book inspired by *Frogs Jump: A Counting Book.*

Bibliography

Aker, Suzanne. *What Comes in 2's, 3's, & 4's?* New York: Scholastic, 1999.

Anno, Mitsumasa. *Anno's Counting Book.* New York: Harper, 1986.

Brett, Jan. *Goldilocks and the Three Bears.* New York: G. P. Putnam's Sons, 1990.

Cherrill, Paul. *Ten Tiny Turtles, a Crazy Counting Book.* Boston: Houghton Mifflin, 1995.

Crews, Donald. *Ten Black Dots.* New York: Mulberry Books, 1995.

Gag, Wanda. *Millions of Cats.* New York: Paper Star, 1996.

Geisel, Theodore (Dr. Seuss). *The 500 Hats of Bartholomew Cubbins.* New York: Random House, 1990.

Lobel, Anita. *One Lighthouse One Moon.* New York: Greenwillow, 2000.

Saul, Carol P. *Barn Cat, a Counting Book.* Boston: Little, Brown, 1998.

Saxton, Freyman, and Joost Elffers. *One Lonely Sea Horse.* New York: Scholastic, 2000.

Schnetzler, Pattie. *Ten Little Dinosaurs.* Denver: Accord, 1999.

Scieszka, Jon. *The True Story of the 3 Little Pigs.* New York: Viking, 1999.

Related Standards 2000

Standard 2: Algebra

Standard 8: Communication

Standard 9: Connections

Standard 10: Representation

Related Standards 1989

Standard 2: Mathematics as Communication

Standard 4: Mathematical Connections

Standard 6: Number Sense and Numeration

Standard 13: Patterns and Relationships

LESSON 3

Count and Add

Baker, Keith. *Quack and Count.* San Diego: Harcourt Brace, 1999.

In Keith Baker's counting and adding book a family of ducklings displays an assortment of sums that add up to seven. "7 ducklings in a row/Count those ducklings as they go!/Slipping, sliding, having fun/7 ducklings, 6 plus 1." Students will repeat the rhyme and rhythm of the text while adding sums of waddling ducks. Baker's bright, uncluttered illustrations make it easy for students to see that no matter how the ducklings are arranged, they still add up to seven.

Time Frame

50 minutes

Materials

For the teacher:

Chalkboard or chart paper, chalk or pen

Figure 1.3.1. *Sample—T-Table*

Figure 1.3.2. *T-Table*

Figure 1.1.4. *Anecdotal Record*

For each student:

Several half sheets of plain white paper (eight sheets per student)

Pencil and crayons

Story and Mini-Lesson

1. **P**review the story by taking a "picture walk" through the book. Encourage students to notice the illustrations and comment about what they see.

2. Ask students to **p**redict what kind of a book this is. Your students will quickly notice that it is a counting and adding book.

3. **R**ead the story. Invite students to join in or repeat after you as you read the story aloud.

4. **R**eview the story by asking students to tell you what they noticed about the number seven. Students might respond by saying, "I counted seven ducklings," or "The ducklings were grouped in different ways but I still counted 7," and "The pictures in the book are addition pictures."

5. Use this student dialog to connect the story to the lesson by saying, "Let's see if we can find all the ways the ducklings added up to seven."

Group Lesson

1. Ask a student to display the pages of the book and to call on other students to tell the sums that add up to seven while you record the sums on the board.

2. When the sums are recorded, ask students if they notice a pattern. Some children may notice that as one addend goes up, the other addend goes down. Draw a T-table next to the list of sums to illustrate this pattern. See **Figure 1.3.1. Sample— T-Table** and **Figure 1.3.2. T-Table.**

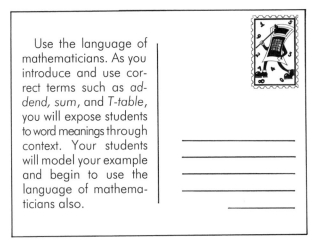

Use the language of mathematicians. As you introduce and use correct terms such as *addend, sum,* and *T-table,* you will expose students to word meanings through context. Your students will model your example and begin to use the language of mathematicians also.

3. Leave the sums and T-table on the chalkboard for reference. Tell the students that it is time for them to draw their own addition problems.

Discovery

▪ Discuss with students what characters or animals they would like to draw. If you are studying a particular theme such as farm animals, your students might choose to draw calves, foals, piglets, or chicks. Make sure each student chooses just one kind of animal for his or her set of addition problems.

▪ Instruct students to draw pictures that illustrate problems to make sums of seven. Tell them to put the answer to each problem on the back of the paper. Later, during an extension activity, they will be able to test their friends with their picture problems.

If a student is fluent in finding addends to make the sum of seven, he or she may draw illustrations of addends to make a higher number such as eight, nine, or ten.

▪ Have one or two students distribute papers. Use this as a math sequencing opportunity. Check to see if the student paper passers distribute papers in a sequential, rather than a random, manner. If not, take time to discuss and model an organized way of distributing papers. Have the rest of the class gather their own pencils and crayons to begin working on addition illustrations.

Reflection

- Allow time for students to share and enjoy each other's illustrations. If you determine that students have a good understanding of the addends that combine to make a sum of seven, extend the lesson by having students play "What is the missing addend?"

- Have students form pairs. Each student will take a turn covering up one of the addends in an illustration. When the addend is hidden, the student asks his or her partner, "What is the missing addend?" For example, because the child's partner knows the sum is seven, and he or she can see just two piglets in the picture, there must be five piglets missing. The missing addend is five.

- Collect students' illustrated problems to post on a bulletin board or to use to review addition sums later.

Assessment

Check students' illustrations to determine whether they followed directions, added sums correctly, and completed the family of addition facts that combine to make seven. Use **Figure 1.1.4.** *Anecdotal Record* to record notes about progress and proficiency.

Special Needs Adaptations

Auditory disability: An interpreter should sign the lesson. Students with auditory disabilities can participate with the class in all the activities for this lesson.

Motor disability: Have these students participate in the activities based on their abilities. If students have difficulty with fine motor coordination and are unable to illustrate addition problems for the number seven, have them record problems into tape recorders. These students could rewind and play back their recordings to partners during the Reflection activity, and they could stop the tape to hide an addend.

Visual disability: Partner these students with sighted peers. Students with visual disabilities could set up problems for both the Discovery and Reflection activities with manipulatives. For example, a child could set out three plastic sheep and add four more sheep to make the sum of seven. Or a partner could ask, "I have seven sheep total, in one of my hands there are three sheep, how many sheep do I have in my other hand?"

English Language Learners: Partner these students with bilingual classmates or volunteers to help with translation during the Story and Mini-Lesson, Group Lesson, and Reflection activities. During the Discovery activity, partner these students with English-speaking peers so all share their native languages as they discuss and illustrate their pictures.

Extensions

- Label the illustrations from the Discovery activity above to make word problems.

- As a class, write and illustrate a word problem book.

- Substitute another number besides seven in the activities above.

- Refer to **Figure 1.3.1.** *Sample T-Table* **and Figure 1.3.2.** *T-Table.* Model for students how to make T-tables for the numbers one through four. Then have students make their own T-tables for addition fact families from one through ten. Students could also make picture T-tables for concrete representations of numbers.

- Have the students explore *The Graph Club* by Tom Snyder Productions, then use this software to create tables and graphs.

- Play "What is the missing addend?" with manipulatives as suggested for students with visual disabilities in the Special Needs Adaptations section.

- Have groups of students play board games with dice.

- Read *Jumanji,* by Chris Van Allsburg, to the class. Together, create a board game and share it with others.

- Have the class play domino addition, matching domino sums to one another.

- Play "sevens" with a deck of cards. Have students remove face cards and other cards with a value above seven. Then play "sevens" with the remaining cards from the deck. Students take turns drawing a card. When a student discovers a combination that adds up to the number seven, he or she gets a match. Continue until all cards are played.

- Adapt the previous game to play "eights," "nines," or "tens."

- Read Loreen Leedy's *Mission: Addition* to find more addition activities.

Bibliography

Leedy, Loreen. *Mission: Addition*. New York: Holiday House, 1997.

Murphy, Stuart J. *Animals on Board.* New York: HarperCollins, 1998.

Van Allsburg, Chris. *Jumanji.* New York: Scholastic, 1993.

Walton, Rick. *One More Bunny*. New York: Lothrop, Lee & Shepard, 2000.

Software

Tom Snyder Productions. 1998. *The Graph Club.* Macintosh and Windows, www.tomsnyder.com. (Accessed February 2001).

Related Standards 2000

Standard 2: Algebra

Standard 8: Communication

Standard 9: Connections

Standard 10: Representation

Related Standards 1989

Standard 2: Mathematics as Communication

Standard 4: Mathematical Connections

Standard 6: Number Sense and Numeration

Standard 7: Concepts of Whole Number Operations

Standard 8: Whole Number Computation

Standard 13: Patterns and Relationships

LESSON 4

Count Back and Subtract

Toft, Kim Michelle, and Allan Sheather. **One Less Fish.** Watertown, MA: Charlesbridge, 1998.

One Less Fish is a cautionary tale about the importance of preserving coral reefs as well as other natural environments. Set in Australia's Great Barrier Reef, the book begins with twelve fish and subtracts one for each page. The story tells about different factors that contribute to the demise of various underwater species. Each page introduces the reader to a species of fish and a threat to its survival. The pages are beautifully illustrated, and the story has an easy-to-read rhythm. The last two pages include a glossary of terms and an explanation of each type of fish featured in the story. When children read this book, they will want to prevent this subtraction story from coming true.

Time Frame

Day One: 50 minutes

Day Two: 50 minutes

Materials

➤ **Day One**

For the teacher:

Several sheets of chart paper and a pen

Chalkboard and chalk

Map of the world (to show Australia and the Great Barrier Reef)

For each student:

Twelve goldfish crackers

White scrap paper

Large sheet of white construction paper

Pencil

➤ **Day Two**

For the teacher:

Crayons

Cups for water (one for every three or four students)

Blue watercolor paint

Newspapers

Paint shirts (optional)

For each student:

Paintbrush

Figure 1.4.1. *Fish Subtraction*

Crayons

One die from a set of dice

Story and Mini-Lesson: Day One

1. Ask students what they know about oceans. Record on chart paper statements that all students agree are true, such as, "We need oceans to survive. Oceans surround all the continents. Fish, whales, and sea lions live in oceans." Remove this paper and store it for future use.

2. Use the map to introduce Australia and the Great Barrier Reef. Give students a brief explanation about a coral reef.

    > A coral reef is a community of ocean animals and plants that live in warm, clear, and shallow water.

3. **P**review the book. Introduce the title of the story and flip through the pages. Have students **p**redict what they think the story will be about and why the authors chose this title.

4. **R**ead the story. Read through each page and take time to discuss the cautionary notes on the bottom of each page.

5. **R**eview and **c**onnect the book to the lesson. Ask students to reflect about their predictions from item 3. Encourage students to discuss how they feel about the loss of each fish.

6. Have students go back to their desks. Pass out twelve goldfish crackers to each student. Be sure to tell them they are not to eat them yet. Have the students help you count as you pass out the goldfish.

7. **R**e-read the story. This time, have the students eat one fish cracker after one fish disappears. It is not necessary to read the footnotes this time. As a class, count how many crackers each student has. On the chalkboard, have a student helper write the subtraction problem, $12 - 1 = 11$.

    > You may also show students how to manually subtract one by using a 12-inch ruler as a calculating tool. Instruct students: "Put your right index finger on the number 12 on your ruler, like this [model]. Hold it there. Then, count back one with your left index finger to number 11, like this." Continue to instruct students in this way to count back one number as you continue to subtract each additional fish in the story.

8. Read the next page and have students eat one more crackers, then have students count the remaining crackers. Your student helper should write the following problem on the board: $11 - 1 = 10$. Continue until there are no more crackers.

9. Compare the number of remaining fish crackers with the fish in the story. Discuss with students how all the fish crackers are gone and cannot come back because they are in students' stomachs. Of course, you can always buy more fish crackers, but the fish in the story will not survive *unless* we learn to protect and save them.

Group Lesson: Day One

1. Tell students they will create their own fish subtraction story problems.

2. Discuss what a story problem is. Create the following example for the class: "Five fish were swimming in the sea." (Write and draw this on the chalkboard.) "A fisherman came along and caught two. How many fish are left?" Count the three remaining fish together.

3. Create another subtraction story problem with the class. Have students suggest the characters and the situation while you record the problem on the board. Continue to model subtraction story problems until the class has a basic understanding of this concept.

4. On chart paper, brainstorm with your students several types of fish they could use in their story problems. On another piece of paper, brainstorm with the class different situations that the fish could get into to create a subtraction story. Post these ideas in a place where all students can refer to them.

5. Tell students that they will now create a story problem of their own. Hand out one piece of white scrap paper to each student.

6. Have each student write and illustrate his or her own fish subtraction story. Students should refer to the "brainstorm charts" for ideas.

7. If you have time, have students share their ideas with partners or the class. Collect the story problems. This is the end of the activities for Day One.

Assessment: Day One

Collect the scrap paper story problems to assess students' understanding of subtraction and of how to write story problems. Note the students who need assistance and support them individually on Day Two.

Story and Mini-Lesson: Day Two

1. **R**eview *One Less Fish* with students. Discuss the pictures and how colorful they are.

2. Tell students they will create a book like *One Less Fish* using their own subtraction story problems from Day One.

3. Return the Day One story problems to the students. Tell them they will now copy their ideas onto a big sheet of construction paper. Direct students to write and illustrate (pencil only) their problems on the paper going the long way (landscape), not the tall way (vertical). Also, tell the students to fill the space well and write large. Tell

students that after they have written, colored, and traced their story problems on paper, they will put a blue wash in watercolor over the entire page. This will make it look like the ocean. You may want to show a sample you have created.

4. After students have completed writing and illustrating in pencil, they may use crayons to color their pages. Tell students to press hard with their crayons and fill in all the spaces they want colored.

5. Students should trace their words in white crayon. Tell them to press hard and make sure to trace each letter.

6. When students have finished coloring and tracing, they are ready to paint. Have newspaper and paint shirts available to protect their desks and clothing. Students should paint a thin layer of blue watercolor over the entire piece of construction paper.

7. Place finished products on a table or in a corner of the room where the illustrations will dry.

8. When all the pages are completed and dried, collect the pages and bind them together to create a class book.

Discovery: Day Two

When students finish painting, have them clean up. Direct students to get their copies of **Figure 1.4.1. *Fish Subtraction,*** one die, and crayons. Model how to do the following activity. First, roll the die. For example, you roll a 3. The number 3 is the answer to one of the problems on the ***Fish Subtraction*** sheet. Now you look for problems on the sheet that equal the number 3. Ah ha! You find, $5 - 2 = $ ____. Since $5 - 2 = 3$, you color that section of the picture. The goal is to color *every* section on the picture, using the die to find the answers.

Reflection: Day Two

Have students share their finished products. Post the chart paper with the "ocean facts" you recorded on Day One. Review the facts, correct misconceptions, and add other facts students learned.

Assessment: Day Two

Evaluate finished products: Did students' illustrations correspond to their problems and answers? Use **Figure 1.1.4. *Anecdotal Record*** to note progress.

Special Needs Adaptations

Auditory disability: An interpreter should sign the story, the teacher's instructions, and students' dialog.

Motor disability: Set up an area where it is comfortable for these students to work. Assign student buddies or aides to assist with writing, coloring, and painting. Students with motor disabilities may assist you as "checkers"; that is, they could check to determine whether other students' story problems make sense.

Visual disability: These students can create a subtraction story scene using clay or plastic fish models. They could dictate story problems into a tape recorder for other students to answer.

English Language Learners: Have these students partner with bilingual or English-speaking buddies. Check that they understand instructions. Provide writing assistance to these students during the Day One story problem activity.

Extensions

- Say, write, or draw more subtraction problems using goldfish crackers as manipulatives. Students may eat the crackers they subtract.

- Model for students how to use a number line as a tool for doing subtraction problems. Have students create their own fish number lines and then use the number lines to work subtraction problems.

- Have students do mini-research projects about species of fish that were introduced in the book.

- Include this book in a unit about oceans, Australia, or the Great Barrier Reef.

Bibliography

Christelow, Eileen. *Five Little Monkeys Jumping on the Bed*. Boston: Houghton Mifflin, 1999.

Dunbar, Joyce. *Ten Little Mice*. San Diego: Harcourt Brace Voyager Books, 1995.

Ehlert, Lois. *Fish Eyes*. San Diego: Harcourt Brace, 1992.

Hulme, Joy N. *Sea Sums*. New York: Hyperion Books for Children, 1996.

Schnetzler, Pattie. *Ten Little Dinosaurs*. Denver: Accord, 1999.

Related Standards 2000

Standard 1: Number and Operations

Standard 2: Algebra

Standard 6: Problem Solving

Standard 7: Reasoning and Proof

Standard 8: Communication

Standard 9: Connections

Standard 10: Representation

Related Standards 1989

Standard 1: Mathematics as Problem Solving

Standard 2: Mathematics as Communication

Standard 3: Mathematics as Reasoning

Standard 4: Mathematical Connections

Standard 6: Number Sense and Numeration

Standard 7: Whole Number Operations

Standard 13: Patterns and Relationships

LESSON 5

Find and Multiply Sets

Leedy, Loreen. *2x2 = BOO! A Set of Multiplication Stories.* New York: Holiday House, 1995.

Your students will not be spooked by multiplication any more! This amusing book introduces the basic concepts of multiplying. The pictures and "comic-like" nature of each story in the book capture the reader's attention until the end. Use this lesson as a stepping stone to higher mathematics, and use Leedy's book as a resource for further multiplication lessons. *2x2 = BOO! A Set of Multiplication Stories* relates well to Halloween, but can be read anytime.

Time Frame

50 minutes

Materials

For the teacher:

Chalkboard or chart paper; chalk or pen

Big bulletin board or large amount of wall space to display completed projects

Orange or yellow chart paper, covering the bulletin board or wall, as a background

Twenty or thirty old magazines

One package of sentence strips

For each student:

Construction paper (various colors)

One piece of white construction paper

Pencils, markers, crayons, scissors, and glue

Story and Mini-Lesson

1. **P**review, **p**redict, and **r**ead the story.

2. Discuss with students what multiplication means (for example, a faster way of adding, a way of grouping items, or repeated addition). Have students give you examples from the story of how multiplication was used (for example, the ghost used the machine to make more bags of candy, and the rooster and the fox used three pumpkins to create a better way to scare away crows).

3. Practice skip counting together to help students warm up to multiplication. Skip count by counting by twos, fives, and tens.

4. Tell students they can use their own bodies to illustrate and solve multiplication problems. Here is an example: Ask students to line up at the door in two equal lines. (If one student is left over, have him or her assist you in creating this problem.) Have the class figure out how many students are in each line. Ask, "How many groups are at the door?" Students will answer, "Two!" Then ask, "How many students are in each group?" Guide the students through the problem. Do the addition problem first. For example, if there are two lines of ten, the problem is 10 (students in one row) + 10 (students in the other row) = 20 students in all. Then do the multiplication problem, 2 (rows or groups of students) × 10 (students in each row) = 20 (students in all). Write these algorithms on the board.

5. Use the problem in item 4 to discuss how addition and multiplication are related. The problem was the same, but it was solved in various ways. Discuss how multiplication is like taking a short cut.

6. Practice other multiplication problems, such as:

   ✓ How many eyes are in the class? Count by twos to figure out the answer (2 × number of students in the class = total number of eyes in the class).

   ✓ How many fingers are in the class? Count by fives and tens to figure out the answer (5 × number of hands in the class = total number of fingers in the class, or 10 × number of students in the class = number of fingers in the class).

   ✓ How many heads are in the class (1 × number of students in the class = number of heads in the class)?

Group Lesson

1. Tell students they will now create a "spooky" multiplication scene.

2. Brainstorm with the class what things you might see in a spooky scene, such as pumpkins, bats, haunted houses, or black cats. Record all items on the chalkboard or chart paper.

3. Divide your class into groups of two or more.

4. Each group will choose one spooky item they will create for the spooky scene. Record the names of the students in each group next to the chosen item on the chart paper.

5. Brainstorm with the class how each group can create a multiplication problem with their spooky item. For example, the bat group could create three bats with two eyes each. They would ask, "How many eyes do three bats have?"

6. Once each group has an idea for a multiplication problem using their spooky item, let them gather construction paper and crayons to create their part of the scene.

7. As groups complete their parts of the scene, have them write their multiplication questions on sentence strips.

8. Assist groups with placing their questions and items on the bulletin board.

Discovery

When students complete their scenes, have them go to a table where you have placed old magazines. Instruct students to make a "multiplication collage." Show students a sample collage and multiplication problem, such as a cutout picture of two trucks with the question, "How many headlights do two trucks have?" and the multiplication problem, 2 (trucks) × 2 (headlights) = 4 (trucks). Students may use the magazines to find pictures to make their own multiplication problems. They should glue the pictures to white construction paper and record the corresponding multiplication problem next to each picture.

Reflection

Gather the class together to review the "spooky scene." Have each group share their problem.

Assessment

■ While groups work on the spooky scene, circulate through the class and take anecdotal notes. Provide assistance as needed. Clarify misunderstandings.

■ Review the multiplication collages for accuracy. Keep anecdotal records. Clarify misunderstandings.

Special Needs Adaptations

Auditory disability: An interpreter should sign the lesson and interpret instructions.

Motor disability: Student buddies or aides may assist these students with the cutting, coloring, writing, and pasting activities.

Visual disability: Peer partners may assist these students in constructing a spooky item out of clay, yarn, or Popsicle sticks to contribute to the "spooky" scene. During the Discovery activity, have these students walk around the room feeling for items such as stuffed animals, groups of desks, groups of cubbies, or book shelves that could be used for multiplication problems. For example, a student could ask, "How many arms do four stuffed teddies have?" or "How many desks are in one group of four desks?"

English Language Learners: Student buddies should partner with these students. Buddies can demonstrate the activities from the lesson to clarify understanding of the instructions. Students should be encouraged to talk about their work to support and practice language skills. Have these students teach the class how to say the numbers one through twenty in their native languages. Place an English-language copy of the book and cassette of *2x2 = BOO! A Set of Spooky Multiplication Stories* at the listening center for English-language reinforcement.

Extensions

- Have each student create his or her own spooky scene with two or three multiplication problems.

- Use graph paper to make patterned sets of multiplication problems, geoboards to make sets of shapes, and other manipulatives such as tiles or rows of plastic figures to create multiplication problems.

- Adapt and change the multiplication scene from the Group Lesson so that it is appropriate to other holidays or seasons of the year, such as winter, Presidents' Day, Valentine's Day, or spring.

- Set up a multiplication center. Provide paper, stamps and stamp pads, or stickers so students can stamp or stick on multiplication problems such as three groups of three stars equals nine stars, or $3 \times 3 = 9$.

Bibliography

Aker, Suzanne. *What Comes in 2's, 3's, and 4's?* New York: Simon & Schuster, 1992.

Anno, Masaichiro, and Mitsumasa Anno. *Anno's Mysterious Multiplying Jar.* New York: Putnam, 1999.

Dixon, Ann. *Trick-or-Treat.* New York: Scholastic, 1998.

Giganti, Paul, Jr. *Each Orange Had 8 Slices.* New York: Mulberry Books, 1999.

Hong, Lily Toy. *Two of Everything.* Morton Grove, IL: Whitman, 1993.

Neuschwander, Cindy. *Amanda Bean's Amazing Dream.* New York: Scholastic, 1998.

Raschka, Chris. *Like, Likes, Like.* New York: DK Publishing, 1999.

Schlein, Miriam. *More Than One.* New York: Greenwillow, 1996.

Recordings

Brown, Ron. *Math Concepts I.* Teachin' Tunes, 1996. (Teachin' Tunes, 12930 Peach Tree Lane, Red Bluff, CA 96080)

Related Standards 2000

Standard 1: Number and Operations

Standard 2: Algebra

Standard 6: Problem Solving

Standard 7: Reasoning and Proof

Standard 8: Communication

Standard 9: Connections

Standard 10: Representation

Related Standards 1989

Standard 1: Mathematics as Problem Solving

Standard 2: Mathematics as Communication

Standard 3: Mathematics as Reasoning

Standard 4: Mathematical Connections

Standard 6: Number Sense and Numeration

Standard 7: Concepts of Whole Number Operations

Standard 13: Patterns and Relationships

LESSON 6

Divide Fare Shares

Hoberman, Mary Ann. *One of Each.* Boston: Little, Brown, 2000.

Oliver Tolliver has one of everything and likes it that way, that is, until he discovers he is very lonely. This is a fable about the importance of sharing. In the end, readers will agree that life is better when it is shared with others!

Time Frame

Day One: 50 minutes

Day Two: 50 minutes

Materials

➤ **Day One**

For the teacher:

One apple	Paper towels
One pear	One sharp knife
One plum	Small cutting board
One peach	

You may substitute fruit in season for this activity. The fruit must be suitable for cutting into slices to be divided among students.

_____

_____

_____

_____

> **Day Two**

For the teacher:

Chart paper or chalkboard, pen or chalk

Overhead transparency of **Figure 1.6.1. *Character Cards,*** cut into squares

Overhead transparency of **Figure 1.6.2. *Record Sheet, Dividing Shares***

For each pair of students:

Figure 1.6.1. *Character Cards*

Figure 1.6.2. *Record Sheet, Dividing Shares*

One small bag of Skittles candy

Pencil, crayons, scissors

Story and Mini-Lesson: Day One

1. **P**review, **p**redict, and **r**ead the story.

2. Ask students, "How did Oliver solve the problem of not having enough fruit for his new friends?" Students will answer, "He cut slices of fruit and shared them." Support students' answers. **C**onnect *One of Each* to the lesson by saying, "Oliver *divided* his fruit into *equal parts* so all could have a *fair share.*"

3. Direct students' attention to the plum, pear, peach, and apple you have. Tell students they will practice dividing the fruit into fair shares.

4. Ask for volunteers, or assign students, to act out the roles of Oliver, Peggoty, the sheep, the snake, the rabbit, the pig, and the goose.

5. Place the plum on the cutting board.

6. Have Oliver and Peggoty come forward and decide how many pieces to cut the plum into, so each will have a fair share. (They may ask for assistance from the audience.) Cut the plum according to their directions (two pieces) and place the plum slices aside for later.

7. Next have the sheep join Oliver and Peggoty. Have them decide how many pieces to divide the pear into so that each of the three will have a fair share. Cut the pear according to their directions (three pieces) and place the pear slices aside.

8. Then have the snake and rabbit join Oliver, Peggoty, and the sheep. They must decide how to divide the peach so that each of the five of them will have a fair share (five pieces). Cut the peach and place the peach slices aside.

9. Finally, have the pig and goose join the rest and decide how to divide the apple so that each of the seven will have a fair share (seven pieces).

10. Place the apple slices with the other fruit slices. Count the total number of fruit slices (28).

11. Discuss with the class how many pieces of fruit you need so everyone in the class gets a piece of fruit. Give each child one slice of fruit.

12. Discuss with the class these questions: "What should we do with the remaining pieces of fruit? Did everyone get a fair share? Why or why not? Which gives you a bigger piece of fruit, a plum divided into two pieces or an apple divided into seven pieces? Is there a better way to divide the fruit?" Discuss. What determines how many pieces of fruit you need to cut?

Reflection: Day One

Students will eat and enjoy the fruit, then have students write responses in their journals to the questions discussed in item 12.

Group Lesson: Day Two

1. **R**eview and **r**eread *One of Each.*

2. Brainstorm about what division means. Record the students' ideas on chart paper or on the chalkboard.

3. Tell the class that today they will get a chance to practice division by dividing Skittles among the different characters so each one receives a fair share. Tell students they may eat the Skittles *after* they complete the entire Group Lesson.

4. Divide the class into partners.

5. Distribute **Figure 1.6.1. *Character Cards*** to each pair of partners.

6. Provide ten minutes for students to color and cut out the characters.

7. Distribute **Figure 1.6.2. *Record Sheet, Dividing Shares*** to each set of partners.

8. Follow the directions in **Figure 1.6.2. *Record Sheet, Dividing Shares.*** Model how to set up the character cards and ask students to give you suggestions for how to divide the Skittles equally among the characters. Students might suggest you deal the Skittles as you deal cards in a card game. Use the overhead transparencies of **Figures 1.6.1.** and **1.6.2.** to demonstrate this.

9. Direct the partners to complete **Figure 1.6.2. *Record Sheet, Dividing Shares.***

10. Let the students eat their Skittles.

Discovery: Day Two

Have students form into groups of various sizes and practice dividing items into fair shares. You may use playing cards; stuffed animals; or manipulatives such as dice, paper clips, tiles, or plastic figurines.

Reflection: Day Two

Ask students to record in their journals responses to one or more of the following questions/assignments:

■ Have you ever had to divide something among friends or family members? Did everyone get a fair share?

- What could you do with leftovers or remainders that cannot be shared equally?

- Write down or illustrate what *divide* or *division* means.

Assessment: Day Two

- Review students' answers to the reflection questions to assess their understanding of division. Review students' answers on **Figure 1.6.2.** *Record Sheet, Dividing Shares* for accuracy.

- Assess students' understanding of division during the class discussions and activities. Use **Figure 1.1.4.** *Anecdotal Record* to write down comments and notes about students' understanding and progress.

Special Needs Adaptations

Auditory disability: An interpreter should sign the lesson and instructions.

Motor disability: Student buddies or an aide may assist these students with dividing the Skittles and sorting manipulatives.

Visual disability: Use stuffed animals to represent the characters of the book, rather than the cutout characters used in the Group Lesson. Assign a buddy or have an aide read the questions and record the answers for **Figure 1.6.2.** *Record Sheet, Dividing Shares.*

English Language Learners: These students should pair up during the lesson with bilingual buddies. Encourage English-speaking partners to speak in English to model correct language use in the context of the lesson. Place a copy of the book and a tape-recorded copy of *One of Each* in the listening center for these students to review later.

Extensions

- Take advantage of serendipitous moments. Together, problem solve situations such as when a child brings cookies to the class and there are remainders left over, or when there are not enough cookies for everyone.

- Read *The Doorbell Rang* by Pat Hutchins. Use paper cutout cookies to represent the cookies in the story. Have children take turns acting out the parts of Mom, Sam, and Victoria, their friends and cousins, and Grandma.

- Plan a tea party for classroom volunteers. Have students determine the number of guests to be invited and how much food and supplies will be needed.

- Select fruit in season. Ask students to tell you how to do problems such as the following:

    ✓ Divide two pears among four people.

    ✓ Divide three plums among nine people.

    ✓ Divide four apples among sixteen people.

- Use fruit to introduce the concept of remainders. For example, divide three apples among ten people. Divide four peaches among six people.

Bibliography

Hutchins, Pat. *The Doorbell Rang.* New York: Mulberry Books, 1999.

Murphy, Stuart. *Divide and Ride.* New York: Scholastic, 1997.

Pfister, Marcus. *The Rainbow Fish.* New York: North South Books, 1992.

Pinczes, Elinor. *One Hundred Hungry Ants.* Boston: Houghton Mifflin, 1999.

———. *A Remainder of One.* New York: Houghton Mifflin, 1995.

Stevens, Janet. *Tops and Bottoms.* San Diego: Harcourt Brace, 1995.

Tatler, Sarah. *We Can Share It!* New York: Addison Wesley Longman, 1995.

Related Standards 2000

Standard 2: Algebra

Standard 6: Problem Solving

Standard 7: Reasoning and Proof

Standard 8: Communication

Standard 9: Connections

Standard 10: Representation

Related Standards 1989

Standard 1: Mathematics as Problem Solving

Standard 2: Mathematics as Communication

Standard 3: Mathematics as Reasoning

Standard 4: Mathematical Connections

Standard 6: Number Sense and Numeration

Standard 7: Concepts of Whole Number Operations

Standard 8: Whole Number Computation

Standard 12: Fractions and Decimals

Standard 13: Patterns and Relationships

LESSON 7

Identify and Build Fraction Models

Adler, David. *Fraction Fun.* New York: Holiday House, 1997.

Fraction Fun is a colorful and informational math book that introduces four fraction activities: 1) making paper plate pizza pies; 2) weighing common classroom items such as pencils, paper, and tissues; 3) weighing coins; and 4) making graph paper fractions. The vivid illustrations by Nancy Tobin provide good models for student fraction finders. Teachers can use a fraction or the whole of this book for math lesson plans.

Time Frame

50 minutes

Materials

For the teacher:

Concrete models and materials to show fractions, such as the following:

Use concrete models of materials that are accessible to you. Please do not feel limited or constrained by the materials list.

- ✓ Pattern blocks (to show that two congruent triangles make a square or that half a square is equal to two triangles)

- ✓ Cuisinaire rods: two yellow and one orange (to show that two yellow rods equal one orange rod)

- ✓ One whole egg carton and two half egg cartons (to show that two half cartons equal one whole carton)

- ✓ Two fifty cent pieces and one dollar bill

- ✓ Two quarters and one fifty cent piece

- ✓ Four quarters and one dollar bill

Chalkboard

Cut colored paper scraps

Beans, pasta, and yarn scraps

Figure 1.7.1. *Assessment, Halves and Wholes*

For each student:

One paper plate	Pencils and crayons
Scissors and glue	Math journal

Story and Mini-Lesson

1. Preview and "picture walk" through the book. As you turn through the pages of the book, ask students if they know or use any fractions. You might get responses such as, "My dog ate half a cake," "I am $7\frac{1}{2}$ years old," "I ate half a bag of popcorn at the movies," or "There is a half moon tonight."

2. Read the first fifteen pages, or the first half ($\frac{15}{30}$ pages) of *Fraction Fun* aloud. This shows how to make paper plate fractions. Choose one paper plate fraction to make per day. Begin the first day with the fraction, $\frac{1}{2}$, and progress to smaller fractions on subsequent days. Omit or add fractions as appropriate for the ages and grades you teach.

3. Brainstorm other items that could be divided into fractions such as $\frac{1}{2}$, $\frac{1}{4}$, or $\frac{1}{8}$. List these on the chalkboard.

4. Introduce and discuss examples of fractions with the concrete models suggested in the materials list above.

Group Lesson

1. Review the illustrated fractions of paper plate pizzas in *Fraction Fun*.

2. Discuss how to make a paper plate pizza.

3. Discuss and problem solve how to divide the pizza into two equal halves. Your students will probably suggest that they fold the paper plates in half through the middle. It is not necessary to cut the paper plates in half.

4. Instruct students to decorate each half of their plates with a different "topping" so that the halves are clearly visible. That is, use cut red scraps and orange scraps for tomato and cheese on one half and green and red strips of cut paper for green and red pepper pizza on the other half.

5. Tell students to select three or more sets of materials to use to decorate their paper plate pizzas.

6. Let students begin making the paper plate pizzas.

Discovery

1. When students have completed their paper plate pizzas, invite them to go on a scavenger hunt throughout the room to find halves and wholes of things.

2. Have students write or draw examples of halves and wholes in their math journals. The list could include: 2 halves of a closet door = 1 whole set of doors; equal pairs of red Cuisinaire rods match the size of 1 yellow rod; 2 frames of a window = 1 whole window; 2 halves of a book make 1 complete book; and 1 shoe on each foot = 1 whole pair of shoes.

Reflection

Instruct students to label each half of their fraction pizzas with the ½ symbol. Share, discuss, and display paper plate pizzas. Share math journal examples of halves and wholes.

Assessment

Use **Figure 1.7.1. *Assessment, Halves and Wholes*** to record students' understanding of halves and wholes.

Special Needs Adaptations

Auditory disability: An interpreter should sign the lesson.

Motor disability: Students with motor impairments could direct students with visual impairments how to decorate their pizzas. A student buddy or aide may assist students with motor disabilities with pizza decorating.

Visual disability: These students should work with concrete models of sets of halves and wholes while you read the book. Have these students build a three-dimensional pizza on an aluminum pan. They can use string to divide the pizza in half, and paper scraps, buttons, twist tops, and magnets to decorate the pizza halves.

English Language Learners: Have a same-language student partner with these students during the story and lesson. Have a volunteer read *Fraction Fun* into a tape recorder for these students to hear English-language repetition.

Extensions

- Continue to read *Fraction Fun*. Do one activity per day until you have completed all the lessons.

- Do activities from Loreen Leedy's *Fraction Action*.

Bibliography

Beil, Karen Magnuson. *A Cake All for Me!* New York: Holiday House, 1998.

Hewitt, Sally. *Making Fractions*. Brookfield, CT: Millbrook Press, 1998.

Leedy, Loreen. *Fraction Action*. New York: Holiday House, 1994.

McMillan, Bruce. *Eating Fractions*. New York: Scholastic, 1991.

Murphy, Stuart J. *Fractions Jump*. New York: HarperCollins, 1999.

———. *Give Me Half*. New York: HarperCollins, 1996.

Pallotta, Jerry. *The Hershey's Milk Chocolate Bar Fractions Book*. New York: Scholastic, 1999.

Related Standards 2000

Standard   2: Algebra

Standard   6: Problem Solving

Standard   7: Reasoning and Proof

Standard   8: Communication

Standard   9: Connections

Standard 10: Representation

Related Standards 1989

Standard   1: Mathematics as Problem Solving

Standard   2: Mathematics as Communication

Standard   3: Mathematics as Reasoning

Standard   4: Mathematical Connections

Standard   6: Number Sense and Numeration

Standard 13: Patterns and Relationships

1   One playful dog

2   Two rabbits dancing

3   Three pies baked

4   Four bottles of pop

5   Five fluffy sheep

6   Six slim cats

7   Seven slimy worms

8   Eight spotted fish

9   Nine noisy bees

10   Ten tiny turtles

Figure 1.1.1. *Ten Tiny Turtles Number Play*

In the table below, strike through the numbers in the columns that each student is able to (1) recognize, (2) match with one-to-one correspondence, and (3) write correctly.

Name	(1) Recognition	(2) Matching	(3) Writing
	1 2 3 4 5 6 7 8 9 10	1 2 3 4 5 6 7 8 9 10	1 2 3 4 5 6 7 8 9 10
	1 2 3 4 5 6 7 8 9 10	1 2 3 4 5 6 7 8 9 10	1 2 3 4 5 6 7 8 9 10
	1 2 3 4 5 6 7 8 9 10	1 2 3 4 5 6 7 8 9 10	1 2 3 4 5 6 7 8 9 10
	1 2 3 4 5 6 7 8 9 10	1 2 3 4 5 6 7 8 9 10	1 2 3 4 5 6 7 8 9 10
	1 2 3 4 5 6 7 8 9 10	1 2 3 4 5 6 7 8 9 10	1 2 3 4 5 6 7 8 9 10
	1 2 3 4 5 6 7 8 9 10	1 2 3 4 5 6 7 8 9 10	1 2 3 4 5 6 7 8 9 10
	1 2 3 4 5 6 7 8 9 10	1 2 3 4 5 6 7 8 9 10	1 2 3 4 5 6 7 8 9 10
	1 2 3 4 5 6 7 8 9 10	1 2 3 4 5 6 7 8 9 10	1 2 3 4 5 6 7 8 9 10
	1 2 3 4 5 6 7 8 9 10	1 2 3 4 5 6 7 8 9 10	1 2 3 4 5 6 7 8 9 10
	1 2 3 4 5 6 7 8 9 10	1 2 3 4 5 6 7 8 9 10	1 2 3 4 5 6 7 8 9 10
	1 2 3 4 5 6 7 8 9 10	1 2 3 4 5 6 7 8 9 10	1 2 3 4 5 6 7 8 9 10
	1 2 3 4 5 6 7 8 9 10	1 2 3 4 5 6 7 8 9 10	1 2 3 4 5 6 7 8 9 10
	1 2 3 4 5 6 7 8 9 10	1 2 3 4 5 6 7 8 9 10	1 2 3 4 5 6 7 8 9 10
	1 2 3 4 5 6 7 8 9 10	1 2 3 4 5 6 7 8 9 10	1 2 3 4 5 6 7 8 9 10
	1 2 3 4 5 6 7 8 9 10	1 2 3 4 5 6 7 8 9 10	1 2 3 4 5 6 7 8 9 10
	1 2 3 4 5 6 7 8 9 10	1 2 3 4 5 6 7 8 9 10	1 2 3 4 5 6 7 8 9 10
	1 2 3 4 5 6 7 8 9 10	1 2 3 4 5 6 7 8 9 10	1 2 3 4 5 6 7 8 9 10
	1 2 3 4 5 6 7 8 9 10	1 2 3 4 5 6 7 8 9 10	1 2 3 4 5 6 7 8 9 10
	1 2 3 4 5 6 7 8 9 10	1 2 3 4 5 6 7 8 9 10	1 2 3 4 5 6 7 8 9 10

Figure 1.1.2. *Number Recognition, Matching, and Writing Assessment*

Code System:

Use the following code system, or one of your own, to record anecdotal notes:

Key:

Math Time Lesson: # 1.1
ML: Mini-Lesson
GL: Group lesson
DL: Discovery lesson
B: Beginning understanding
D: Developing understanding
P: Proficient and is able to generalize and apply knowledge

Name: Abby

Date: **Lesson:** **GL:** *P, numbers 1–5; B, numbers 5–10* **DL**: *D, able to match symbols to same number of concrete models; unable to sequence concrete models*	Date: **Lesson:** **GL:** **DL:**	Date: **Lesson:** **GL:** **DL:**
Date: **Lesson:** GL: **DL:**	Date: **Lesson:** GL: **DL:**	Date: **Lesson:** GL: **DL:**

Figure 1.1.3. *Sample—Anecdotal Record*

Name: _____

Date: Lesson: GL: DL:	Date: Lesson: GL: DL:	Date: Lesson: GL: DL:
Date: Lesson: GL: DL:	Date: Lesson: GL: DL:	Date: Lesson: GL: DL:
Date: Lesson: GL: DL:	Date: Lesson: GL: DL:	Date: Lesson: GL: DL:

Figure 1.1.4. *Anecdotal Record*

Code System:

Use the following code system, or one of your own, to record anecdotal notes:

Key:

Math Time Lesson:
ML: Mini-Lesson
GL: Group lesson
DL: Discovery lesson
B: Beginning understanding
D: Developing understanding
P: Proficient and is able to generalize and apply knowledge

Name: Leo

Date: 9/6 Lesson: 1.2 GL: *P—sequences numbers in successive order to 12* *D—learning to sequence numbers in reverse order, not yet fluent, lost track of reverse order sequence and said the following: 12, 11, 12, self-corrected, then down to 11 again, several starts and restarts.* DL: *P—one-to-one correspondence with number card symbols and concrete objects*	Date: Lesson: GL: DL:	Date: Lesson: GL: DL:

Figure 1.1.5. *Sample—Anecdotal Record*

List of Numbers and Animals

Post the following list of numbers and animals on the chalkboard or on chart paper prior to the lesson.

1	frog	7	geese
2	ducks	8	monkeys
3	elephants	9	spiders
4	rabbits	10	snakes
5	bats	11	pigs
6	pelicans	12	whales

Group Assignments

Assign each student to work in one of the following four groups. Students will draw the number symbols and the corresponding number of animals for each section of the class mural.

Group 1 Draw 1 frog, 2 ducks, 3 elephants, 4 rabbits, 5 bats *(15 animals total)*

Group 2 Draw 6 pelicans, 7 geese, 8 monkeys *(21 animals total)*

Group 3 Draw 9 spiders, 10 snakes *(19 animals total)*

Group 4 Draw 11 pigs, 12 whales *(23 animals total)*

Figure 1.2.1. *List of Numbers, Animals, and Group Assignments*

Addends for the sum of 7, so that X + Y = 7

X	Y
0	7
1	6
2	5
3	4
4	3
5	2
6	1
7	0

Figure 1.3.1. *Sample—T-Table*

Name: _____   **Date:** _____

Addends for the sum of _____, so that X + Y = _____

X	Y

Figure 1.3.2. *T-Table*

Directions:

Roll the single die to color the fish subtraction picture. For example, if you roll a 3, find a problem that equals 3, such as 5 – 2 = ___. Then color in that section of the picture. Color only one section for each roll of the die. You may choose any colors you like. Keep rolling the die until you have colored every section.

7 – 1 = ___   8 – 2 = ___   6 – 0 = ___   9 – 3 = ___   6 – 1 = ___   7 – 2 = ___

10 – 5 = ___   5 – 0 = ___   5 – 1 = ___   6 – 2 = ___   8 – 4 = ___   4 – 0 = ___

4 – 1 = ___   5 – 2 = ___   6 – 3 = ___   3 – 0 = ___   3 – 1 = ___   4 – 2 = ___

5 – 3 = ___   2 – 0 = ___   2 – 1 = ___   1 – 0 = ___   3 – 2 = ___   4 – 3 = ___

Figure 1.4.1. *Fish Subtraction.* Illustration by Cherie Blackmore.

Directions: Color each animal, then cut on the dotted lines.

Oliver

Peggoty

Snake

Sheep

Rabbit

Pig

Goose

Figure 1.6.1. *Character Cards.* Illustration by Cherie Blackmore.

Name: _____

Name: _____

Directions: Use your character cards to help you figure out the answers, then write them in the blanks.

1. Give Oliver all the Skittles.

   Oliver has _____ Skittles.

2. Divide the Skittles between Oliver and Peggoty. Give each a fair share; if any are left over, put them aside.

   Oliver has _____ Skittles. Peggoty has _____ Skittles.

   There are _____ Skittles left over.

3. Divide the Skittles among Oliver, Peggoty, and the snake. Give each a fair share.

   Oliver has _____ Skittles. Peggoty has _____ Skittles.

   The snake has _____ Skittles. There are _____ Skittles left over.

4. Divide the Skittles evenly among Oliver, Peggoty, the snake, and the sheep.

   Oliver has _____ Skittles. Peggoty has _____ Skittles.

   The snake has _____ Skittles. The sheep has _____ Skittles.

   There are _____ Skittles left over.

5. Divide the Skittles evenly among Oliver, Peggoty, the snake, the sheep, and the rabbit.

   Oliver has _____ Skittles. Peggoty has _____ Skittles.

   The snake has _____ Skittles. The sheep has _____ Skittles.

   The rabbit has _____ Skittles. There are _____ Skittles left over.

6. Divide the Skittles evenly among Oliver, Peggoty, the snake, the sheep, the rabbit, and the pig.

   Oliver has _____ Skittles. Peggoty has _____ Skittles.

   The snake has _____ Skittles. The sheep has _____ Skittles.

   The rabbit has _____ Skittles. The pig has _____ Skittles.

   There are _____ Skittles left over.

Figure 1.6.2.—Continues

7. Divide the Skittles evenly among Oliver, Peggoty, the snake, the sheep, the rabbit, the pig, and the goose.

   Oliver has _____ Skittles. Peggoty has _____ Skittles.

   The snake has _____ Skittles. The sheep has _____ Skittles.

   The rabbit has _____ Skittles. The pig has _____ Skittles.

   The goose has _____ Skittles. There are _____ Skittles left over.

8. Now, divide the Skittles evenly among Oliver, Peggoty, the snake, the sheep, the rabbit, the pig, the goose, and YOU!

   Oliver has _____ Skittles. Peggoty has _____ Skittles.

   The snake has _____ Skittles. The sheep has _____ Skittles.

   The rabbit has _____ Skittles. The pig has _____ Skittles.

   The goose has _____ Skittles. YOU have _____ Skittles.

   There are _____ Skittles left over.

9. Good job! You may now eat or save the Skittles!

Figure 1.6.2. *Record Sheet, Dividing Shares*

Use the following checklist to assess student understanding of halves:

Name: _____ **Date:** _____

Labeled paper plate pizza showing two halves make one whole. _____ (1)

Demonstrated two halves equal one whole with at least three sets of manipulatives. _____ (3)

Total: _____ (4)

Beginning: 0–4; Developing: 2–4; Proficient: 4

Anecdotal notes:

_____

_____

_____

Name: _____ **Date:** _____

Labeled paper plate pizza showing two halves make one whole. _____ (1)

Demonstrated two halves equal one whole with at least three sets of manipulatives. _____ (3)

Total: _____ (4)

Beginning: 0–4; Developing: 2–4; Proficient: 4

Anecdotal notes:

_____

_____

_____

Name: _____ **Date:** _____

Labeled paper plate pizza showing two halves make one whole. _____ (1)

Demonstrated two halves equal one whole with at least three sets of manipulatives. _____ (3)

Total: _____ (4)

Beginning: 0–4; Developing: 2–4; Proficient: 4

Anecdotal notes:

_____

_____

_____

Figure 1.7.1. *Assessment, Halves and Wholes*

Chapter 2

Algebra

Dear Math Teacher,

What! Teach Algebra in primary school? Of course, yes! Primary students gain background knowledge for formal algebra when they repeat and predict patterns, create models and pictures, interpret symbols, and observe change in the world around them. The lessons in this chapter provide opportunities for students to repeat, predict, and create patterns. Students chant rhymes and stomp rhythms when you read Margaret Wise Brown's *Little Scarecrow Boy*. They observe growth and change when Scarecrow Boy finally triumphs over his pesky enemies, the crows. During the lesson inspired by *The Talking Cloth,* students interpret patterned symbols, and later, create their own symbols and patterns. After you read *The Teeny Tiny Teacher* by Stephanie Calmenson, students map and build a miniature town on grid lines. And, when you read *A String of Beads* by Margarette Reid, your students will classify, sort, mold, arrange, and string an assortment of beads.

Patterns and change are all around us,
Caroline

LESSON 1

Discover and Repeat Patterns

Brown, Margaret Wise. *The Little Scarecrow Boy.* New York: Joanna Cotler Books, HarperCollins, 1998.

Caldecott Medal recipient and illustrator David Diaz introduces a long-forgotten manuscript by Margaret Wise Brown, the beloved author of *Goodnight Moon. The Little Scarecrow Boy* has the same style, charm, and lyrical language that has made *Goodnight Moon* a classic among children's literature. *The Little Scarecrow Boy* is painted in the reds, oranges, and yellows of a summer cornfield. In this story, a scarecrow boy is anxious to grow up and frighten crows, just as his father does. The story is replete with patterns and repetitions in threes and sixes that children will enjoy reciting. And, what do you think? Yes, the scarecrow boy *does* grow up. He learns six fierce faces to frighten the crows away and surprises both the crows and his parents.

Time Frame

50 minutes

Materials

For the teacher:

Chart paper or chalkboard

Figure 2.1.1. *Assessment, Three-Element Pattern*

For each student:

Math journal

Pencil and crayons

Story and Mini-Lesson

1. **P**review the book by sharing the title, author, illustrator, and book cover.

2. Invite students to describe what is on the cover and to state their **p**redictions about what the book will be about.

3. Take a "picture walk" through the pages of the book.

4. **R**ead the story aloud and encourage students to chime in as they quickly learn the patterns of repetition, such as, "Oh, Oh, Oh!/Time to go!" and, "No/No little boy./You can't go./You're not fierce enough/ to scare a crow./Wait until you grow."

5. Invite student **r**esponse by having students imitate each one of the six terrible faces that Father Scarecrow teaches his son.

Group Lesson

1. Discuss, review, and repeat word patterns that students heard in the story.

2. Model how students can make word patterns in repetitions of threes, such as, "Yes, yes, yes!" and with a three-word phrase such as, "I will grow!" The entire chant could sound like this, "Yes, yes, yes!/I will grow."

3. Divide students into groups of three or six and invite them to work together to make up their own patterns and chants.

4. Have students practice repeating and clapping the chants in their groups.

5. Have all the groups return to the community center to perform their chants. Make sure every group has an opportunity to share at least one chant.

Discovery

Groups that finish creating and practicing chants more quickly than others may continue creating new chants.

Reflection

Have students write their chants and other chants they have learned in their math journals.

Assessment

Use **Figure 2.1.1. *Assessment, Three-Element Pattern*** to assess students' responses.

Special Needs Adaptations

Auditory disability: A sign language interpreter should interpret the book and the lesson. Encourage these students to draw, stomp, or act out patterns. These students should draw their own patterns or match patterns with dried ears of corn, magazine pictures, postcards, dominoes, or dice.

Motor disability: No adaptations needed.

Visual disability: These students may record chants into a tape recorder or dictate patterns to an aid, student partner, volunteer, or teacher. They could use cubes, stuffed animals, or varied-textured cloth to create patterns in groups of three.

English Language Learners: Have these students repeat the phrases used in the activities above in English and encourage them to make up their own patterned phrases in their native languages.

Extensions

- Have students create and write more rhythmic chants in their math journals.

- Ask students to draw a sequence of six pictures of scarecrows with different scary faces.

- Invite students to draw a sequence of three pictures of the Scarecrow Boy growing from big, to bigger, to biggest.

- Model for students how to write word problems that require completion of the third sequence in a set of three, such as:

  ✓ Hey, hey, _____! One fine _____.

  ✓ One, two, _____! Look at _____.

- Encourage students to identify and discuss the geometric patterns and shapes in *The Little Scarecrow Boy* such as triangles, squares, circles, rectangles, and ellipses (ovals).

- Have the students use *Kid Pix Deluxe* by Broderbund Software, Inc., to design and print patterns.

- Ask the students to make mosaic or patchwork scarecrows inspired by David Diaz's illustrations.

- Make a Little Scarecrow Boy and Girl class mural. Have the students design and repeat patterns across the mural.

- Have a scary face contest. Have the students act out scary faces or draw scary faces on paper plates. Arrange them in sequence from least scary to scariest.

- Do a problem-solving activity by asking children to divide themselves into groups of three or six.

- As a class, write and illustrate a Little Scarecrow Girl story.

Bibliography

Bartch, Marian R. *Math Stories*. Glenview, IL: Good Year Books, 1996.

Brown, Margaret Wise. *Another Important Book*. New York: HarperCollins, 1999.

London, Jonathan. *The Village Basket Weaver*. New York: Dutton Children's Books, 1996.

Mosel, Arlene. *Tikki Tikki Tembo*. New York: Henry Holt, 1995.

———. *Tikki Tikki Tembo,* Spanish ed. New York: Lectorum Publications, 2000.

Sloat, Teri. *There Was an Old Lady Who Swallowed a Trout*. New York: Henry Holt, 1998.

Smoothey, Marion. *Let's Investigate Number Patterns*. New York: Marshall Cavendish, 1993.

Taback, Simms. *There Was an Old Lady Who Swallowed a Fly*. New York: Viking Children's Books, 1997.

Tafuri, Nancy. *Snowy, Flowy, Blowy*. New York: Scholastic, 1999.

Software

Broderbund Software, Inc. 1998. *Kid Pix Deluxe*. Macintosh and Windows.

Related Standards 2000

Standard 1: Number and Operations

Standard 3: Geometry

Standard 4: Measurement

Standard 6: Problem Solving

Standard 8: Communication

Standard 9: Connections

Standard 10: Representation

Related Standards 1989

Standard 1: Mathematics as Problem Solving

Standard 2: Mathematics as Communication

Standard 3: Mathematics as Reasoning

Standard 4: Mathematical Connections

Standard 6: Number Sense and Numeration

Standard 9: Geometry and Spatial Sense

Standard 10: Measurement

LESSON 2

Create Symbols and Patterns

Mitchell, Rhonda. *The Talking Cloth.* New York: Orchard, 1997.

Amber's Aunt Phoebe is a collector of "things" from Africa. During a visit to Aunt Phoebe's house, Amber learns about her Ashanti ancestors through her aunt's collection. Of particular interest to Amber is a "Talking Cloth," which "speaks" of the wearer's feelings by its colors and symbols. Many patterned designs decorate the "Talking Cloth," as well as the pages of the book.

Time Frame

Day One: 50 minutes

Day Two: 50 minutes

Materials:

➤ Day One:

For the teacher:

Set up printmaking workstations to accommodate four students each. Cover each workstation with newsprint to protect table surfaces. Each workstation should include:

> Four or more printmaking tools, such as *egg carton bottoms, jar lids, pieces of cut sponge, forks, pieces of rope, perforated spice jar lids,* and *toothbrushes*

> One color (black, blue, yellow, or green) of tempera paint in a paint pan

> Two 1-inch paintbrushes for painting the printmaking tools

> Several sheets of chart or scrap paper (at least one sheet per student)

Set up one separate workstation for potato carving. This workstation should have:

> One pre-carved potato as a model

> Ten or more pre-cut potatoes (both ends cut so the potatoes are easy to handle)

> Carving tools such as spoons, forks, bottle openers, potato peelers, and paper clips

For each student:

Paint shirt

➤ Day Two:

One week prior to this lesson, send parents **Figure 2.2.1. *Letter Home and Wish List*** to enlist their support and to gather materials and tools for this project. Plan to provide the paint and brushes from school supplies.

Make your own *Talking Cloth* T-shirts! Have students create their own designs and patterns on scrap paper as in Day One. Then, on Day Two, use T-shirts (cotton preferable) and *fabric paint*, rather than scrap cloth and acrylic paint. You will also need cardboard sections (approximately 9 by 9 inches each) to stuff inside the T-shirts to keep the shirts from wrinkling and to keep paint from bleeding through to the back of the shirts.

For the teacher:

Set up printmaking workstations as in Day One. (There is no need to set up the potato carving workstation.) This time, use blue, yellow, and green *acrylic paint* rather than tempera paint. Use strips of cloth or cut-up sheets and pillowcases rather than chart or scrap paper. Make a list on the chalkboard with the following colors and symbols from *The Talking Cloth*:

Blue = love

Yellow = wealth

Green = newness, growth

White = joy

For each student:

Paint shirt

Use fabric with *all* or at least *some* cotton content because cotton *absorbs* rather than *repels* paint.

Story and Mini-Lesson: Day One

1. **P**review, **p**redict, **r**ead, and **r**eview *The Talking Cloth*.

2. After you **p**review the book with students, ask them to **p**redict which math concept they will be studying *(patterns)*.

3. As you **r**ead the story, invite students to be ready to raise their hands when they see a pattern.

4. Call on children to describe the patterns they see.

5. Stop reading after the twenty-second page.

The pages of the book are not numbered, so mark this page with a sticky note prior to reading the story to your students. On this page, Amber and Aunt Phoebe imagine the patterned cloth Amber's little brother and her daddy would wear.

6. The colors of the cloth symbolize the following:

    Blue = love

    Yellow/gold = wealth

    Green = newness, growth

    White = joy

7. Discuss why Amber and Aunt Phoebe chose the colors and patterns they did for Little Brother and for Daddy. For example, Little Brother could wear the green cloth for newness and growth, and the handprints might represent how his hands are always into things. Daddy might wear black lines and squares on gray because Amber and Aunt Phoebe tease him for being kind of a square.

8. Ask students to close their eyes and imagine the color and pattern *they* would choose to design or wear. Encourage students to share their ideas.

9. Finish reading *The Talking Cloth.* Connect the story to the lesson by telling students they will make their own "talking cloth" patterns. Today they will experiment with making and stamping designs onto paper. Then, on Day Two, they will choose favorite designs and colors to print patterns onto cloth.

Group Lesson: Day One

1. Demonstrate how to carve a design into a pre-cut potato. Use the bottle opener to carve lines or notches, and a potato peeler to carve holes or circles, in the potato.

2. Show students how to paint the bottom of the carved potato. Then demonstrate how to stamp potato print patterns onto scrap paper.

3. Show students the other printmaking tools, such as the egg carton bottoms, jar lids, pieces of cut sponge, forks, pieces of rope, perforated spice jar lids, and toothbrushes. Paint the bottom of one of these printmaking items, then model how to stamp it onto scrap paper to make a pattern. Repeat this several times to make repeated patterns.

4. Allow students to experiment with printmaking tools and practice making their own designs and patterns on paper.

Discovery: Day One

Have students wear paint shirts. Position one group of four students at the potato carving workstation, where they will choose a tool to carve a design in a potato bottom. Position the rest of the students at the printmaking workstations. There, they will experiment with printmaking tools and with pattern making. Tell students you would like them to be bold and to experiment with many different tools and patterns. Periodically switch the potato-carving group with a printmaking group so all students participate in both potato carving and printmaking. Circulate throughout the room to support and encourage students' work.

Allow time for students to clean up their workstations before reflecting about printmaking.

Reflection: Day One

Gather students together to show and talk about their patterns. Conclude this lesson by telling students to save today's printmaking papers. They must choose one or two of their own favorite patterns from today's work to repeat during tomorrow's project.

Story and Mini-Lesson: Day Two

1. **R**eview and reread *The Talking Cloth.* Encourage students to notice patterns they did not notice on Day One.

2. When you have finished reading *The Talking Cloth*, discuss new patterns students noticed during this reading of the book.

3. **R**eview and discuss the printmaking techniques learned from Day One. Point out effective printmaking strategies that you observed children using.

4. Refer to the posted list of colors and symbols from *The Talking Cloth*. Tell students to decide on one or two colors of paint to use to symbolize their own mood or message.

5. Ask students to refer to their printmaking papers from Day One and to circle their two or three favorite patterns with a pencil or marker. Students will use these patterns as a reference when they print their "talking cloths." Now it is time to make "talking cloth" patterns.

Discovery: Day Two

Have students put on paint shirts before working at the printmaking stations. Have each student print his or her own design on a section of fabric or a T-shirt to make a personal "talking cloth." Circulate throughout the room and support students as needed.

Direct students to clean up before they meet for the reflection activity.

Reflection: Day Two

Gather students together to observe and enjoy each other's "talking cloths." Invite students to tell what their cloths say about themselves. Share and discuss. Let the cloths dry, then piece them together on a bulletin board. If students have made T-shirts, they may wear them proudly after the paint has dried.

Assessment: Day Two

When you circulate throughout the room, check that students make repeated patterns rather than random designs. Write notes in **Figure 1.1.4. *Anecdotal Record*** (found at the end of chapter 1).

Special Needs Adaptations

Auditory disability: An interpreter should sign the book and the lesson. Have demonstration samples available for students to see while they work on the group activity. Provide simple step-by-step instructions on the chalkboard. Display *The Talking Cloth* and open to pages showing cloth patterns.

Motor disability: Provide an aid or buddy to assist students with motor impairments during the Group activity.

Visual disability: Have samples of textured and patterned cloth available for these students to explore tactilely as you read the story aloud. Visually impaired students could make an auditory message with a rhythmic or "talking beat" rather than do the patterned cloth project. These students may record verbal patterns into a tape recorder or dictate patterns to an aide, student partner, volunteer, or teacher.

English Language Learners: Check for understanding. Have students partner with a bilingual buddy.

Extensions

- Invite a speaker from Africa, or one who has visited Africa, to share patterned designs from native artwork.

- Invite musicians who play percussion instruments to play repeated rhythmic beats.

- Have students make percussion instruments out of recyclable materials and make up and play rhythmic patterns.

- Set up a center in the room where students can experiment with making patterns on scrap paper. Make "talking cloth" wrapping paper.

Bibliography

Buckley, Richard. *The Foolish Tortoise*. New York: Little Simon, 1998.

Carle, Eric. *Pancakes, Pancakes*. New York: Aladdin, 1998.

Jonas, Ann. *Bird Talk*. New York: Greenwillow, 1999.

Martin, Bill, Jr. *Polar Bear, Polar Bear*. New York: Houghton Mifflin, 1991.

Murphy, Stuart J. *Beep Beep, Vroom Vroom!* New York: HarperCollins, 2000.

Raschka, Chris. *Like, Likes, Like*. New York: DK Publishing, 1999.

Schwartz, Amy. *Old MacDonald*. New York: Scholastic, 1999.

Related Standards 2000

Standard 1: Number and Operations
Standard 3: Geometry
Standard 6: Problem Solving
Standard 8: Communication
Standard 9: Connections
Standard 10: Representation

Related Standards 1989

Standard 1: Mathematics as Problem Solving
Standard 2: Mathematics as Communication
Standard 3: Mathematics as Reasoning
Standard 4: Mathematical Connections
Standard 5: Estimation
Standard 6: Number Sense and Numeration
Standard 9: Geometry and Spatial Sense

LESSON 3

Design and Build a Town

Calmenson, Stephanie. *The Teeny Tiny Teacher.* New York: Scholastic, 1998.

This story is based on an English folktale in which a teeny tiny woman discovers and takes home a teeny tiny bone. The owner then comes to retrieve its bone. In this new version, the teeny tiny woman is a schoolteacher who collects a bone while taking her class on a walk. Students will enjoy this teeny tiny spooky ghost story.

If you cannot find *The Teeny Tiny Teacher*, you may substitute the following books for this lesson:

Galdone, Paul. *The Teeny Tiny Woman, a Ghost Story*. New York: Houghton Mifflin, 1993.

Robins, Arthur. *The Teeny Tiny Woman: A Traditional Tale*. New York: Candlewick, 1998.

Winters, Kay. *The Teeny Tiny Ghost*. New York: Harper-Collins, 1999.

Time Frame

Day One: 50 minutes

Days Two, Three, and Four: 50 minutes each; build a Tiny Town

Materials

Prior to the lesson, send home **Figure 2.3.1. *Letter to Parents***

➤ **Day One**

For the teacher:

Transparency of **Figure 2.3.2. *Sample—Words That Describe Size***

Transparency of **Figure 2.3.3. *Sample—Pattern Story***

Transparency of **Figure 2.3.4. *My Pattern Story***

Figure 2.3.5. *Assessment, Pattern Story*

Transparency of **Figure 2.3.6. *Words That Describe Size***

Overhead projector and screen

For each student:

Copy of **Figure 2.3.6. *Words That Describe Size***

Copy of **Figure 2.3.4. *My Pattern Story***

➤ **Days Two, Three, and Four**

For the teacher:

Figure 2.3.7. *Sample—Grid Pattern*

Large rectangular or square table for project display

Large sheet of chart paper marked with grid, **Figure 2.3.7.,** to cover the table

Figure 2.3.8. *Sample—Tiny Town Grid Assignments*

Figure 2.3.9. *Tiny Town Grid Assignments*

Pencils, paints, paint trays, and paintbrushes

For each student:

Material brought from home, including:

- ✓ Boxes of various sizes and shapes

- ✓ Various manipulatives, including chess pieces, erasers, pennies, paints, used postage stamps, dominoes, dice, or Scrabble letters

- ✓ One small plastic figurine (Lego type or other) representing the student

Story and Mini-Lesson: Day One

1. **Preview.** Ask students to notice the objects in the book that make the teeny tiny school and town, for example: an eraser as a doorstep, a spool of thread for jumping rope, a Lincoln penny symbol for Lincoln School, and Scrabble pieces for stepping stones. Ask students how they know that the people in this story are teeny tiny. They might answer that the blades of grass are like trees, the dominoes are used for students' desks, and a postage stamp is a poster on the wall.

2. **Predict** the teeny tiny things the students might find on a walk.

3. **Read** the story. Tell students they will get a chance to participate by chiming in with the words, "teeny tiny ___" each time you read them.

4. When you reach the pages where the ghost says, "Give me my bone!" have students say this in a spooky whisper. As you read the following pages, have the students make their voices increasingly louder (crescendo). When the teeny tiny teacher has had enough, you will say in a very loud voice, "Take it!"

5. **R**eview and discuss. When you finish reading the story, ask students if they noticed any patterns or "teeny tiny" repetitions.

Group Lesson: Day One

1. Ask students to tell you the pattern words that described the teacher (*teeny* and *tiny*).

2. Use a transparency of **Figure 2.3.2. Sample—Words That Describe Size** on the overhead projector.

3. Students can complete their copy of **Figure 2.3.6. Words That Describe Size**.

4. Show a transparency of **Figure 2.3.3. Sample—Pattern Story** to give an example of a completed pattern story.

5. Then show a transparency of **Figure 2.3.4. My Pattern Story.** Model how to complete the story by doing the following:

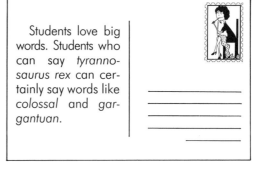

> ✓ Choose a character together.

> ✓ Choose describing words from **Figure 2.3.2. Sample—Words That Describe Size.**

> ✓ Call on students to help you fill in the pattern story.

6. When you have completed the transparency of **Figure 2.3.4. My Pattern Story** together, tell students they will write their own pattern stories. They must choose a character or animal first, then choose two describing words from one column of their completed list in **Figure 2.3.6. Words That Describe Size.**

Reflection: Day One

When students have completed their pattern stories, have them gather together to share them. Post pattern stories on a bulletin board for all to admire.

Assessment: Day One

Use **Figure 2.3.5. Assessment, Pattern Story** to evaluate students' completed copies of **Figure 2.3.4. My Pattern Story.**

Story and Mini-Lesson:
Days Two, Three, and Four, Build a Tiny Town

1. **R**ead and **r**eview the *Teeny Tiny Teacher.* Encourage students to chime in again as you read.

2. **R**eview patterns students hear in the story.

3. Introduce a new pattern, **Figure 2.3.7. Sample—Grid Pattern.**

4. Discuss the grid. Ask students what they notice about the pattern of lines.

5. Model how to find specific locations on the grid, for example, "Find and point to B-3."

6. Have students practice and quiz each other on reading the grid.

Group Lesson:
Days Two, Three, and Four, Build a Tiny Town

1. Tell students they will make a teeny tiny town with the objects and manipulatives they brought from home.

2. Explain that many towns and cities are set up in a grid pattern.

3. Brainstorm what buildings, parks, roads, and houses your tiny town needs. List these suggestions on chart paper. Discuss how students would make buildings and houses; for example, a milk carton could be a house.

4. Decide collectively where to place the buildings on the grid. Use **Figure 2.3.7. Sample—Grid Pattern** to record this information. Encourage students to use grid terminology by saying, "We will put our school on C-4."

5. Discuss and complete **Figure 2.3.9. Tiny Town Grid Assignments.** (See **Figure 2.3 8. Sample—Tiny Town Grid Assignments** for your own reference.)

6. Have students work with partners or independently on their building assignment for the tiny town.

7. Once the students have completed the buildings, each student will place his or her building on the chart paper grid on the assigned location. Students can refer to **Figure 2.3.9. Tiny Town Grid Assignments** to determine their buildings' placement.

Discovery:
Days Two, Three, and Four, Build a Tiny Town

When the building assignments are completed and have been placed on the correct grid location, each student may then place his or her figurine on a free space on the town site.

Reflection:
Days Two, Three, and Four, Build a Tiny Town

Display, share, and admire building projects. Discuss whether your tiny town would be a good design for people to live in. Talk about your own town. Was it designed with a grid pattern? Do you know any grid pattern towns? Discuss the advantages and disadvantages of a grid pattern town.

Assessment:
Days Two, Three, and Four, Build a Tiny Town

Check that building projects are completed and placed correctly on the grid.

Special Needs Adaptations

Auditory disability: An interpreter should sign the book and the lesson.

Motor disability: A partner or volunteer may assist students with motor impairments.

Visual disability: Have these students partner with other students and record responses into a tape recorder. Add string to the grid lines so these students can locate where to place their buildings on the tiny town grid.

English Language Learners: Check for understanding. Have these students partner with a bilingual buddy. These students could generate a list of words that describe size (see **Figure 2.3.6.**) in their native languages.

Extensions

- Continue working on the tiny town as class time allows.

- Have students locate maps of their home towns to practice map skills. Have them compare and contrast the design of the tiny town with their home towns.

- Ask students to continue to identify and chart the locations of new buildings or structures added to the grid.

- Have students use a grid pattern to develop new maps of their classroom, town, bedrooms, or neighborhoods.

- Explore the *Neighborhood MapMachine* software program. Students can follow cardinal directions and travel through towns along gridlines as well as along crooked roads and curvy paths.

- Readers and writers can find and write more pattern stories based on patterns similar to that of the *Teeny Tiny Teacher*.

Bibliography

Sloat, Teri. *There Was an Old Lady Who Swallowed a Trout*. New York: Henry Holt, 1998.

Taback, Simms. *There Was an Old Lady Who Swallowed a Fly*. New York: Viking Children' Books, 1997.

Software

Tom Snyder Productions. 1997. *Neighborhood MapMachine*. Version 1.22. Macintosh and Windows 95, www.tomsnyder.com. (Accessed February 2001).

Related Standards 2000

Standard 1: Number and Operations

Standard 3: Geometry

Standard 4: Measurement

Standard 6: Problem Solving

Standard 8: Communication

Standard 9: Connections

Standard 10: Representation

Related Standards 1989

Standard 1: Mathematics as Problem Solving

Standard 2: Mathematics as Communication

Standard 4: Mathematical Connections

Standard 5: Estimation

Standard 6: Number Sense and Numeration

Standard 9: Geometry and Spatial Sense

Standard 10: Measurement

LESSON 4

Classify and Sort Beads; Model and String Bead Necklaces

Reid, Margarette S. *A String of Beads.* New York: E. P. Dutton, 1997.

"We're beaders Grandma and I." So begins this story told by a young child about the craft she and her grandmother share. Together they collect, sort, and make their own beads. Beads dance gaily across the pages of this book in a multitude of patterns of colors, shapes, and sizes. After reading *A String of Beads*, you and your students will want to become beaders, too.

Time Frame

Day One: 50 minutes, classifying and sorting beads

Day Two: 50 minutes, making beads

Day Three: 50 minutes, stringing beads in patterns

For a substitute activity, you could omit Day Two, making beads, and skip to Day Three to string patterned necklaces with Cheerios, Fruit Loops, or pasta.

Materials

➢ **Day One**

For the teacher:

Chart paper or chalkboard

Transparency of **Figure 2.4.1. Sorting Mat**

Overhead projector and screen

Figure 2.4.2. Assessment, Anecdotal Notes

For each student:

One or two handfuls of beads to classify and sort

Copy of **Figure 2.4.1. Sorting Mat**

➢ **Day Two**

For the teacher:

Bamboo skewers to poke holes through beads

One or two parent volunteers to help with bead making (optional)

Baking tray for baking Sculpey

Conventional oven for baking Sculpey (follow directions on package)

For each student:

1 ounce Sculpey (variety of colors)

Scoring tools such as toothpicks or pencils

1 paper plate

Sculpey comes in individual 2 oz. packets. Unwrap each packet and cut the Sculpey into eighths. Sort by color, then have each student take four cubes of Sculpey in colors they choose.	

➢ **Day Three**

For the teacher:

One sample patterned, beaded necklace (illustrations from *A String of Beads* will suffice)

A parent or older student helper to assist in stringing beads and tying necklaces

Figure 2.4.3. Assessment, Patterns with Beads

For each student:

Handful of beads made during Day Two, or cheerios, fruit loops, or pasta

One length of string, quilting thread, or nylon cord, 33 inches long

One blunt-ended needle for stringing beads

Story and Mini-Lesson: Day One

1. **P**review the book. Encourage students to comment about the colors, shapes, and sizes of the beads.

2. **P**redict. Ask, "What do you think this book will be about?"

3. **R**ead the story aloud to students.

4. **R**eview the story by asking students, "Who likes to sort, string, and make beads?" They may answer, "Beaders," "The girl and her grandmother," "I do," "Native Americans," "Egyptians," "Ancient peoples," or "Everyone."

5. Ask how beaders sort their beads. Make a list of students' responses on chart paper or on a chalkboard. Your list should look something like this:

   Size
   Color
   Shape
   Nationality (Native American, Egyptian, African)
   Plastic
   Animal, vegetable, or mineral
   Shell
   Pasta

Group Lesson: Day One

1. Tell students they will get a chance to examine, classify, and sort beads. Show them a transparency of **Figure 2.4.1. Sorting Mat**. Ask, "If I wanted to sort these beads by size, what should I do?" Your students will probably decide that you should use one circle for big beads, one for medium-sized beads, and one for small beads. Sort the beads accordingly.

2. Ask students to direct you in sorting the same beads by shape. They will probably choose to put round beads in one circle, square beads in another, and cylindrical beads or "other" in the last circle.

3. As you do this together, monitor students' answers for understanding.

Discovery: Day One

1. Invite students to sort their own beads.

2. Distribute beads and copies of **Figure 2.4.1. Sorting Mat.**

3. Students must choose at least three ways to sort their beads.

4. Encourage students to sort beads in as many ways as they can think of. Have the student-generated sorting list visible (from **r**eview above) as a reminder to students of the many ways to sort beads.

Reflection: Day One

Take time before cleaning up materials to have students walk around the room and observe the ways others sorted their beads. Encourage students to tell about their sorting methods.

Assessment: Day One

Circulate throughout the room while students sort beads. Make anecdotal records about students' work. Use **Figure 2.4.2. *Assessment, Anecdotal Notes.***

Story and Mini-Lesson: Day Two

1. **R**eview *A String of Beads.*

2. **R**eview the different ways students sorted beads on the previous day.

3. Tell students that today they will make their own beads.

Introduce the lesson as directed, but be sure to plan at least 30 minutes for bead making.

Group Lesson: Day Two

1. Show students the bead-making material.

2. Model various ways of rolling, twisting, cubing, flattening, and scoring beads.

3. Demonstrate appropriate use of the bamboo skewers and how to poke a hole through a bead.

4. Instruct students to make *pairs* of beads that match in size, color, or shape.

5. Tell them the beads will be used to make patterned necklaces on the following day.

6. Distribute materials.

Discovery: Day Two

1. Have students use the paper plates as work mats.

2. Allow at least 30 minutes for students to shape, score, and poke holes in their beads.

3. When students have completed their beads, have them write their names on their paper plates and line up their beads on the bamboo skewers. This will help you keep track of each student's beads when you put them in the oven.

To bake the beads, follow the directions on the Sculpey package. To keep students' beads separate, take the beaded skewers off the paper plates and line them up on the baking sheet. Pile the paper plates in sequential order so that you can return the skewers to the appropriate plates when you take them out of the oven.

Reflection: Day Two

Allow students to walk around the room to admire each other's handiwork.

Assessment: Day Two

Check that students made beads in matching pairs.

Story and Mini-Lesson: Day Three

1. Take a "picture walk" through *A String of Beads* and pause to identify patterned necklaces.

2. Re-read the nineteenth page (the pages are not numbered), which shows the child stringing an assortment of beads.

3. Ask students to recall useful information from the child's instructions, such as, "Start with a big bead in the center" and, "On either side match and march beads, two by two."

4. Remind students that they must be able to show a pattern when their necklaces are complete.

5. Demonstrate bead stringing and tying. (Ask a parent or older student helper to assist in threading needles and tying off beads.)

6. Distribute materials.

Discovery: Day Three

Have the students string beads in patterns and tie them off.

Reflection: Day Three

Let the students sport their new patterned-bead apparel.

Assessment: Day Three

Have students identify the patterns on each other's bead necklaces. Use **Figure 2.4.3.** *Assessment, Patterns with Beads*.

Special Needs Adaptations

Auditory disability: An interpreter should sign the book and the lesson.

Motor disability: A partner or volunteer may assist students with bead making, stringing, and tying off.

Visual disability: A partner or volunteer may assist students with bead making, stringing, and tying off. Encourage these students to verbalize their sorting methods. Have a parent or volunteer read the story into an audiotape so these students may hear repeated readings.

English Language Learners: Check for understanding. Have these students partner with other students. Allow these students time to read and re-read the story onto an audiotape.

Extensions

- Invite a Native American bead maker to your class as a special guest to share beadwork and tell about the history and uses of beads in Native American societies.

- Use the last two pages of *A String of Beads*, entitled, *"Here is more information about beads,"* as a springboard for research projects regarding the history and origin of beads.

- Show how an abacus is used as a calculator. Make a shoebox abacus. Refer to pages 42–45 in *Math Art* by Carolyn Ford Brunetto to learn how to construct one.

- Have a "Barter and Trade Day." Students purchase crafts and items made by other students with beads as "wampum" or money.

Bibliography

Brunetto, Carolyn Ford. *Math Art.* New York: Scholastic, 1997.

Conner, Wendy Simpson. *The Children's Beading Book.* New York: Interstellar, 1998.

Gibbons, Gail. *Tool Book.* New York: Holiday House, 1988.

MacDonald, Sharon. *Squish, Sort, Paint and Build.* New York: Griffon House, 1996.

McGrath, Barbara Barbieri. *Cheerios Counting Book.* New York: Scholastic, 2000.

———. *M&M's Brand Chocolate Candies Counting Book.* New York: Charlesbridge, 1996.

Pluckrose, Henry Arthur. *Sorting.* New York: Children's Press, 1995.

Ryan, Pam Munoz. *The Crayon Counting Book.* New York: Charlesbridge, 1996.

Schreiber, Anne. *Shoes, Shoes, Shoes.* New York: Millbrook Press, 1998.

Shannon, David. *A Bad Case of Stripes.* New York: Scholastic, 1998.

Winthrop, Elizabeth. *Shoes.* New York: HarperCollins, 1999.

Related Standards 2000

Standard 1: Number and Operations

Standard 3: Geometry

Standard 4: Measurement

Standard 6: Problem Solving

Standard 8: Communication

Standard 9: Connections

Standard 10: Representation

Related Standards 1989

Standard   1: Mathematics as Problem Solving

Standard   2: Mathematics as Communication

Standard   3: Mathematics as Reasoning

Standard   4: Mathematical Connections

Standard   5: Estimation

Standard   6: Number Sense and Numeration

Standard   9: Geometry and Spatial Sense

Standard 10: Measurement

Assess the oral or written responses to the *Little Scarecrow Boy* activity with the following rubrics and suggested scoring system:

Name: _____**Date:** _____

1. Repeats a three-word repetition and a three-word phrase.   _____ (1)

2. Matches word patterns with rhythmic hand clapping.   _____ (1)

3. Completed a word pattern or chant in his or her math journal.   _____ (1)

4. Completed additional word patterns, or picture patterns.   _____ (1)

Total: _____ (4)

Beginning: 0–1; Developing: 2–3; Proficient: 4

Anecdotal notes:

_____

_____

_____

Name: _____**Date:** _____

1. Repeats a three-word repetition and a three-word phrase.   _____ (1)

2. Matches word patterns with rhythmic hand clapping.   _____ (1)

3. Completed a word pattern or chant in his or her math journal.   _____ (1)

4. Completed additional word patterns, or picture patterns.   _____ (1)

Total: _____ (4)

Beginning: 0–1; Developing: 2–3; Proficient: 4

Anecdotal notes:

_____

_____

_____

Figure 2.1.1. *Assessment, Three-Element Pattern*

Dear Parents,

Next week during math, we will read *The Talking Cloth* by Rhonda Mitchell. This is a story about the Ashanti people, who printed patterned designs on cloth to represent their history. Students will notice the many patterns illustrated in the book and then will print their own patterned designs on paper and cloth.

We need volunteers to help with this project on (___date___) at (___time___) and on (___date___) at (___time___). Please contact me at (___phone number___) if you will be able to help.

In addition, we need several items and tools. Together with your child, please do a treasure hunt in your home to find *at least one* item from the list below:

Old, solid-colored cotton sheets or pillowcases to cut up

Newspapers to reuse

Printmaking tools such as egg carton bottoms, jar lids, pieces of cut sponge, forks, pieces of rope, perforated spice jar lids, and toothbrushes

One potato

Carving tools such as spoons, forks, bottle openers, and potato peelers

One old shirt to wear while painting

Please have your child bring item(s) to school by (___date___).

Thanks for your help,

Figure 2.2.1. *Letter Home and Wish List*

Dear Parents,

Next week our class will build a miniature town, inspired by the book, *The Teeny Tiny Teacher* by Stephanie Calmenson. As we build our town, we will learn about grid patterns, how to locate and fix places on a grid, and about mapping. Please help your child find several of the items listed below:

Small boxes, assorted shapes

Odds and ends such as erasers, pennies, toothpicks, orphan chess or game pieces, used postage stamps, dominoes, dice, or Scrabble letters

One small figurine (Lego type or similar) to represent your child.

Please send these materials to school on _____.

Thanks for your help. Please stop in and see our Tiny Town on _____.

Sincerely,

Figure 2.3.1. *Letter to Parents*

Small	Medium	Large
Teeny	Average	Big
Tiny	Ordinary	Enormous
Miniature	Standard	Colossal
Petite	Regular	Gigantic
Minute	Usual	Huge
Infinitesimal	Moderate	Immense
Miniscule		Massive
Little		Gargantuan
		Titanic

Figure 2.3.2. *Sample—Words That Describe Size*

Once there was a <u>massive, monstrous monster</u> who lived in a <u>massive, monstrous marsh</u>. One morning, she decided to take a <u>massive, monstrous march</u>. On the <u>massive, monstrous march,</u> she found a <u>massive, monstrous mushroom.</u> She decided to take it home and put it in a pot. Then she took a nap.

During her nap she heard a <u>massive, monstrous moan,</u> "Give me back my mushroom."

The <u>massive, monstrous, monster</u> thought the moan was a dream, so she kept napping.

Next, she heard a more <u>massive, monstrous moan,</u> "Give me back my mushroom."

She threw mud on her head and went back to sleep.

Then she heard an *even* more <u>massive, monstrous moan,</u> "Give me back my mushroom!"

So, the <u>massive, monstrous monster</u> said in her most <u>massive, monstrous</u> roar, "Take it!"

Figure 2.3.3. *Sample—Pattern Story*

_____'s pattern story
Name

Once there was a _____, _____ _____ who lived in a

_____, _____ _____. One morning, she decided to take a

_____, _____ walk. On the, _____, _____ walk she

found a _____, _____ bone. She decided to take it home

and put it in a pot. Then she took a nap. During her nap she

heard a _____, _____ moan, "Give me back my bone."

The _____, _____ _____ thought the moan was a

dream, so she kept napping.

Next, she heard a more _____, _____ moan, "Give me

back my bone."

She threw mud on her head and went back to sleep.

Then she heard an even more, _____, _____ moan,

"Give me back my bone!"

So, the _____, _____ _____ said in her most

_____, _____ roar, "Take it!"

Figure 2.3.4. *My Pattern Story*

Name: _____ **Date:** _____

Did the student choose a character or animal for his or her story?   _____ (1)

Did the student use two words that describe size?   _____ (1)

Did the student choose the describing words from only one column?
*This is critical because if a student chooses one from one column and
one from another, the description of the character's size would be contradictory, such as a little huge dinosaur.*   _____ (1)

Did the student complete his or her pattern story?   _____ (1)

Did the student repeat the chosen pattern throughout the story?   _____ (1)

Total: _____ (5)

Beginning: 0–1; Developing: 2–4; Proficient: 5

Anecdotal notes:

_____

_____

_____

Name: _____ **Date:** _____

Did the student choose a character or animal for his or her story?   _____ (1)

Did the student use two words that describe size?   _____ (1)

Did the student choose the describing words from only one column?
*This is critical because if a student chooses one from one column and
one from another, the description of the character's size would be
contradictory, such as a little huge dinosaur.*   _____ (1)

Did the student complete his or her pattern story?   _____ (1)

Did the student repeat the chosen pattern throughout the story?   _____ (1)

Total: _____ (5)

Beginning: 0–1; Developing: 2–4; Proficient: 5

Anecdotal notes:

_____

_____

_____

_____

Figure 2.3.5. *Assessment, Pattern Story*

Small	Medium	Large

Figure 2.3.6. *Words That Describe Size*

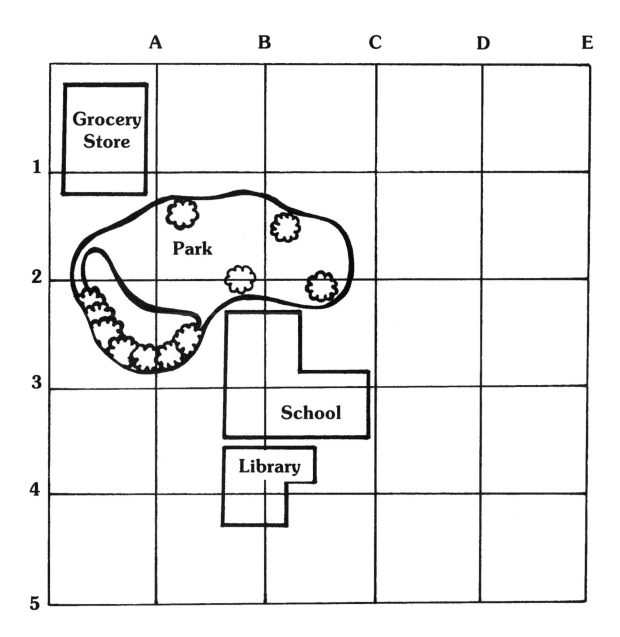

Figure 2.3.7. *Sample—Grid Pattern*

Building	Builder/s	Location
School	Latisha and Brent	B-3
Library	Landon	B-4
Park	Ashley, Roberto	A-2, B-2
Grocery Store	Diego	A-1

Figure 2.3 8. *Sample—Tiny Town Grid Assignments*

Building	Builder/s	Location

Figure 2.3.9. *Tiny Town Grid Assignments*

Figure 2.4.1. *Sorting Mat*

Use a code system like the following to minimize notetaking time:

Key:

 ML: Mini-Lesson
 DL: Discovery
 R: Reflection
 B: Beginning understanding (1)
 D: Developing understanding (2)
 P: Proficient (3)

Name: _____ **Date:** _____

ML: ____

DL: ____

R: ____

Additional Notes:

_____
_____
_____

Use a code system like the following to minimize notetaking time:

Key:

 ML: Mini-Lesson
 DL: Discovery
 R: Reflection
 B: Beginning understanding (1)
 D: Developing understanding (2)
 P: Proficient (3)

Name: _____ **Date:** _____

ML: ____

DL: ____

R: ____

Additional Notes:

_____
_____
_____

Figure 2.4.2. *Assessment, Anecdotal Notes*

Use a code system like the following to minimize notetaking time:

Key:

ML: Mini-Lesson
DL: Discovery
R: Reflection
B: Beginning understanding (1)
D: Developing understanding (2)
P: Proficient (3)

Name: _____   **Date:** _____

Strings beads in matching pairs.   _____ (1)

Strings beads in an identifiable pattern.   _____ (1)

Able to repeat the pattern aloud.   _____ (1)

Total score: _____ (3)

Anecdotal notes:

_____
_____
_____

Use a code system like the following to minimize notetaking time:

Key:

ML: Mini-Lesson
DL: Discovery
R: Reflection
B: Beginning understanding (1)
D: Developing understanding (2)
P: Proficient (3)

Name: _____   **Date:** _____

Strings beads in matching pairs.   _____ (1)

Strings beads in an identifiable pattern.   _____ (1)

Able to repeat the pattern aloud.   _____ (1)

Total score: _____ (3)

Anecdotal notes:

_____
_____
_____

Figure 2.4.3. Assessment, Patterns with Beads

Chapter 3

Geometry

Dear Math Teacher,

In this chapter, students learn about geometric shapes and structures in their world. Students will notice, describe, draw, classify, sort, and construct two- and three-dimensional shapes. In the first lesson, *When a Line Bends . . . A Shape Begins,* students learn to recognize and identify two-dimensional geometric shapes, then search for these shapes in their environment. In the second lesson, *Bear in a Square,* students illustrate and label two-dimensional shapes to make a "Hide and Seek Shapes Book." In the lesson corresponding to *Spaghetti and Meatballs for All,* they compose and decompose arrangements of square tiles, then determine the area and perimeter for each arrangement. During the last lesson, *Clay Ladies,* students identify, compare, and construct three-dimensional shapes.

Get ready to shape it up!
Anne

LESSON 1

Discover, Identify, and Label Two-Dimensional Shapes

Greene, Rhonda Gowler. *When a Line Bends . . . A Shape Begins.* Boston: Houghton Mifflin, 1997.

Children will be fascinated with the colorful illustrations and rhyming text in *When a Line Bends . . . A Shape Begins.* As you turn each page, students will see new ways a line can turn into a simple shape. Teachers and children alike will enjoy locating triangles, circles, stars, squares, octagons, diamonds, rectangles, hearts, crescents, and ovals in this book, as well as thinking of other ways to curve and bend lines to make different shapes.

Time Frame

50 minutes

Materials

For the teacher:

Figure 3.1.1. *Two-Dimensional Shapes Assessment Checklist*

Old magazines to cut up

Chart paper or chalkboard

Index cards (any size)

Ten shoebox-sized boxes, labeled for each of the following shapes: triangle, circle, star, square, octagon, diamond (rhombus), rectangle, heart, crescent, and oval (ellipse)

For each student:

Figure 3.1.2. *Two-Dimensional Shapes*

One zipping storage bag

Ten Popsicle sticks

Scissors, crayons, glue, and a pencil

Story and Mini-Lesson

1. Introduce the story by showing the students the cover and title of the book.

2. Invite students to predict what they think the title means. Ask, "Why do you think the author chose this title for the book?" Ask students if they think the author is correct. "Do you begin making a shape when you bend a line?" Allow a few minutes for discussion, then open the book, and say, "Let's see what the author wants to tell us about how we can make shapes."

3. **P**review the book by showing a few pages you selected prior to the lesson. Ask children to notice the shapes on these pages. What do they notice about the shapes? Are the shapes on each page similar to others on that same page?

4. Next, **r**ead the story. As you read, ask students to be sure to notice different shapes throughout the book.

5. **R**eview the story by asking students to explain the author's meaning when she wrote, "When a line bends . . . A shape begins." You, or one of your students, may demonstrate what can happen to a line when you bend it to make a curve or a corner. First draw a line on the chalkboard, then bend the line to make a circle or an oval. Next draw another line and bend it at a corner. Finish that shape by making a square.

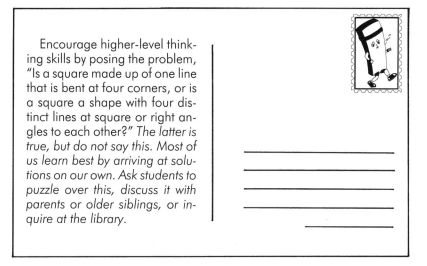

Encourage higher-level thinking skills by posing the problem, "Is a square made up of one line that is bent at four corners, or is a square a shape with four distinct lines at square or right angles to each other?" *The latter is true, but do not say this. Most of us learn best by arriving at solutions on our own. Ask students to puzzle over this, discuss it with parents or older siblings, or inquire at the library.*

6. Model how to draw an imaginary line in the air with your finger. Together, draw squares in the air. Then have students draw several other shapes in the air with their fingers, such as triangles, rectangles, and circles.

7. Use chart paper or the chalkboard to record the names and descriptions of shapes students know.

8. Challenge students to notice and name objects in the classroom that have specific shapes, such as the stars and the stripes *(rectangles)* on the flag.

9. **R**e-read the story and encourage students to locate shapes on each page to reinforce their shape recognition and geometric vocabulary.

Group Lesson

1. Give each student a copy of **Figure 3.1.2. *Two-Dimensional Shapes.*** Have students color, cut out, and label the ten different shapes: heart, circle, triangle, octagon, crescent, rectangle, square, star, diamond *(rhombus),* and oval *(ellipse).*

2. To reinforce color recognition and students' abilities to follow directions, have them color each shape the color you specify. For example, "Color the heart red. Color the circle blue." List these directions on the chalkboard.

3. While students work, give each child ten Popsicle sticks and one zipping storage bag.

4. When students have colored, cut, and labeled their shapes, instruct them to glue each shape onto a Popsicle stick.

Discovery

When students have completed their shapes, have them locate shapes in magazine pictures. Students should cut out the shapes they find, then glue each shape onto a separate index card. Students should then categorize each card by placing it in the box with the appropriate shape label. For example, if a student cuts out a picture of a television, he or she would glue the picture onto an index card and place it in the container labeled "rectangles" because it is a rectangular object.

You may use these shape cards later for a center activity. Students may mix up the cards, then sort them back into the appropriate boxes. Or, turn the cards face down and students can play shape concentration.

Reflection

Direct students to return to their seats with their shape cards. Invite student to share an object they cut out of a magazine and explain what shape it is. Ask students if they discovered any different shapes that weren't mentioned in the book. Were some shapes hard to find? Discuss. Conclude this lesson by asking students to be on the lookout for shapes in the classroom, school, at home, and outdoors. The world is full of shapes.

Assessment

As students work on the discovery activity, assess individual students to evaluate their shape recognition skills. Use **Figure 3.1.1. *Two-Dimensional Shapes Assessment Checklist*** to record results. Note students who need assistance and clarification in shape recognition. Provide many opportunities for these students to find, manipulate, and identify shapes in your classroom.

Special Needs Adaptations

Auditory disability: An interpreter should sign the story and lesson.

Motor disability: A partner or teacher's aide can assist these students with coloring or cutting.

Visual disability: The teacher or classroom helper can laminate and pre-cut the shapes from **Figure 3.1.2. *Two-Dimensional Shapes*** for these children. Invite these students to touch and identify the shapes and match them with pattern blocks or two-dimensional shapes in the classroom.

English Language Learners: Identify colors and shapes in the students' native languages as well as in English, and have these students share the shape names from their native languages with classmates.

Extensions

- Have the students stretch and bend rubber bands and make two-dimensional shapes on geoboards.

- Ask the students to write rhymes about shapes.

- Re-read the book. Estimate the number of shapes on each page, then count the shapes. Or, invite students to hold up their Popsicle stick shapes to match those shown on each page of the book.

- Have the students draw shape pictures of houses, buildings, or make believe creatures.

- Choose shape stamps from the *Kid Pix Deluxe* software program and have the students create pictures with shapes.

- Introduce Tangrams, or pattern blocks. Allow time for students to sort, combine, rotate, and design patterns, structures, and pictures with Tangrams and blocks.

- Make a list of shapes found on a playground, in the classroom, or at home.

Bibliography

Adler, David. *Shape Up! Fun with Triangles and Other Polygons.* New York: Holiday House, 2000.

Burns, Marilyn. *The Greedy Triangle.* New York: Scholastic, 1995.

Dotlich, Rebecca Kai. *What Is a Square?* New York: HarperCollins, 1999.

Hewitt, Sally. *Shapes.* New York: Raintree Steck-Vaughn, 1996.

Rotner, Shelley, and Richard Olivo. *Close, Closer, Closest.* New York: Simon & Schuster, 1997.

Software

Broderbund Software, Inc. 1998. *Kid Pix Deluxe.* Macintosh and Windows.

Related Standards 2000

Standard 2: Algebra

Standard 7: Reasoning and Proof

Standard 9: Connections

Standard 10: Representation

Related Standards 1989

Standard 2: Mathematics as Communication

Standard 5: Estimation

Standard 8: Whole Number Computation

Standard 13: Patterns and Relationships

LESSON 2

Illustrate and Hide Two-Dimensional Shapes

Blackstone, Stella. *Bear in a Square.* New York: Scholastic, 1998.

Find a jolly bear in a square. Then, join Bear during the course of a day as he hunts for shapes in the world around him. This easy-to-read book not only serves as an introduction to two-dimensional shapes, but also serves as a book of colors, rhymes, and numbers.

Time Frame

Day One: 50 minutes
Read the story and begin illustrating a "Hide and Seek Shape Book."

Day Two: 50 minutes
Re-read the story, complete illustrations, and then write illustration labels.

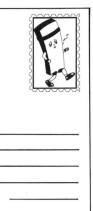

You and your students could produce a "Hide and Seek Shape Book" on the computer. Use *Kid Pix Deluxe* to draw shape pictures, then label the shape pictures with the text tool. Print students' work or save it in *Microsoft PowerPoint* to make a "Hide and Seek Shape Slide Show."

Materials

➤ **Day One**

For the teacher:

Index cards from the previous lesson, or models or pattern blocks of everyday two-dimensional shapes such as squares, hearts, circles, crescents, rectangles, triangles, ovals (ellipses), and diamonds (rhombuses)

Chart paper or chalkboard

For each student:

One sheet of 8½-by-11-inch white paper

Pencils, crayons, and rulers (optional)

Materials

➤ **Day Two**

For the teacher:
Brightly colored 12-by-18-inch construction paper
Chalkboard

For each student:
Illustrations from Day One
Pencils and crayons
Lined writing paper

Story and Mini-Lesson: Day One

1. **R**ead the title and **p**review the book by doing a "picture walk" through the pages.

2. Encourage students to tell what they notice about the book. Some will notice the bright colors, others the shapes, and others the progressive number pattern.

3. Invite students to **p**redict what the story will be about. Support all predictions.

4. **R**ead aloud *Bear in a Square*. As this book has large type, encourage students to chime in when they recognize words and become accustomed to the rhyming pattern of the story.

5. **R**e-read the story and enlist the support of all students in identifying the "hidden" shapes.

6. Display the last two pages of the book. **R**eview by asking children to name the shapes. Record the shape names on chart paper or on the chalkboard as students say them aloud. Students may also hold up shape cards from the previous lesson as they say the shape names.

Group Lesson: Day One

1. Brainstorm and list other two-dimensional shapes students know.

2. Tell students they will each illustrate a page for a class "Hide and Seek Shape Book." You may choose a theme for the illustrations that complements a unit you are currently studying, such as "Forest Animals," or you may allow students to draw a picture of whatever suits their fancy.

3. Provide the following instructions for the "Hide and Seek Shape Book" illustrations:

   ✓ Include at least four different kinds of two-dimensional shapes in your picture.

   ✓ Draw from one to twenty of each of the different shapes you choose.

   ✓ Color and fill in your entire illustration with crayons.

   ✓ Outline your shapes with marker when you have completed your picture.

Discovery: Day One

Allow time for students to draw their pictures. Have students clean up materials before gathering to share and reflect about their illustrations.

Reflection: Day One

Gather together and encourage students to point out and identify the shapes in their illustrations. Reinforce the geometric vocabulary of mathematicians with shape words like *rhombus* (diamond), *crescent* (moon), *ellipse* (egg-shaped or oval), and *polygon* (a shape with many sides.) Collect students' illustrations to review and save for the Day Two lesson.

Assessment: Day One

Check that students followed the instructions from Group Lesson item 3 above. Write notes regarding your observations of students' work and progress on **Figure 1.1.4.** *Anecdotal Record.*

Story and Mini-Lesson: Day Two

1. **Re**-read the story. Encourage students to join in reading aloud with you.

2. **R**eview the two-dimensional shape names.

3. **R**eturn students' illustrations.

Group Lesson: Day Two

1. Tell students that today they will identify, name, and count the different shapes in their pictures. For instance, Rylea's forest scene might include nine hearts, three rectangles, twelve triangles, and three polygons. Together, identify and count the shapes in Rylea's illustration.

2. Discuss how a reader of the "Hide and Seek Shape Book" will know what to look for in a picture. Encourage all suggestions and ideas for solving this problem. Students might come up with a solution like the following: Rylea could label her illustration with these words, "Find 9 hearts, 3 rectangles, 12 triangles, and 3 polygons." As a class, agree upon this or another format for labeling the illustrations.

3. Write an example of the chosen format on the board for students to use as a model for their written work.

4. Post the two-dimensional shape word list from Day One for students' reference.

Discovery: Day Two

Have the students write labels for their shape illustrations. Correct students' spelling, grammar, and punctuation on rough drafts because students will publish this class "Hide and Seek Shape Book" to read over and over again. Have students rewrite corrected copies. Then have students mount their illustrations and corresponding labels onto brightly colored 12-by-18-inch construction paper. Finally, publish the class "Hide and Seek Shape Book" by having a parent volunteer or classroom aide laminate and bind students' work.

Reflection: Day Two

Display the book where it is accessible for all students to read proudly.

Assessment: Day Two

Use **Figure 3.1.1.** *Two-Dimensional Shapes Assessment Checklist* to reassess students' ability to recognize and identify shapes.

Special Needs Adaptations

Auditory disability: An interpreter should sign the story, lesson, and instructions. Provide a visual display of the two-dimensional shapes and corresponding labels.

Motor disability: Partner these students with other children so they may collaborate in directing and drawing the illustrations during the discovery activity. If these students are able to manipulate pattern blocks, they may illustrate their own pictures by arranging blocks into shape pictures or patterns. These children may dictate labels for other students or an aide to inscribe.

Visual disability: As you read *Bear in a Square*, have another child or classroom aide pass pattern blocks of each shape described in the story to these children. Encourage them to feel and then describe each shape in their own words. After they learn to recognize and identify each shape, play a hide-and-seek game in which they touch, describe, and identify each shape. Rather than illustrate a page for the "Hide and Seek Shape Book," these children can make a "Peek-a-Boo" box for other students. An aide or student volunteer can help design a shoebox with a hole in it just big enough for a child's hand. These students can challenge sighted students to identify the shapes in the box by touch.

English Language Learners: Second Language learners will easily understand the meaning of *Bear in a Square* because it has clear, easy-to-understand illustrations. Partners or bilingual buddies should team up with these students to translate the lesson instructions. On the chalkboard or chart paper, write shape words in these students' native languages. Encourage these students to share the words in their native languages with English-speaking students.

Extensions

- Make shape "Peek-a-Boo" boxes as described for students with visual disabilities.

- Play "Guess-My-Shape" with pattern blocks. Students play this game with partners. One partner hides a shape behind his or her back. He or she tells what the shape feels like by using words to describe how many sides, corners, or curves it has, and if the sides have the same or different lengths. Partners switch tasks when one partner correctly guesses the shape.

- Play "Match-My-Shape" with partners. Students sit back-to-back so they cannot see each other's work. One student draws a shape on a piece of paper. Then he or she describes that shape to his or her partner using shape vocabulary as in "Guess-My-Shape." Have students compare shapes, then switch tasks.

- Take a photographic walk around the school. Take snapshots of the shapes you see. Have students use the photos to illustrate and label a "Shapes in My School" class book.

- Suggest that children use chalk to draw and number crazy hopscotch shapes (draw other shapes besides squares or rectangles) on the playground sidewalk, then play hopscotch.

- Choose five of your favorite two-dimensional shapes. Survey at least five class members to find out which of these shapes is their favorite. Record their answers, then use *The Graph Club* software to make graphs that represent the results of the survey.

- Introduce symmetry. Discuss and provide examples of symmetrical two-dimensional objects such as hearts, squares, rectangles, and rhombuses. Compare symmetrical and asymmetrical two-dimensional objects. Ask, "Can hearts be divided in such a way that they are no longer symmetrical?" Discuss.

- Read *Three Pigs, One Wolf, and Seven Magic Shapes* by Grace Maccarone and Marilyn Burns or *Grandfather Tang's Story* by Ann Tompert. Make sets of Tangrams for each student. Have them manipulate, rotate, and flip Tangrams and move them into picture or animal shapes, as described in either book.

Bibliography

Geisel, Theodore (Dr. Seuss). *The Shape of Me and Other Stuff.* New York: Random House, 1999.

Hoban, Tana. *So Many Circles, So Many Squares.* New York: Greenwillow, 1998.

Maccarone, Grace. *The Silly Story of Goldie Locks and the Three Squares.* New York: Scholastic, 1999.

Maccarone, Grace, and Marilyn Burns. *Three Pigs, One Wolf, and Seven Magic Shapes.* New York: Scholastic, 1997.

Tompert, Ann. *Grandfather Tang's Story.* New York: Crown, 1997.

Software

Broderbund Software, Inc. 1998. *Kid Pix Deluxe.* Macintosh and Windows.

Microsoft Corporation. 1999. *Microsoft PowerPoint.* Windows 98.

Tom Snyder Productions. 1998. *The Graph Club.* Macintosh and Windows, www.tomsnyder.com. (Accessed February 2001).

Related Standards 2000

Standard 2: Algebra

Standard 6: Problem Solving

Standard 7: Reasoning and Proof

Standard 9: Connections

Standard 10: Representation

Related Standards 1989

Standard 1: Problem Solving

Standard 2: Mathematics as Communication

Standard 8: Whole Number Computation

Standard 13: Patterns and Relationships

LESSON 3

Arrange Shapes; Measure Sides and Space (Perimeter and Area)

Burns, Marilyn. ***Spaghetti and Meatballs for All: A Mathe-matical Story.*** New York: Scholastic, 1997.

> Mrs. Comfort is having a family get together. She has everything organized, that is, until the guests start arriving and mess up her seating arrangements by pushing together tables and moving chairs! This book challenges students to consider alternative ways to seat the guests so that everyone is comfortable and happy, especially Mrs. Comfort! This engaging and funny story is an excellent tool to help elementary students develop spatial sense and to work with and measure perimeter and area.

Time Frame

50 minutes

Materials

For the teacher:

Overhead projector and pen

Small tiles (transparent overhead tiles preferable) or square pattern blocks

Transparency of **Figure 3.3.1. *Mrs. Comfort's House***

Figure 3.3.2. *Answers, Seating Arrangements at Mrs. Comfort's House*

For each student:

Copy of **Figure 3.3.1. *Mrs. Comfort's House***

Figure 3.3.3. *Seating Arrangements at Mrs. Comfort's House*

Pencil and crayons

Eight or ten tiles or square pattern blocks to manipulate

Story and Mini-Lesson

1. **P**review the story by showing the book cover and taking a "picture walk" through *Spaghetti and Meatballs for All.* Point out the part of the title where it says, "A Mathematical Story."

2. Invite students to **p**redict what might happen in this story. Ask, "How do you think this story will be mathematical?" Accept all predictions.

3. Tell students that when you finish reading the story, you will ask them if their predictions held up. Then **r**ead the story.

4. When you have finished reading the story, connect the book to the following math lesson by asking students, "Did your predictions hold up? What did you like about the story? Why was it funny? What was the problem in the story? (Mrs. Comfort wanted everyone to have a place to sit. When the relatives pushed the tables together, there were not enough places for all the guests.) How did the relatives solve the problem? (They moved the tables back to the way Mrs. Comfort originally had them.)

5. Write the words *perimeter* and *area* on the chalkboard. Ask, "Does anyone know the meaning of these words?" Confirm answers, or teach these definitions to the class: Perimeter is the total distance around the outside of an object. Area is the total space inside an object.

6. Demonstrate perimeter by holding up a tile or square pattern block. Ask how many sides the tile has (four) Together, count the sides of the square. Tell students they have just determined perimeter! Each side of the square is one unit. To determine the perimeter one must count and add up each unit.

7. Demonstrate area by holding up the tile once again. The area of the tile is the space within the sides of the tile. The area of the square tile is one unit. Then hold up two tiles. Pose this problem, "If the area of one square tile is one unit, what is the area of two square tiles" (two)?

Group Lesson

1. Tell children they are going to re-create *Spaghetti and Meatballs for All* by using square tiles to represent the tables in Mrs. Comfort's house. Distribute copies of **Figure 3.3.1. *Mrs. Comfort's House*** and eight or ten tiles to each student.

2. Ask students to position the tiles on their paper just as Mrs. Comfort had arranged the tables at the beginning of the story. (See page 7 of *Spaghetti and Meatballs for All* or Figure 1 at the end of the book.) Position your own tiles on the overhead projector in the same way that Mrs. Comfort arranged her tables.

3. Ask students to count how many people could sit at the tables in this arrangement (32). Ask if anyone can tell the perimeter of each table. When a child answers, "Four," have all students count the sides of the table. "Yes, the perimeter is four because there are four units, and four people could fit around each table." Then ask if anyone can tell the area of each table. When a child answers, "One," have all the students point to the one square unit or one tile that represents one table.

4. Ask students what happened next in the story. Students may say that the relatives came and moved the tables. Have students put their tiles together to represent the new way the relatives arranged the tables. Do the same on the overhead.

5. Count how many people can sit at the tables when they are arranged this way (30). Question students about why this number or perimeter is smaller than the first table setup. (There aren't as many sides when the tables or tiles are pushed together.) Ask what the area of the two tables that are pushed together is. (The answer is two; count each tile for the area.)

6. Continue to manipulate the tiles to represent all the many table configurations from *Spaghetti and Meatballs for All*.

7. After each manipulation, ask students to count the number of available seats or perimeter of the tables. Also, ask students the area of the tables when the tiles are pushed together in groups. (Count each tile used for the area.)

8. Compare the perimeter or seats available for each design and discuss which would be most useful to Mrs. Comfort and why.

Reflection

Invite students to retell the events of the story in sequence to their neighbors. Encourage them to think of other ways to set up the seating arrangements for Mrs. Comfort's dinner party. Use the tiles to represent these different table setups.

Assessment

Distribute **Figure 3.3.3. Seating Arrangements at Mrs. Comfort's House.** Support students by reading the questions aloud. Encourage students to determine their answers by using the tiles to represent the seating arrangements. Refer to **Figure 3.3.2. Answers, Seating Arrangements at Mrs. Comfort's House** when you assess students' work. Jot down notes regarding any confusion students experienced.

If this is the first time your students have worked with the concepts of *area* and *perimeter*, do the assessment on a later day or omit this part of the lesson. Provide students with several opportunities to tell their own dinner party stories and to set up their own tiles to make seating arrangements. Encourage students to use the words *perimeter* and *area* while telling their stories.

Special Needs Adaptations

Auditory disability: An interpreter should sign the story and directions for the lesson.

Motor disability: A student friend or aide may assist with manipulation of the tiles and written work.

Visual disability: Partner these students with buddies. These students may need help placing and arranging tiles during the lesson and the assessment.

English Language Learners: Assign a student or ELL teacher to interpret the story and directions during the lesson and the assessment (use **Figure 3.3.3.**).

Extensions

■ Use tiles to make table settings. Have partners then quiz each other about perimeter and area.

■ Design a bird's-eye view of a one-story dream house. As a class, make a list of the different rooms such as the kitchen, bedrooms, bathrooms, living room, and garage. Provide paper with centimeter or inch grid lines on which students may design floor plans. Students may design their houses as they wish, but they must stay on the grid lines so they can figure the area and perimeter for each room and for the entire house. Review with students that the area of a room equals the number of the squares in that room. The perimeter equals the number of units that are around each room, or the number of units around the entire house. When students complete their projects, encourage them to share their dream house designs and measurements with others.

■ Let the students play *Lego Chess*. They can join the ranks of pawns, castles, knights, bishops, queen, and king as they strategize, plan moves, and navigate across this chessboard.

Bibliography

Axelrod, Amy. *Pigs on the Ball.* New York: Simon & Schuster, 2000.

Carle, Eric. *The Secret Birthday Message.* New York: Harper & Row, 1999.

Dewan, Ted. *The Sorcerer's Apprentice.* New York: Bantam Doubleday Dell, 1998.

Macaulay, David. *Pyramid.* Boston: Houghton Mifflin, 1999.

Morris, Ann. *Houses and Homes.* New York: Mulberry Books, 1995.

Neitzel, Shirley. *The House I'll Build for the Wrens.* New York: Greenwillow, 1997.

Van Cleave, Janice. *Geometry for Every Kid.* New York: John Wiley & Sons, 1994.

Software

Lego Media International, Inc. 1998. *Lego Chess.* 555 Taylor Road, Enfield, CT 06082-3298

Related Standards 2000

Standard 1: Number and Operations

Standard 4: Measurement

Standard 6: Problem Solving

Standard 7: Reasoning and Proof

Standard 9: Connections

Standard 10: Representation

See Chapter 2, Lesson 3, for an activity that uses coordinate geometry. In *The Teeny Tiny Teacher* lesson, students design a town where they place and map buildings on a grid system.

Related Standards 1989

Standard 1: Mathematics as Problem Solving

Standard 2: Mathematics as Communication

Standard 3: Mathematics as Reasoning

Standard 4: Mathematical Connections

Standard 5: Estimation

Standard 10: Measurement

LESSON 4

Identify and Model Three-Dimensional Shapes and Sculptures

Bedard, Michael. *The Clay Ladies.* Ontario: Tundra Books, 1999.

What about reading a book about the lives of two famous sculptors? This true story, told through the eyes of a little girl, introduces readers to the amazing lives of Frances Loring and Florence Wyle. Loring and Wyle lived in an old, tumbledown church in Toronto from 1920 to 1960. There, they shaped and sculpted clay and inspired others to become artists and sculptors as well. In this story, a young girl discovers that Frances and Florence, her eccentric neighbors, have a love for animals. Through this shared love, the girl is drawn into their sanctuary of beauty and sculpture. Once inside, the child learns to work, mold, smooth, and sculpt clay with the artists' guidance.

Time Frame

Day One: 50 minutes
Introduce *The Clay Ladies* and three-dimensional geometric shapes.

Day Two: 50 minutes
Model clay into three-dimensional shapes and objects.

Materials

➤ Day One

For the teacher:

Examples of a sphere, cone, cylinder, cube, and rectangular prism (wooden blocks, or objects such as a ball, an ice cream cone, a paper towel tube, and a cereal box)

For each student:

Two and one-half sticks of clay (about one 5-pound box of non-hardening modeling clay)

Wax paper to use as a work mat

➤ Day Two

For the teacher:

Three-dimensional shapes from Day One

You may find this clay in any art store, or ask your school art teacher to help you order some. It is reusable, so you only have to buy it once.

For each student:

Clay pieces from Day One

Wax paper to use as a work mat

Figure 3.4.1. *Three-Dimensional Shapes Assessment*

Story and Mini-Lesson: Day One

1. **P**review the story by showing the cover and reading the book title. Take a "picture walk" through the story by showing several pages of the book. Ask students to point out things they notice in the story, such as the sculptures and animals.

2. Invite students to **p**redict what the story will be about.

3. **R**ead the story aloud.

4. When you finish reading the book, invite students to **r**etell events and to summarize the story. Ask students, "What did you like about this story?" Accept all answers. Ask, "What did the little girl learn from the ladies?" (The little girl learned to notice the beauty in the world around her and to re-create it with clay in her own hands.) Ask, "How do sculpture and art relate to math?" (Sculpture and art use geometric shapes and lines.)

5. Review geometric vocabulary by having students describe two-dimensional shapes such as a square, a triangle, and a circle. Have students explain the properties of these shapes; for example, a student might say that a triangle has three sides and a square has four equal sides.

6. Introduce three-dimensional shapes. Tell students that three-dimensional shapes have volume or depth, or space inside. They are not flat.

7. Show your example of a sphere. Ask students to describe and identify this three-dimensional shape. Many students will call it a ball. Tell them that it is indeed a ball, but mathematicians call it a sphere. Ask students to tell you the difference between a circle and a sphere. (A circle is round and flat, and a sphere is round and has volume or depth.) Ask students to brainstorm other real life items that are spheres (a globe, a snowball, a baseball, and a basketball). Continue to share the other three-dimensional shapes as you did the sphere.

8. Take a "picture walk" through the story again. This time, have students point out how the illustrator used shapes in her drawings. For example, the window is square, and the girl's legs are cylinders. Some students might notice techniques artists use to show depth in their paintings, such as shadowing and curved or diminishing lines.

Group Lesson: Day One

1. Explain to students that they will use clay just like the little girl in the book, to create geometric shapes.

2. Hand out clay to each child and tell the students to work the clay between their hands for about five minutes to soften it and to get rid of the air bubbles.

3. Direct students to make a sphere using all or some of their clay. Have students discover the best way to make a sphere and share their techniques with others, such as rolling clay in a circle in the palm of one's hand. When students have completed the spheres, have them hold them up for others to see. Explain that although the spheres are not exactly the same size, they are all spheres.

4. Instruct students to make the rest of the three-dimensional shapes (cone, cylinder, cube, and rectangular prism) following the same method used to make the sphere. Support students who need direction and help in molding the clay shapes. For example, to make a cone students will need to take the sphere and roll it on just one side. To make the cylinder, students can roll the cone on both sides to make them even, then flatten the ends by pressing them onto the table. To make the cube, they should make a sphere and flatten it on the table on each side. To make a rectangular prism, students should take the cylinder and flatten it on all sides.

5. Continue to have students share their shapes and discuss the similarities and differences between the shapes.

6. Clean up materials before meeting to review three-dimensional shapes. Save out clay shapes to share during the reflection activity.

Reflection: Day One

Have students present their clay shapes to one another and share their discoveries about techniques for molding clay. Conclude today's lesson by telling students that on Day Two they will each make a sculpture by forming and combining shapes they learned today.

Group Lesson: Day Two

1. Select half a dozen or so illustrations from *The Clay Ladies* to share and admire with students. Encourage students to notice the three-dimensional shapes illustrated in the pictures. Discuss how an artist makes a flat picture appear to have depth. (Artists shade objects and curve or diminish lines. They narrow lines and bring lines together to make them appear far away. Artists overlap foreground objects in front of the background and make objects in the foreground appear larger than those in the background.)

2. Exhibit and review three-dimensional shapes learned on Day One.

3. Review and practice techniques for molding and shaping clay from items 3 and 4 in the Group Lesson from Day One.

4. Tell students they are going to create a sculpture. A sculpture is three-dimensional art.

Discovery: Day Two

Students should use the clay they worked during Day One to make today's sculpture. Direct students to sculpt an object that contains some or all of the three-dimensional shapes they have just learned. When students have completed their sculptures, have them clean up and put away their materials before meeting to reflect about their work.

Reflection: Day Two

Invite students to present their sculptures. Commend and support students for using vocabulary such as *sphere, cone, cylinder, cube,* and *rectangular prism* to describe their work.

Assessment: Day Two

Hand out **Figure 3.4.1.** *Three-Dimensional Shapes Assessment.* Read the questions aloud together, then direct students to complete the assessment independently.

Special Needs Adaptations

Auditory disability: An interpreter should sign the story and lesson.

Motor disability: A student helper or aide may need to assist these students while they manipulate the clay.

Visual disability: Distribute samples of three-dimensional objects to these students. Instruct these students to find, touch, describe, and identify three-dimensional shapes located around the room. You, or an assistant, should help these students as they manipulate clay and build a sculpture.

English Language Learners: Assign a student partner or teacher to check that these students understand the story and lesson instructions. Encourage these students to share native language vocabulary for three-dimensional terms.

Extensions

- Invite your school art teacher to observe or assist with the Group Lessons or to teach one of these extension activities.

- Discuss and provide examples of symmetrical three-dimensional objects. Make symmetrical sculptures.

- Read *The Tyger* by William Blake, illustrated by Neil Waldman. Ask students why they think Blake described Tyger as *symmetrical.* What is symmetrical about a tiger? Discuss. Have students use clay to sculpt a three-dimensional symmetrical tiger.

- As a class, estimate, then count, the number of shapes in students' sculptures.

- Have the students give their sculptures names, then write stories about how the sculptures came to exist, that is, either give step-by-step directions for sculpture making or write a fictional story about the sculpture.

- Have the students draw the sculptures as still lifes on paper.

- Ask students to replicate someone else's sculpture.

- Have students make an animal, house, or automobile out of three-dimensional shapes.

- Host a Math Night and invite family and friends to view the sculptures or to participate in making their own sculptures.

- Make a shape sorting game. For example, have students sort objects by attributes such as shape, size, symmetry, or color.

- Make an "In-the-Bag-Game." Place several three-dimensional shapes in a bag. Have students close their eyes and feel inside the bag, then guess the identity of the shapes before pulling them out.

- Ask students to describe how various three-dimensional shapes are alike and different.

Bibliography

Anno, Mitsumasa. *Anno's Math Games III.* New York: Paper Star, 1997.

Blake, William. *The Tyger.* New York: Harcourt Brace, 1993.

Geisel, Theodore (Dr. Seuss). *The Shape of Me and Other Stuff.* New York: Random House, 1999.

Macaulay, David. *City.* Boston: Houghton Mifflin. 1983.

Related Standards 2000

Standard 7: Reasoning and Proof

Standard 8: Communication

Standard 9: Connections

Standard 10: Representation

Related Standards 1989

Standard 1: Math as Problem Solving

Standard 2: Math as Communication

Standard 4: Mathematical Connections

Standard 5: Estimation

Standard 10: Measurement

Standard 13: Patterns and Relationships

Name	Shape Recognition	Verbal Identification	Color Recognition
	♡ ☐ □ ☾ ⬡ ☆ △ ◇ ⬭ ○	♡ ☐ □ ☾ ⬡ ☆ △ ◇ ⬭ ○	red, orange, yellow, green, blue, purple, brown, black, gray, pink
	♡ ☐ □ ☾ ⬡ ☆ △ ◇ ⬭ ○	♡ ☐ □ ☾ ⬡ ☆ △ ◇ ⬭ ○	red, orange, yellow, green, blue, purple, brown, black, gray, pink
	♡ ☐ □ ☾ ⬡ ☆ △ ◇ ⬭ ○	♡ ☐ □ ☾ ⬡ ☆ △ ◇ ⬭ ○	red, orange, yellow, green, blue, purple, brown, black, gray, pink
	♡ ☐ □ ☾ ⬡ ☆ △ ◇ ⬭ ○	♡ ☐ □ ☾ ⬡ ☆ △ ◇ ⬭ ○	red, orange, yellow, green, blue, purple, brown, black, gray, pink
	♡ ☐ □ ☾ ⬡ ☆ △ ◇ ⬭ ○	♡ ☐ □ ☾ ⬡ ☆ △ ◇ ⬭ ○	red, orange, yellow, green, blue, purple, brown, black, gray, pink
	♡ ☐ □ ☾ ⬡ ☆ △ ◇ ⬭ ○	♡ ☐ □ ☾ ⬡ ☆ △ ◇ ⬭ ○	red, orange, yellow, green, blue, purple, brown, black, gray, pink
	♡ ☐ □ ☾ ⬡ ☆ △ ◇ ⬭ ○	♡ ☐ □ ☾ ⬡ ☆ △ ◇ ⬭ ○	red, orange, yellow, green, blue, purple, brown, black, gray, pink
	♡ ☐ □ ☾ ⬡ ☆ △ ◇ ⬭ ○	♡ ☐ □ ☾ ⬡ ☆ △ ◇ ⬭ ○	red, orange, yellow, green, blue, purple, brown, black, gray, pink
	♡ ☐ □ ☾ ⬡ ☆ △ ◇ ⬭ ○	♡ ☐ □ ☾ ⬡ ☆ △ ◇ ⬭ ○	red, orange, yellow, green, blue, purple, brown, black, gray, pink

Figure 3.1.1. *Two-Dimensional Shapes Assessment Checklist*

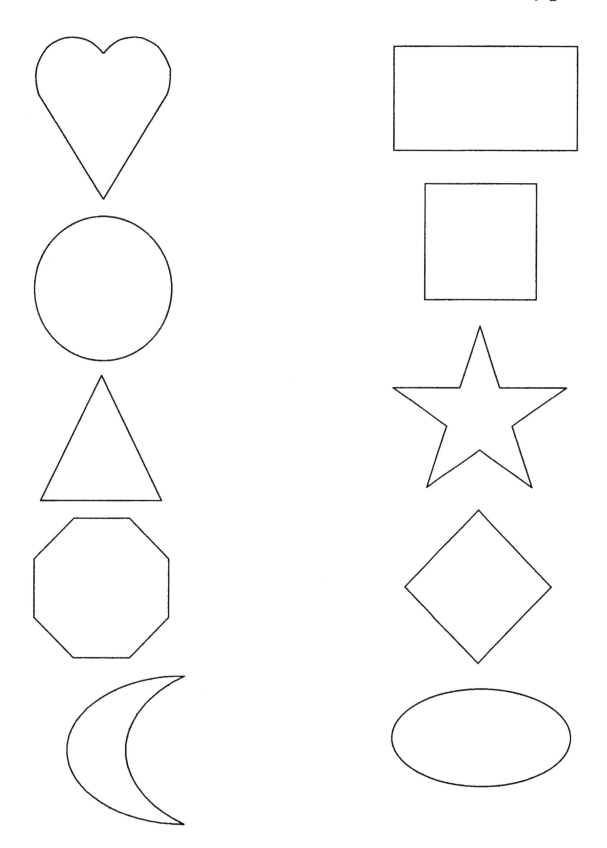

Figure 3.1.2. *Two-Dimensional Shapes*

Figure 3.3.1. Mrs. Comfort's House

1. How many people did Mrs. Comfort expect for the family reunion? (32)

2. How many small square tables did Mrs. Comfort figure she needed to seat all her guests? (8)

3. Draw a picture of Mrs. Comfort's seating arrangement.

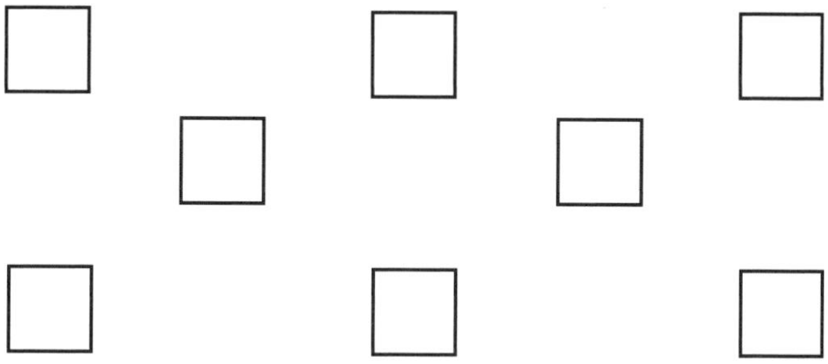

4. If the top of each table has the area of one square unit, how much is the perimeter of one table? (4 units)

5. When the Comforts' daughter, her husband, and their two children arrived, they pushed two tables together so that the four of them could sit with Mr. and Mrs. Comfort. Draw this seating arrangement.

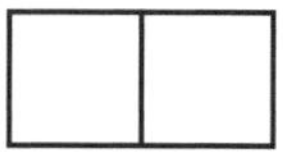

6. What are the area and perimeter of the "new" rectangular table? (area = 2 units, perimeter = 6 units)

7. What are the area and perimeter of these arrangements?

   (area = 8 units, perimeter = 12 units)

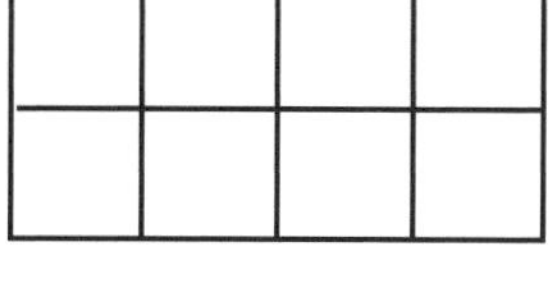

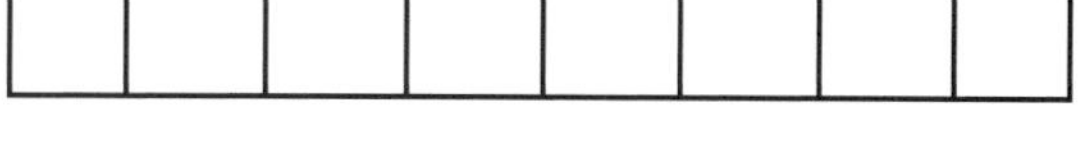

   (area = 8 units, perimeter = 18 units)

Figure 3.3.2. *Answers, Seating Arrangements at Mrs. Comfort's House*

Name: _____   **Date:** _____

1. How many people did Mrs. Comfort expect for the family reunion? _____

2. How many small square tables did Mrs. Comfort figure she needed to seat all her guests? _____

3. Draw a picture of Mrs. Comfort's seating arrangement.

4. If the top of each table has the area of one square unit, how much is the perimeter of one table? _____

5. When the Comforts' daughter, her husband, and their two children arrived, they pushed two tables together so that the four of them could sit with Mr. and Mrs. Comfort. Draw this seating arrangement.

6. What are the area and perimeter of this "new" rectangular table? _____

7. What are the area and perimeter of these arrangements?

    area _____ perimeter _____

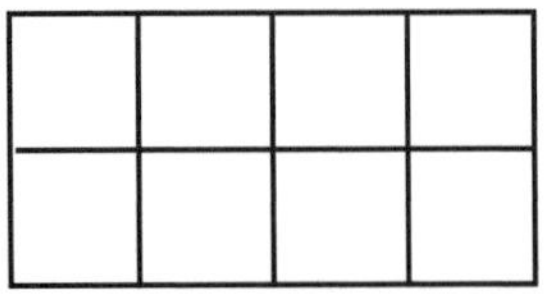

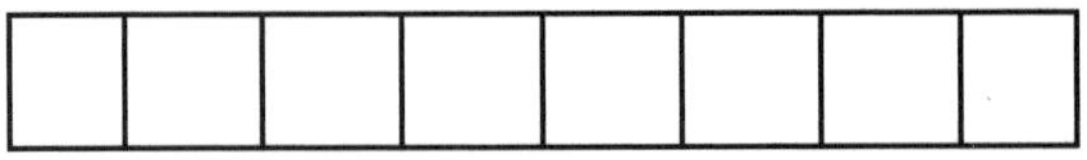

    area _____ perimeter _____

Figure 3.3.3. *Seating Arrangements at Mrs. Comfort's House*

Name: _____

1. Draw and label a picture of a toy or other object that is the shape of a sphere:

2. Draw and label a picture of a toy or other object that is the shape of a cone:

3. Draw and label a picture of a toy or other object that is the shape of a cylinder:

4. Draw and label a picture of a toy or other object that is the shape of a cube:

5. Draw and label a picture of a toy or other object that is the shape of a rectangular prism:

Figure 3.4.1. *Three-Dimensional Shapes Assessment*

Chapter 4

Measurement

Dear Math Teacher,

In this chapter, students participate in hands-on activities to develop a basic understanding of measurement. They learn about the attributes of length, weight, time, and capacity.

In the following lessons, students use standard and nonstandard units to estimate and measure classroom objects. They weigh and measure carrots and use carrots to measure themselves. They estimate and measure the length of time it takes to do bedtime routines and they determine how many things they can do in one minute. Students measure, mix, time, and bake strawberry shortcake in the culminating activity of this unit. By the end of this chapter, students will understand that measurement is an important part of everyday life.

This chapter measures up to be full of great activities.

Anne

LESSON 1

Measure Length with Nonstandard and Standard Measuring Tools

Hightower, Susan. ***Twelve Snails to One Lizard, a Tale of Mischief and Measurement.*** New York: Simon & Schuster, 1997.

> Milo Beaver has a dilemma, and Bubba Bullfrog is a great help. Or is he? Milo is desperate to measure a log that he will use to patch a hole in his dam. But what should he use to measure the hole? Follow Milo and Bubba in this humorous book as they try to measure the log, using one animal after another as a measuring tool.

Time Frame

50 minutes

Prior to the lesson: Set up a Measurement Scavenger Hunt. Choose ten different objects in your classroom that you want students to measure. Label each object with a letter, using the letters A through J. These letters and corresponding objects will be used as measuring stations during the scavenger hunt.

Materials

For each student:

Figure 4.1.1. *How Long Is Your Desk?*

Pencil

Measuring tools such as paper clips, straws, crayons, pencils, erasers, tiles, and rods

Centimeter or inch ruler

Math journal

Figure 4.1.2. *Measurement Scavenger Hunt!*

Story and Mini-Lesson

1. **P**review the story by taking a "picture walk" through the book. Introduce the word *measure*. Ask students to share with you what they think the word means. Confirm correct answers.

2. **P**redict the events in the story. Ask the class, "What do you think is going on in this story?"

3. **R**eview the story by re-reading it. Have the class keep track of all the different animals that Milo uses to measure the log and how many of each animal he uses.

4. Discuss how an object can be measured with various measuring tools (or animals), with the results from each measuring tool being different.

5. **C**onnect the story to the lesson. Ask students to tell about when they measured something. Ask, "What did you measure? What did you use for a measuring tool?"

Group Lesson

1. Choose an item to measure and model how to measure that item with a measuring tool. Give students an opportunity to practice measuring several items with that tool.

> This could be a team activity if your seating arrangement is in teams, or an individual activity for students to work on independently. Decide beforehand which way you want your students to work.

2. Show students **Figure 4.1.1.** *How Long Is Your Desk?* Tell students they will choose four classroom items as measuring tools (for example, paper clips, straws, crayons, and pencils) to measure the length of their tables or desks.

3. Hand out **Figure 4.1.1**. and model for students how to fill in this measurement recording sheet.

4. Direct students to work in teams or independently, as you have decided previously.

5. When students have completed their measurements with nonstandard measuring tools, show them how to measure their tables or desks with standard centimeter and inch rulers. Then have students complete **Figure 4.1.1.**

Discovery

When students have completed the Group Lesson activity, have them begin the Measurement Scavenger Hunt. First have students choose a measuring tool. Then direct them to find the objects at the stations marked A through J. At each letter, they must measure the object they find, then record that measurement on **Figure 4.1.2.** *Measurement Scavenger Hunt!* Tell students that no more than two students are allowed at each station at the same time.

Reflection

Have students or teams share the data they collected with the rest of the class. Students should then reflect in their math journals on the following questions: Which measuring tool was the easiest to use? Why? Which was the most difficult to use? Why? Explain why you think people have come up with standard units of measurement (centimeters and meters, or inches, feet, and yards).

Assessment

Observe how students use their measuring tools. Spot-check measurements for accuracy. Check students' record sheets and math journals. Did students give logical reasons to explain why people use standard measuring tools? Keep anecdotal records of your observations.

Special Needs Adaptations

Auditory disability: An interpreter should sign the story and lesson for these students. This lesson provides many visual cues and kinesthetic activities that are appropriate for those with auditory disabilities.

Motor disability: Some students may need assistance with the activities in this lesson. You may need to assign a student partner or an aide to help these students move about the classroom, manipulate the measuring tools, and record information.

Visual disability: Orient these students to the locations of the measuring tools and scavenger hunt objects. Have these students work with an aide or a partner during the measuring and recording activity. These students may record their measurements into a tape recorder.

English Language Learners: Partner these students with same-language-speaking buddies. Demonstrate how to do each activity. Check to ensure that these students understand the instructions.

Extensions

- Change the objective of the measurement scavenger hunt; for example:

    ✓ Have students hunt for items to measure throughout the school.

    ✓ Have students create their own measurement scavenger hunt in the classroom.

- Set up a measurement center where students can engage in free exploration using standard and nonstandard units of measurement.

- Use *Interactive Math Journey* to reinforce measurement skills. Go to *Log Cabin Measurement*.

Bibliography

Adler, David. *How Tall, How Short, How Faraway?* New York: Holiday House, 2000.

Briggs, Raymond. *Jim and the Beanstalk.* New York: Putnam, 1997.

Browning, Dave. *Marvin Measures Up.* New York: William Morrow, 2000.

Leedy, Loreen. *Measuring Penny.* New York: Henry Holt, 2000.

Ling, Bettina. *The Fattest, Tallest, Biggest Snowman Ever.* New York: Scholastic, 1996. (Math activities by Marilyn Burns included.)

Software

The Learning Company. 1996. *Interactive Math Journey.* Macintosh and Windows 95, Windows 3.1.

Related Standards 2000

Standard 1: Number and Operations

Standard 2: Algebra

Standard 3: Geometry

Standard 6: Problem Solving

Standard 7: Reasoning and Proof

Standard 8: Communication

Standard 9: Connections

Standard 10: Representation

Related Standards 1989

Standard 1: Mathematics as Problem Solving

Standard 2: Mathematics as Communication

Standard 3: Mathematics as Reasoning

Standard 4: Mathematical Connections

Standard 6: Number Sense and Numeration

Standard 10: Measurement

LESSON 2

Measure Length, Weight, Volume, and Time

Peck, Jan. *The Giant Carrot.* New York: Dial Books for Young Readers, 1998.

The Giant Carrot, an adaptation of the Russian folktale *The Enormous Turnip,* is a story about a family that plants a carrot seed. Each member of the family hopes to be the one to prepare a special treat from the carrot after it is harvested. They all work together to care for the carrot, but it grows the most when Little Isabelle sings and dances for it. Soon the carrot is so big that the entire family must heave together to pull it up. There is enough carrot for each member of the family to prepare his or her favorite carrot meals. A recipe for Little Isabelle's Carrot Puddin' is in the back of the book.

Time Frame

50 minutes

Materials

For the teacher:

Five bags of large carrots (approximately 50)

Chart paper or chalkboard

Measuring instruments: weighing scale (pounds), ruler with inches and centimeters, paper clips, Unifix cubes, and beans

Recipe for Carrot Puddin' from the back of the book, two copies (optional; see extensions)

Ingredients for the pudding, doubled (optional; see extensions)

Figure 4.2.1. *Measuring Carrots and Measuring Me*

For each student:

Figure 4.2.1. *Measuring Carrots and Measuring Me*

Pencil

One scraped and washed carrot for the final Discovery activity

Copy of the recipe for Carrot Puddin' (to take home).

Prior to the lesson, set up the following measuring centers around the room:

♦ A weighing scale for estimating and weighing five carrots

♦ Paper clips for estimating and measuring the length of one carrot

♦ Beans for estimating and measuring the length of one carrot

♦ Inch rulers for estimating and measuring the length of one carrot

♦ Centimeter rulers for estimating and measuring the length of one carrot

♦ A basket of fifteen carrots for estimating and measuring the height of each student in carrots

Plan at least 30 minutes for students to spend on this activity.

Story and Mini-Lesson

1. **P**review and **p**redict the story. Take a "picture walk" through the story and have the students make predictions about what they think will happen in the story.

2. **R**ead the story. As you read, have students identify what each character does to help the carrot grow.

3. **R**etell the story. Ask for volunteers to explain the main idea of the story or to tell what happened at the beginning, middle, and end of the story.

4. **R**eview the author's note in the beginning of the book. Explain to students that this story is an adaptation of the Russian folktale *The Enormous Turnip*.

Group Lesson

1. **C**onnect *The Giant Carrot* to the math lesson by explaining to students that they will do estimation activities with carrots. **R**eview what *estimation* means (for example, making smart guesses). Discuss examples of things students estimate, such as the number of beans in a jar, how long it takes to drive from school to home, or how much a box of books weighs.

2. Show the class the measuring centers you have set up throughout the room. Model what to do at each center; for example, at the weight scale center, make an estimate, then weigh six carrots. Demonstrate how to fill out the first row of **Figure 4.2.1.** *Measuring Carrots and Measuring Me.*

3. Review the names of the standard measuring tools, then model the correct use of each tool.

4. Distribute copies of **Figure 4.2.1**.

5. Divide students into six groups, then direct groups to the various measuring centers.

6. Students should work together. Have them discuss and record their estimations, then measure and record the actual measurements.

7. Allow approximately five minutes at each station. Ring a bell or flash the lights to signal groups to rotate clockwise to the next measuring center.

Discovery

When all groups have participated at each measuring center, gather students together to answer the last question, "How long does it take you to eat a carrot?" Pass out one scraped and washed carrot to each child. Have each student record how long he or she estimates it will take to eat one carrot. Direct students' attention to the classroom clock. Model how to use the second hand of a clock to count minutes. Have each student record the actual amount of time it takes to eat his or her carrot.

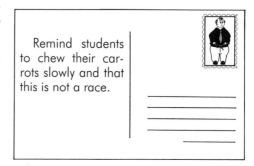

Remind students to chew their carrots slowly and that this is not a race.

Reflection

Lead a discussion about the results of the measuring activities. Were students' estimations close, way off, or exact? Which estimation was the easiest to determine? Which was the hardest? Did discussing estimates with one another help students make accurate or close estimations? Why or why not? Which measuring tool was the easiest to use? Which tool was the hardest to use? Which measuring tool had they used before?

Assessment

As students work at the estimation centers, observe and record their abilities to estimate with reasonable accuracy. Assist students in using measuring tools appropriately. Check the accuracy of students' measurements.

Special Needs Adaptations

Auditory disability: An interpreter should sign the story and give directions throughout the lesson. Provide visual aids to support these students, such as printing instructions for each activity on the chalkboard.

Motor disability: An aide or student helper should assist students with motor disabilities in moving about the room, in using the measuring tools, and with recording data.

Visual disability: Have partners assist students with visual disabilities by orienting these students to the location of the estimating centers, the objects to measure, and the measuring tools. Partners may help by placing measuring instruments and materials to be estimated within easy reach of these students. Visually impaired students can record their estimations and subsequent measurements on a tape recorder.

English Language Learners: Record or locate a recording of *The Giant Carrot* in these students' native languages. These students can also share the words in their native languages for the measuring tools, *carrot*, and the numbers used in each estimating activity. Post these words on a chalkboard or bulletin board.

Extensions

- Re-read the story and have five students play the parts of the carrot, Papa Joe, Mama Bess, Brother Abel, and Sweet Little Isabelle. The rest of the class can choose a song to sing while Isabelle does her dance.

- Ask the students to make up a song that corresponds to the events in the story.

- Have the students make up movements to Isabelle's dance.

- Plant carrot seeds and watch them grow. Ask the students to estimate how long it will take. They should also make and record observations of actual growth.

- Have students draw a picture of a carrot and measure the drawing.

- Compare and contrast different variations of this traditional folktale.

- Have the students write a story about "The Giant . . . Tomato," or other vegetables such as pumpkins, eggplants, or radishes.

- Arrange to use a kitchen. Make Little Isabelle's Carrot Puddin'. Divide the class into two groups. One group has the recipe and the ingredients; the other group has only the ingredients. Both groups make Carrot Puddin'. The group with the ingredients only must estimate how much of each ingredient to put in the recipe, based on prior cooking experience or knowledge. Compare the two finished products. Have students do a taste test to see if the estimating group was close to estimating the correct amounts for the real recipe!

Bibliography

Kroll, Steven. *The Biggest Pumpkin Ever.* New York: Scholastic, 1993.

Tolstoy, Alexei. *The Gigantic Turnip.* New York: Barefoot Books, 2000.

White, Linda. *Too Many Pumpkins.* New York: Holiday House, 1998.

Related Standards 2000

Standard 1: Number and Operations

Standard 2: Algebra

Standard 5: Data Analysis and Probability

Standard 6: Problem Solving

Standard 7: Reasoning and Proof

Standard 8: Communication

Standard 9: Connections

Standard 10: Representation

Related Standards 1989

Standard 1: Mathematics as Problem Solving

Standard 2: Mathematics as Communication

Standard 3: Mathematics as Reasoning

Standard 10: Measurement

Standard 12: Fractions and Decimals

LESSON 3

Measure Time

Rathmann, Peggy. *Ten Minutes Till Bedtime.* New York: Putnam, 1998.

Caldecott Medal-winning author Peggy Rathmann brings together a brigade of hamsters and a young boy whose bedtime is approaching. The hamster family parades through the young boy's house while he gets ready for bed. Will he make it to bed on time? Or will the hamsters distract him from his bedtime routine? This book is filled with detailed illustrations that children will want to look at again and again.

Time Frame

Day One: 30 minutes

Day Two: 50 minutes

Materials

For the teacher:

Stopwatch

Chart paper (3 to 4 feet in length) or chalkboard labeled with graph; refer to **Figure 4.3.1. Our Bedtime Routines**

Stop! The Watch: A Book of Everyday, Ordinary, Anybody Olympics (see bibliography) (optional)

For each student:

Pencil

Figure 4.3.1. *Our Bedtime Routines*

Figure 4.3.2. *My Bedtime Routines* (to be started at school and completed as homework)

Figure 4.3.3. *One-Minute Activities*

Five sticky notes

Math journal

Story and Mini-Lesson: Day One

1. **P**review, **p**redict, and **r**ead the story.

2. **R**eview the story. Ask students to tell you all the things the hamsters did in the ten minutes before bedtime.

3. Connect the story to the lesson by discussing bedtime routines. Ask students, "What do you do to get ready for bedtime?"

4. Direct students to look at the graph in **Figure 4.3.1. *Our Bedtime Routines.***

5. Introduce possible choices for bedtime activities. Ask students to think about which of these bedtime activities they do daily.

6. Give each student five sticky notes. Have each student label each sticky note with his or her name.

7. Have students place their labeled sticky notes on the columns corresponding to the bedtime routines in which they participate. For example, if a student reads a book before bedtime, he or she would place a sticky note in the column that corresponds to reading a book before bedtime. After all students have placed their sticky notes on the graph, discuss the results.

8. Have students estimate how long they think it would take to do each one of these activities.

9. Give each child a copy of the record sheet, **Figure 4.3.2. *My Bedtime Routines.***

10. Have the students record their estimations on the record sheet.

Discovery: Day One

Discuss the estimations. Encourage students to tell why they estimated as they did. Ask students to share any other bedtime routines they have. Today, they will take home their copies of **Figure 4.3.2. *My Bedtime Routines*** to complete as homework. With help from parents, students will measure and record the actual time it takes to complete each bedtime routine. Students should return the record sheets to school on the following day.

Group Lesson: Day Two

1. Re-read and review *Ten Minutes Till Bedtime*. Have students compare the bedtime activities they do with the activities Milo does.

2. Connect the story to today's lesson. Have students discuss the homework from the previous night. Were they surprised at the actual time it took to do each activity? Were their estimations correct?

3. Share *Stop! The Watch: A Book of Everyday, Ordinary, Anybody Olympics*. If this book is not available, brainstorm activities that could be timed in a minute, such as hopping on one foot, saying the alphabet, or tying one's shoes. Refer to **Figure 4.3.3. *One-Minute Activities,*** which suggests activities to be timed and recorded.

4. Tell students that they will now see what they can do in one minute.

5. Give each child a copy of **Figure 4.3.3.**

6. Discuss the first activity. Have students estimate how many times they think they can tie and untie their own shoes in one minute. Have students record their estimations in the box provided, then encourage students to share their estimations.

7. Start the stopwatch and have students begin shoe tying. Say, "Stop!" when one minute is over. Have students record the actual number of times they did the activity in the box provided.

8. Discuss the estimations. Which were close, and which were far off from the actual time it took?

9. Continue to follow this procedure throughout the rest of the activities.

Discovery: Day Two

When students finish the activities listed in **Figure 4.3.3.** *One-Minute Activities,* have them brainstorm their own one-minute activities. Show students how to use the classroom clock and second hand to time one minute. (The second hand should be on the 12 to start, and return to the 12 to stop.)

Have each student choose a partner, then take turns timing each other as each one does a one-minute activity. Students may use the back of **Figure 4.3.3.** to record the activity and the estimated number of times and actual number of times they did the activity in one minute.

Reflection: Day Two

Lead a classroom discussion about time and how it can feel fast or slow depending on what you are doing. Ask, "What activity did you do that made one minute feel long? What activity did you do that made one minute feel short? How many times do you think you could do the activities in an hour? A day? How do you know when one minute has passed?"

Assessment: Day Two

Have students turn in their estimation papers. Review journal work and make anecdotal notes regarding students' understanding of estimation and time. Check students' homework, **Figure 4.3.2.** *My Bedtime Routines.*

Special Needs Adaptations

Auditory disability: An interpreter should sign the story and the directions for the activities. Students with auditory disabilities can participate with the class in all the activities.

Motor disability: Have these students participate in activities based on their abilities. These students may also choose alternate activities to time, such as clapping hands, blinking eyes, or stomping feet for one minute. A student who is unable to do vigorous exercise such as jumping jacks could be the official class timer and could announce, "Start!" and "Stop!" for the other students.

Visual disability: Provide assistance for these students by a peer or adult. Peer helpers should assist these students in labeling and placing their sticky notes in the appropriate boxes on the class graph, **Figure 4.3.1.** *Our Bedtime Routines.* Use string to divide the columns and rows of the graph so visually disabled students can run their hands up and down the graph to feel where other students have placed their notes. Have a peer helper read aloud the labels for the columns. For **Figure**

4.3.3. *One-Minute Activities,* these students could record their estimates and the actual time they took to do activities into tape recorders.

English Language Learners: Partner these students with bilingual classmates or a teacher. Have these students teach counting words in their native languages to the class.

Extensions

- Keep a running record of how long it takes the class to line up before recess and hang up coats after recess. Check if these times decrease over the school year.

- Have students estimate and measure the actual time it takes to perform routine activities at home, such as eating, sleeping, watching TV, and doing chores.

- Have the class make an estimation book. Have students draw pictures of themselves doing an activity they choose to estimate, write the estimate below each picture, and then record the actual time on the back of the page.

- Post an estimation bulletin board outside the room for other students to guess the amount of time it takes to do certain activities, such as walk to the cafeteria, eat lunch, and play at recess. Use a flip card for them to open and see the actual time.

- Use the *Reader Rabbit Personalized Math, Ages 6–9* software to reinforce clock reading skills. Instruct students to go to *Pirate Lookout.*

Bibliography

Bourde, Linda. *Eye Count: A Book of Counting Puzzles.* San Francisco: Chronicle Books, 1995.

Brett, Jan. *The Mitten.* New York: Putnam, 1996.

Chouinard, Roger, and Mariko Chouinard. *One Magic Box.* New York: Doubleday, 1989.

Keenan, Sheila. *What Time Is It? A Book of Math Riddles.* New York: Cartwheel Books, 2000.

Stop! The Watch: A Book of Everyday, Ordinary, Anybody Olympics. Palo Alto, CA: Klutz Press, 1993.

Software

The Learning Company. 1999. *Reader Rabbit Personalized Math, Ages 6–9.* Macintosh and Windows.

Related Standards 2000

Standard   1: Number and Operations

Standard   2: Algebra

Standard   5: Data Analysis and Probability

Standard   6: Problem Solving

Standard   7: Reasoning and Proof

Standard   8: Communication

Standard   9: Connections

Standard 10: Representation

Related Standards 1989

Standard   1: Math as Problem Solving

Standard   2: Math as Communication

Standard   3: Math as Reasoning

Standard 10: Measurement

LESSON 4

Measure Capacity

Stevens, Janet, and Susan Stevens Crummel. *Cook-a-Doodle-Doo!* San Diego: Harcourt Brace, 1999.

"Cook-a-Doodle-Doo!" crows Big Brown Rooster. He is tired of the same old chicken feed every day. Suddenly, Rooster remembers that he is descended from a proud line of baking roosters. After all, his great-grandmother was the Little Red Hen! He decides to take matters into his own hands and bake up a batch of strawberry shortcake, an old family recipe. Will anyone help? Many animals are eager to help, but there is just one problem: They don't know how to bake! Read along and you will discover that learning to measure is an important part of cooking and baking.

Time Frame

Day One: 50 minutes

Day Two: 50 minutes

Materials

➤ Day One

For the teacher:

Teachers, if parents are unable to send the necessary supplies for this project, take a field trip to your school cafeteria or to a local bakery.

Send **Figure 4.4.1. *Parent Letter*** home to parents one week prior to the lesson.

Chart paper or chalkboard with heading; refer to **Figure 4.4.2. *Items Needed, Amounts Needed***

Marker

One bag of flour

One large bowl

One small bowl

One sifter

One piece of waxed paper

Measuring cups

Measuring spoons

One stick of butter (optional)

One egg (optional)

One egg beater

Liquid measuring cup

One big spoon

One timer

Whipping cream or pre-made whipped cream (optional)

Oven mitt

Strawberries (optional)

One 8-inch round pan, $\frac{1}{2}$ inch deep

For each student:

Math journal

Pencil

➤ **Day Two**

> There are a lot of ingredients, and it takes much preparation to get ready for this lesson, but I believe it will be time well spent. Take any shortcuts you think necessary. For example, use pre-made whipped cream and previously sliced strawberries. You will be surprised to find out how many parent and community volunteers are willing to gather and prepare the materials, tools, and ingredients. Just ask!

For the teacher:

One volunteer for each group of four students (optional)

Access to an oven

For each group of four:

Figure 4.4.3. *Directions for Baking Strawberry Shortcake*

Zipping storage bag containing several cups of flour, labeled "Flour"

Zipping storage bag containing 1 cup of sugar, labeled "Sugar"

Zipping storage bag containing 2 tablespoons of baking power, labeled, "Baking Powder"

Zipping storage bag containing 2 teaspoons of salt, labeled "Salt"

One stick of butter

One egg

One-quarter pint of milk (school lunch size)

One pint container of strawberries, or bag of frozen strawberries, thawed

One-half pint of whipping cream or pre-made whipped cream

One large bowl

One small bowl

Sifter

One large piece of waxed paper

One set of measuring cups: 1 cup, $\frac{1}{2}$ cup, $\frac{1}{3}$ cup, and $\frac{1}{4}$ cup

Set of measuring spoons: 1 tbsp., 1 tsp., $\frac{1}{2}$ tsp., and $\frac{1}{4}$ tsp.

Two table knives

One handheld eggbeater or one fork

One liquid measuring cup

One large spoon

One 8-inch round pan, $\frac{1}{2}$-inch deep

One kitchen timer

One potholder or oven mitt

One large paper plate

One sticky note with group members' names on it

For each student:

Paper plate

Fork

Napkin

Figure 4.4.4. *Review*

Story and Mini-Lesson: Day One

1. **P**review the story. Show students the book cover and read them the title. Ask, "Why do you think the title is *Cook-a-Doodle-Doo!*? Do you know any other stories in which an animal cooks or bakes?"

2. **P**redict. Take a "picture walk" through the book with the class. Call on the children to tell you what they think the story is about.

3. If it has not come up already, remind students of the story *The Little Red Hen.* Ask for volunteers to summarize the story for the rest of the class. If needed, fill in the missing parts of the story. Tell children that *Cook-a-Doodle-Doo!* is similar to and different than *The Little Red Hen* in many ways. Tell students to look and listen for these similarities and differences as you read aloud *Cook-a-Doodle-Doo!*

4. **R**ead the story. Do not read the side-notes in the book at this time.

5. **R**eview the story. Discuss the similarities and differences between the two stories.

6. Introduce cooking and baking. Ask the class, "How many of you have helped cook or bake something?" Call on several students to share how they have cooked or baked. Then ask, "Is baking *easy*? Why or why not?" Discuss. Tell the class that they will all have the opportunity to bake strawberry shortcake, just like Big Brown Rooster, Turtle, Iguana, and Pig. But first they need to learn some important things about baking. Tell students, "Today we will be making a list of ingredients and the tools we will use for baking. Listen carefully as I read because I will ask you to help make the list after I finish."

7. **R**e-read *Cook-a-Doodle-Doo!,* but this time just read the notes on the side. This part of the book gives information about baking.

8. Ask students to recall what was first needed to make strawberry shortcake. Refer to pages 11 and 12 (where Iguana turns on the oven). Record the items needed, and the quantity (oven, 1) on the chart paper or chalkboard. Continue to read the side notes throughout the book. Record the items and quantities needed. As you go, talk about each item. Show the sample items and measuring tools to students and demonstrate how the tools work so children become familiar with them. Discuss and explain the abbreviations for *tablespoon* and *teaspoon*.

9. Tell your students that tomorrow they'll bake strawberry shortcake!

Reflection: Day One

Have students return to their desks and take out their math journals. Write one or more of the following questions on the board: Does baking involve measuring? How? Is it important to measure correctly when cooking or baking? Why? What do you think your strawberry shortcake will look like when it is finished? Have the students draw pictures.

Story and Mini-Lesson: Day Two

Before you start today's lesson, divide your students into groups of four. Assign each group member a role: Rooster (the chef), Turtle (the reader), Iguana (the supplier), or Pig (the taster and checker). Set up baking stations with all the supplies each group will need. The school cafeteria is a great place to do this.

Make copies of **Figure 4.4.3. *Directions for Baking Straw- berry Shortcake*** for each group to follow. Enlist the support of parents or community volunteers to help with this project. Coach the parent or community volunteers be- forehand and let them know their job is to assist, not take over.

1. **R**eview *Cook-a-Doodle-Doo!* with the class. Discuss with students what the story was about.

2. **R**e-read the story.

3. Ask the students to recall the ingredients and tools needed to make strawberry short- cake. Refer to the chart you made yesterday.

4. Discuss the characters in the story. Ask students to tell you what each character's job was. (Rooster was the chef, Turtle was the reader, Iguana was the "getter" or sup- plier, and Pig was the taster. Pig also asked questions and kept everyone on track.)

5. Discuss teamwork. Turn to page 11 in the book. Read this page, then ask, "Why does Rooster say they are a team?" Discuss with students how they will be working in teams just like the animals in the book and they must be good team workers. Tell students that each one of them will have a job, just like the characters in the book.

6. Assign each student a group and a job. Send each group to wash their hands and then to find their baking station.

7. Have students find all the ingredients and the direction sheet.

8. Tell students to begin.

9. Observe groups at work, and assist when needed.

Discovery: Day Two

As groups put their strawberry shortcakes in the oven, have each group member get **Figure 4.4.4 *Review*** and work quietly until their shortcake is done baking.

Reflection: Day Two

When all the shortcakes are out of the oven, put them on a table. Put a sticky note with group member names next to each shortcake. As a class, look at all the shortcakes and discuss their similarities and differences. Discuss problems groups encountered and ask groups to share how they solved those problems. Now you may eat and enjoy!

Assessment: Day Two

Collect students' copies of **Figure 4.4.4. *Review*** and check them for understanding.

Special Needs Adaptations

Auditory disability: An interpreter will need to sign the story and assist with the lesson. This is a visual and kinesthetic lesson that students with auditory disabilities will enjoy.

Motor disability: A student buddy or aide may assist these students with the writing and cooking portion of the lesson. Assign these students to be either a Turtle (reader) or a Pig (taster and checker).

Visual disability: This is a visual lesson, so make sure these students comprehend the lesson. Pass around the bags of ingredients and tools during the Story and Mini-Lessons so that these students get to feel each item. With volunteer assistance, these students would be good Iguanas (suppliers) during the cooking process. During the Discovery activity, have these students orally answer the questions and record their answers into a tape recorder.

English Language Learners: Have student partners check for understanding. These students would be good Roosters or Iguanas. Post the recipe in these students' native languages.

Extensions

■ Set up a measuring center in your classroom with measuring cups, spoons, and sand. Put the sand in big basins or tubs. Allow students to use the cups and spoons to measure and pour the sand.

■ Have students bring in favorite family recipes to create a class cookbook.

■ Take a field trip to a local bakery or restaurant to learn about how cooks and chefs use measuring in baking and cooking.

■ Use the *Interactive Math Journey* software. Have students work in the *Sugarcane Bakery*.

Bibliography

Beil, Karen Magnuson. *A Cake All for Me!* New York: Holiday House, 1998.

Brink, Carol. *Goody O' Grumpity.* New York: North South Books, 1996.

Krudwig, Vickie Leigh. *Cucumber Soup.* Golden, CO: Fulcrum, 1998.

Miranda, Anne. *To Market, To Market.* San Diego: Harcourt Brace, 1997.

Software

The Learning Company. 1996. *Interactive Math Journey.* Macintosh and Windows 95, Windows 3.1.

Related Standards 2000

Standard 1: Number and Operations

Standard 2: Algebra

Standard 3: Geometry

Standard 6: Problem Solving

Standard 7: Reasoning and Proof

Standard 8: Communication

Standard 9: Connections

Standard 10: Representation

Related Standards 1989

Standard 1: Math as Problem Solving

Standard 2: Math as Communication

Standard 3: Math as Reasoning

Standard 4: Mathematical Connections

Standard 6: Number Sense and Numeration

Standard 13: Patterns and Relationships

Name: _____ **Date:** _____

Find four different items from your classroom to use as measuring tools. List each item in the left column below. Then measure the length of your desk or table with each measuring tool, one at a time. In the right column below, write the number of units of each item you used to measure the length of your desk or table.

Item used as a measuring tool   **How many units for each item?**

1. _____   1. _____

2. _____   2. _____

3. _____   3. _____

4. _____   4. _____

Now measure your desk with a **centimeter ruler**. How many **centimeters** long is your

desk? _____

Now measure your desk with an **inch ruler**. How many **inches** long is your desk?

_____

Figure 4.1.1. *How Long Is Your Desk?*

Name: _____ **Date:** _____

Directions: Choose a measuring tool. Then find the following letters arranged throughout your classroom. When you find the letter, measure the length of the object next to the letter with your measuring tool. Record your measurements next to the corresponding letters below.

A. _____   **B.** _____

C. _____   **D.** _____

E. _____   **F.** _____

G. _____   **H.** _____

I. _____   **J.** _____

I used the following item as a measuring tool: _____

Figure 4.1.2. *Measurement Scavenger Hunt!*

Name: _____   Date: _____

Measuring Tool	Estimated Measurement of Carrot	Actual Measurement of Carrot
Weight scale	_____ pounds	_____ pounds
Paper clips	_____ paper clips	_____ paper clips
Beans	_____ beans	_____ beans
Unifix cubes	_____ cubes	_____ cubes
Inch ruler	_____ inches	_____ inches
Centimeter ruler	_____ centimeters	_____ centimeters

	Estimated Measurement	Actual Measurement
How many carrots tall am I?	I think I am _____ carrots tall.	I am _____ carrots tall.
How long does it take for me to eat a carrot?	I think it will take me _____ minutes to eat a carrot.	It took me _____ minutes to eat a carrot.

Figure 4.2.1. *Measuring Carrots and Measuring Me*

20				
19				
18				
17				
16				
15				
14				
13				
12				
11				
10				
9				
8				
7				
6				
5				
4				
3				
2				
1				
Brush my teeth	Read a story	Take a bath	Clean my room	Say "Goodnight"

Figure 4.3.1. *Our Bedtime Routines*

Name: _____   **Date:** _____

My bedtime routines	My estimate of the time it takes to do my bedtime routines	The actual time it takes to do my bedtime routines
Brush my teeth	_____ minutes	_____ minutes
Read a story	_____ minutes	_____ minutes
Take a bath	_____ minutes	_____ minutes
Clean my room	_____ minutes	_____ minutes
Say "Goodnight"	_____ seconds	_____ seconds
	_____ minutes	_____ minutes
	_____ minutes	_____ minutes
	_____ minutes	_____ minutes
	_____ minutes	_____ minutes

Use this space to draw a picture of you in bed.

Figure 4.3.2. *My Bedtime Routines*

Name: _____ **Date:** _____

What can you do in one minute? Look at the following activities and estimate how many times you can do the following activities in one minute. Now see how long each one actually takes! Record your results.

Activity	The estimated number of times I can do the activity in one minute:	The actual number of times I can do the activity in one minute:
Tie a shoe		
Write my name		
Sing the Alphabet Song		
Read a poem		
Do jumping jacks		
Line up in a straight line with my class		
Count to 100		
My choice		

Figure 4.3.3. One-Minute Activities

Dear Parents,

Let's get cooking! Next week, our class will use measuring tools and measure ingredients during a baking activity. We will read the story *Cook-a-Doodle-Doo!* by Janet Stevens and Susan Stevens Crummel, then bake up a batch of strawberry shortcake. The baking date is _____ at _____:_____. Not only will students learn more about measuring, but they will also practice working together in teams.

We need your help! May we borrow several items for this lesson? Please label with your name and send any of the items listed below to school with your child. We will take good care of them and wash them before we return them to you. Also, we need several parent volunteers to help out! If you will join us, please make note of this below.

Thanks for your help and support! "Cook-a-Doodle-Doo!"

Sincerely, _____

Items needed:

Large mixing bowl

Waxed paper

Measuring cups

Measuring spoons

Liquid measuring cup

Mixing spoon

Kitchen timer

Oven mitt

Sifter

One 8-inch round pan, $\frac{1}{2}$ inch deep

Small mixing bowl

_____ **I will be able to attend the baking session.**

_____ **I will not be able to attend the baking session.**

_____ **I am sending the items to school that I have circled above.**

Figure 4.4.1. *Parent Letter*

Items Needed	Amounts Needed

Figure 4.4.2. Items Needed, Amounts Needed

1. Read all the directions before starting.
2. Wash your hands.
3. Heat the oven to 450 degrees Fahrenheit.
4. Put a piece of waxed paper on the table.
5. Sift the flour.
6. Measure 2 cups of flour. Pour the flour into the measuring cup and level it off with the straight edge of a knife. Put the 2 cups of flour into the big bowl.
7. Add 2 tablespoons of sugar.
8. Add 1 tablespoon of baking powder.
9. Add $\frac{1}{2}$ teaspoon of salt.
10. Sift all the dry ingredients together.
11. Add one stick of butter. Save the wrapper for later.
12. Cut in the butter. Use the two table knives and cut the butter into tiny pieces.
13. Crack the egg and put it into the small bowl.
14. Beat the egg using a fork or an eggbeater.
15. Pour the beaten egg into the big bowl.
16. Add $\frac{2}{3}$ cup of milk to the big bowl.
17. Mix the dough.
18. Take the round baking pan and grease it. You may use the wrapper from the butter and spread it all over the inside of the pan.
19. Pour the dough into the baking pan.
20. Put it in the oven.
21. Turn the kitchen timer to fifteen minutes.
22. Wash the strawberries and slice them if needed. Remember to cut off the stems and tops!
23. Whip the cream if needed. Wash the big bowl and use it to whip the cream.
24. Clean up.
25. When the kitchen timer goes off, put on the oven mitt and take the shortcake out of the oven. Check to see if the shortcake is done. Stick the knife into the center and see if it comes out clean. If it does, the shortcake is done. If not, put the cake back in the oven and set the kitchen timer for four minutes. Take the cake out using the oven mitt when the timer goes off.
26. Turn off the oven.
27. Let the shortcake cool for five minutes. While waiting, finish cleaning up.
28. Take the shortcake out of the pan. Turn the shortcake over and tap on the bottom until the cake comes out. Do this over the large paper plate.
29. Slice the cake in half, lengthwise.
30. Stack one layer of cake; spread half of the whipped cream on top, and then half of the strawberries.
31. Repeat.
32. Cut into equal slices.
33. Eat and enjoy!

Figure 4.4.3. *Directions for Baking Strawberry Shortcake*

Name: _____   **Date:** _____

Circle the correct answer.

1. Which is more?   cup   teaspoon

2. Which is more?   tablespoon $\frac{1}{2}$ teaspoon

3. Which would you use to measure flour?   ruler   cup

4. Which would you use to cut butter?   scissors   two knifes

5. What is the best way to time what   kitchen timer   count out loud
   you are cooking or baking?

6. Below, draw a picture of three measuring tools you used while baking.

Figure 4.4.4. Review

Chapter 5

Data Analysis and Probability

Dear Math Teacher,

During the lessons in this chapter, students collect, organize and interpret data, and examine concepts of chance and probability. In the first lesson, introduced by Robert Louis Stevenson's *Where Go the Boats?*, students build boats, launch them, and wonder where their boats will land. Students pose questions such as, "Did my boat land here by chance or probability?"

The second lesson uses *A Cheese and Tomato Spider*, a crazy flipbook, to challenge students to discover how many picture combinations can be made from six silly drawings. The third lesson challenges children to pursue the realm of the probable and the improbable after reading Laura Numeroff's *If You Give a Pig a Pancake*. The fourth and final lesson introduces the work of *Snowflake Bentley*, whose life effort was a model for how to collect and record data and to draw conclusions from those data.

Chances are, your students will take a liking to data analysis and probability.

Caroline

LESSON 1

Build and Launch Boats; Learn about Probability

Stevenson, Robert Louis. *Where Go the Boats?* New York: Harcourt Brace, 1998.

Max Grover has published a newly illustrated version of Robert Louis Stevenson's beloved poem, *Where Go the Boats?* In this classic poem, originally published in *A Child's Garden of Verses*, a young boat-maker sends "Boats of mine a-boating" down a river to unknown destinations and wonders, "Where will all come home?" Although your students will enjoy Grover's bright and contemporary illustrations, it is not necessary to have this particular edition of Stevenson's classic poem to do the following chance and probability lesson.

Time Frame

➤ Pre-Activity Homework

50 minutes

At least one week before teaching this lesson, send **Figure 5.1.1. *Letter Home*** to your students' parents. Along with the letter, include a boat number (one number for each student in your class) and your school's field trip permission form with pertinent data such as the date, time, and place for the boat launching as well as information about what students should wear for the event.

Day One: 50 minutes

Day Two: 50 minutes

Materials

➤ Pre-Activity

Figure 5.1.1. *Letter Home*

Boat number for each child

Your school's field trip permission form

➤ **Day One**

For the teacher:

Figure 5.1.2. *Where Go the Boats?*

Posted large print chart paper copy of *Where Go the Boats?* from **Figure 5.1.2.**

Chalkboard with math vocabulary words: *chance* and *probability*

Local area map that includes a stream, river, or lake where you will launch your boats

Chalkboard or chart paper

If you don't have a river or lake nearby, have children make a map of a nearby swimming pool, then have a boat launching at the pool. Discuss how to make an artificial current so the boats will do more than bob about. Students might choose to sit at the side of the pool and kick their feet in the water to get the boats to go from one side of the pool to the other. Have students predict where their boats will land.

For each student:

Paper and pencil

One dot sticker, assorted colors ($\frac{1}{4}$ to $\frac{1}{2}$ inch in diameter) (*Note:* Set aside one color such as red to use for found boats after the boat launching.)

➤ **Day Two**

For the teacher:

Local area map from Day One

For each student:

Signed field trip permission slip

Boat, made at home during pre-activity

Suitable clothing for outing

Math journal

Story and Mini-Lesson: Day One

1. **P**review and make **p**redictions about the book. Encourage children to notice and comment on the illustrations. Ask questions such as, "What do you notice? What are the boats passing by? Where are they going?"

2. **R**ead the poem aloud once. **R**e-read it with your students' help, using the large print chart paper copy of *Where Go the Boats?*

3. **R**eview. Ask students to tell what the poem is about and to describe where they imagine the boats went.

4. Tell them that today they will **p**redict and mark on the local map where their own boats will go after they have been launched.

5. Next tell them that tomorrow they will launch their boats and then wait to find out the outcome of their boats' voyages.

Group Lesson: Day One

1. Discuss the posted vocabulary words, *chance* and *probability*. Ask, "What is chance? What is probability?" (Chance is something that may or may not happen. Probability is the likelihood of whether something will happen or not.)

2. Discuss what is likely to happen to boats launched from the marked launching spot. Ask the students if it is probable that *all* the boats will be found after they are launched. Discuss why or why not. List all suggestions on the chalkboard or chart paper.

3. Demonstrate how to put one's initials and boat number on the dot sticker provided for each student.

4. Refer to the map and invite each student to place a dot sticker on a spot which he or she thinks is a probable place for his or her boat to land or "come home."

Discovery: Day One

■ Distribute materials.

■ Have students initial and number their dot stickers, then place them on the map.

Reflection: Day One

Have students write in their math journals about what they think will happen to their boats.

Group Lesson: Day Two

1. Go to the chosen launching site.

2. Choral read *Where Go the Boats?*

3. Launch the boats. Launch again boats that drift immediately back to shore. Ask students to notice and talk about where their boats are going.

4. To generate discussion, ask students questions such as the following: Do you feel a breeze? Do you see which direction the stream is flowing? Is there a current? Where are the currents? What causes currents? Do winds, gravity, or obstructions cause currents? Do boats swirl about near obstacles in the water? Do you see an eddy? What causes an eddy? Are there any other factors that could affect the course of the boats?

5. Be safe. Celebrate. Have fun!

    Back at school, following the launch:

1. When a boat is reported found, record the boat number and date found on a color-coded (red) dot sticker. Place it on the map where that boat was found.

2. Compare the actual site where the boat was found to the predicted sight.

3. As more boats are reported found, ask students what they notice about the sites where the boats were found. Ask, "Do you see any patterns?" Remind students of their observations at the launching site made in item 4 in the Day One Group Lesson. Discuss.

4. Have the students predict where the remaining boats might turn up, based on the information acquired about the boats already found.

5. As boats continue to be found, ask students if their predictions are closer now that they have more information with which to work.

6. Together, discuss students' observations and draw conclusions based on reported data. For example, if five out of twenty boats landed near the Drake Eddy, it is probable that under similar conditions, five out of twenty boats or one out of four boats would land near the Drake Eddy if boats were launched again. Or, if none of the boats landed near each other, students could conclude that the boats landed according to chance and that an accurate prediction would be improbable.

Assessment: Day Two

Make anecdotal records based on students' class participation, journal entries, and use of introduced vocabulary.

Special Needs Adaptations

Auditory disability: An interpreter should sign the story and assist with the lesson.

Motor disability: Students with motor impairments will need assistance with marking and placing location dots and with the boat building and launching.

Visual disability: Students with visual disabilities will need assistance during the boat launching.

English Language Learners: Send home letters and instructions in students' native languages. During activities, English Language Learners should partner with other students or volunteers.

Extensions

- Launch a class boat and make predictions about its journey based on prior data gathered in the preceding lesson.

- Invite teachers and students from the entire school to be involved in the boat building and launching project. Bring garbage bags and do a River Clean-up.

- Have each student draw a map of his or her boat's journey.

- Make a class mural or draw a map of your waterway using the *Neighborhood MapMachine* software.

Bibliography

Holling, Holling C. *Paddle to the Sea*. New York: Houghton Mifflin, 1999.

Murphy, Stuart. *The Best Vacation Ever*. New York: HarperCollins, 1997.

Vorderman, Carol. *How Math Works*. New York: Putnam, 1999.

Software

Tom Snyder Productions. 1997. *Neighborhood MapMachine*. Version 1.22. Macintosh and Windows 95, www.tomsnyder.com. (Accessed February 2001).

Related Standards 2000

Standard 1: Number and Operations

Standard 2: Algebra

Standard 3: Geometry

Standard 4: Measurement

Standard 6: Problem Solving

Standard 8: Communication

Standard 9: Connections

Standard 10: Representation

Related Standards 1989

Standard 1: Mathematics as Problem Solving

Standard 2: Mathematics as Communication

Standard 3: Mathematics as Reasoning

Standard 4: Mathematical Connections

Standard 5: Estimation

Standard 6: Number Sense and Numeration

Standard 7: Concepts of Whole Number Operations

Standard 8: Whole Number Computation

Standard 9: Geometry and Spatial Sense

Standard 10: Measurement

Standard 13: Patterns and Relationships

LESSON 2

Make a Flipbook and Determine Combinations

Sharratt, Nick. *A Cheese and Tomato Spider.* Hauppauge, NY: Barron's Educational Series, 1998.

This book is just plain fun! Remember the flipbooks, in which you could change and mix up ordinary subject matter and turn it into something crazy, exciting, or weird? Nick Sharratt does just this with *A Cheese and Tomato Spider*. Sharratt begins with, "Eek!! A wriggly spider!," which metamorphoses with a flip of a page into, "Eek!! A wriggly ice cream!" or, "Yummy! A strawberry flavored spider!" You and your students can make over 100 crazy combinations with Sharratt's book, then make your own flipbooks. You'll all have fun being silly. Oh, and by the way, how many crazy combinations can you make?

Time Frame

Day One: 50 minutes

Day Two: 50 minutes

Day Three: 50 minutes

Materials

➤ **Day One**

> Have a volunteer put together construction paper flipbooks from **Figure 5.2.1. Flipbook Model** two or three days in advance. Have a sample ready for Day One and one book per student for Day Two. If you don't have time or means to make individual flipbooks, make a class or team flipbook using big chart paper. Divide students into small groups and assign one page to each group to complete.

<u>For the teacher:</u>

Blank spiralbound 8½-by-11-inch flipbook sample, three pages long, each page split in half horizontally, from **Figure 5.2.1. *Flipbook Model***

Figure 5.2.2. *Sample—Prediction Graph*

Chart paper bar graph from **Figure 5.2.3. *Prediction Graph***

Chalkboard with the following math vocabulary words:

Combinations—different ways to put things together

Data—information

Graph—a number picture

Estimation—a smart guess

Range—lowest to highest number

For each student:

One sticky note

Pencil

Math journal (optional)

➢ Day Two

For the teacher:

Completed graph from Day One

Completed sample three-page flipbook plus cover from Day One

For each student:

Blank spiralbound flipbook, three pages long plus cover, from **Figure 5.2.1. Flipbook Model**

Crayons and pencil

Markers and colored pencils (optional)

➢ Day Three

For the teacher:

Chart paper bar graph from **Figure 5.2.3. Prediction Graph**

Figure 5.2.4. Flipbook Assessment Checklist

For each student:

Completed flipbooks

Pencil

Story and Mini-Lesson: Day One

1. **P**review, **p**redict, and flip through A Cheese and Tomato Spider.

2. Because the print is large, choral **r**ead the book as you would a Big Book. There is no need to read all the combinations. Leave some of the combinations undiscovered so that children will be tempted to read this book over and over again during independent reading time.

3. **R**eview. Ask children to describe the book and tell about some of the silly combinations they enjoyed.

Group Lesson: Day One

1. Tell students that the author says kids can make more than 100 combinations of crazy pictures with this eleven-page book.

2. Show students your sample book of three pages plus the front and back cover.

3. Tell students they will each make an estimate about how many combinations a kid could make with the three-page sample book. (The answer is 9; don't give it away.)

4. Discuss reasonable guesses. Would 100 be a reasonable guess? Would three or fewer be a reasonable guess? Why or why not?

5. Encourage students to discuss the range of reasonable guesses for the three-page book. Explain that the range includes the lowest number to the highest number that they might guess. For example, a range of 1 to 100 would not be reasonable. One combination of silly pictures would be too low because there are three pages in the book, which already makes three silly picture combinations. 100 would be too high, because that was close to the number of combinations for the eleven-page picture book.

6. Show the chart paper sample estimation graph with a range of three to fifteen. Ask students if they think the range shown by the graph is a reasonable one.

7. Demonstrate how to fill out a sticky note with your name and an estimate between three and fifteen. Then place your sticky note on the bar graph.

8. Distribute sticky notes and have each student write his or her name and estimate on the note, then have students take turns placing their sticky notes on the graph next to the appropriate numbers.

9. After the sticky notes are in place, discuss the data on the graph. Which number got the most estimates? Which got the least?

10. Tell students that later they will determine the correct number of combinations for the three-page sample book. Challenge students to problem solve and puzzle out how to determine the correct number of combinations on their own.

Reflection: Day One

■ Conclude today's lesson by reviewing vocabulary such as *combinations, data, graph, estimation,* and *range.*

■ If there is time, have students write a sentence about today's activity in their math journals. They must use at least one of the math vocabulary words.

Story and Mini-Lesson: Day Two

1. **R**eview *A Cheese and Tomato Spider.*

2. Choral **r**ead a few of the flip page combinations as in Day One.

Group Lesson: Day Two

1. Show the sample three-page flipbook and remind students that today they will make their own flipbooks.

2. Guide a brainstorming session to generate ideas for pictures you and your students would like to make. For example, if you are doing a desert unit, you might encourage students to draw desert animals. Working together, come up with ideas for the sample book. For example, draw on the first page and label accordingly, "A slithery, scaly snake," and on the second page, "A furry, gray coyote," and on the third page, "A black, feathery raven."

3. Show students some of the combinations they could make from the sample, such as "A slithery, scaly coyote" or "A furry, gray snake."

4. After you and your students have generated ideas for pictures to draw, give students instructions for how to make their own books. Pass to each student one pre-made spiralbound flipbook.

5. Show students the pre-measured markings on their flipbooks (see **Figure 5.2.1. Flipbook Model**). Tell students to align their pictures to the width between the vertical marks shown in **c)** in the figure. Their pictures must be $6\frac{1}{2}$ inches wide where the top and bottom halves of the page meet in the middle, so that the pictures will match up when combined with other flipbook pictures (see **e)** and **f)** in the figure).

6. Tell students to draw one picture at a time.

Discovery: Day Two

Distribute materials and use the remaining time for students to work on their own flipbooks. As students complete their pictures, show them how to label them. Note that the words go on the left cover and subsequent left-hand pages, opposite the pictures. The adjectives or describing words go on the top left, and the noun or object goes on the bottom left, as in the book and sample.

Story and Mini-Lesson: Day Three

1. In your group gathering place, ask students to share and admire each other's flipbooks.

2. Review the chart paper bar graph from Day One.

3. Ask students if they solved the puzzle about how many combinations of silly pictures there are in a three-page flip book. (The answer is 9; remember, don't tell until students have solved the problem for themselves.)

4. Discuss students' answers. Ask students how they solved the problem and have them share their problem-solving methods, such as, " I counted as many pictures as I could beginning with the first three pictures," with the rest of the class.

Reflection: Day Three

- Celebrate students' problem-solving strategies by repeating and practicing those methods.

- Read and enjoy each other's flipbooks.

Assessment: Day Three

Review students' flipbooks. Use **Figure 5.2.4.** *Flipbook Assessment Checklist* to record notes regarding students' understanding of the lesson.

Special Needs Adaptations

Auditory disability: An interpreter should sign the story and assist with the lesson. List vocabulary words on the chalkboard as directed above. Post the chart paper graph. Display a pre-made flipbook sample. Highlight the pre-marked measurements on the flipbook pages.

Motor disability: Students with motor impairments may need assistance with writing the sticky note and preparing the flipbook.

Visual disability: Students with visual disabilities may need assistance with writing sticky notes and creating flipbooks. Provide materials for a textured paper or cloth flipbook for visually impaired students.

English Language Learners: Students needing help with English could partner up with other students or classroom volunteers. Allow English Language Learners to label their flipbooks in their primary language and encourage them to share their pictures and say the labels in their primary language as well as in English.

Extensions

- As a class, estimate the number of silly picture combinations for *A Cheese and Tomato Spider* and do a sticky note prediction graph.

- Have students problem solve exactly how many silly picture combinations could be made from *A Cheese and Tomato Spider*.

- Have the class make flipbooks for other thematic units.

- Increase the number of flipbook pages to increase the number of combinations.

- Predict, graph, and determine the number of combinations.

- Have students make a series of flipbooks with increasing numbers of pages and graph the increasing number of combinations. Look for a pattern.

- Have students make a flipbook illustrated with pictures of classmates.

Bibliography

Murphy, Stuart. *The Best Vacation Ever*. New York: HarperCollins, 1997.

Vorderman, Carol. *How Math Works*. New York: Putnam, 1999.

Related Standards 2000

Standard 1: Number and Operations

Standard 2: Algebra

Standard 3: Geometry

Standard 4: Measurement

Standard 6: Problem Solving

Standard 8: Communication

Standard 9: Connections

Standard 10: Representation

Related Standards 1989

Standard 1: Mathematics as Problem Solving

Standard 2: Mathematics as Communication

Standard 3: Mathematics as Reasoning

Standard 4: Mathematical Connections

Standard 5: Estimation

Standard 6: Number Sense and Numeration

Standard 7: Concepts of Whole Number Operations

Standard 8: Whole Number Computation

Standard 9: Geometry and Spatial Sense

Standard 10: Measurement

Standard 13: Patterns and Relationships

LESSON 3

What Will Happen "If . . . "?
Is the Future a Matter of Chaos, Chance, or Probability?

Numeroff, Laura. *If You Give a Pig a Pancake.* New York: HarperCollins, 1998.

The author and illustrator duo, Laura Numeroff and Felicia Bond, have done it again! Is it probability, chance, or chaos that causes things to happen when Numeroff and Bond's characters have company? Just as in their previous books, *If You Give a Mouse a Cookie* and *If You Give a Moose a Muffin,* an amazing chain of events occurs when a young hostess gives an animal friend a tasty treat. You may use any one of the books from this series to accomplish the following lesson, so choose one that is handy, and your students will probably ask for more.

Dear Math Teacher,

Before the lesson, arrange for a partner class to do the same two-day lesson your class is going to do. Choose a class that has about the same number of students as yours; this will be important when you compare class stories on Day Two. We recommend a class at a different grade level to promote interaction between grades.

You and your partner teacher must agree on the same story lead-in, such as *If You Give a Bear a Bicycle* for the Day One writing assignment, for the Day Two Ratio Comparison to make sense.

Your class and your partner class will do the entire Day One lesson and the Day Two Story and Mini-Lesson separately. Then, your partner class will join your class for the Day Two Group Lesson.

Caroline

Time Frame

Day One: 50 minutes

Day Two: 50 minutes

Materials

➤ Day One

For the teacher:

Sealed envelope with enclosed note, "Probably everyone in the class will like *If You Give a Pig a Pancake*."

One large piece of chart paper

Twenty or thirty sentence strips

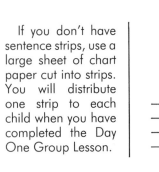

> If you don't have sentence strips, use a large sheet of chart paper cut into strips. You will distribute one strip to each child when you have completed the Day One Group Lesson.

For each student:

One piece of white paper

Pencils, crayons, and markers

➤ Day Two

For the teacher:

Overhead projector and screen

Transparency of **Figure 5.3.1.** *Ratio Comparison*

A large area on which to line up all the completed sentence strips and illustrated events from the two participating classes

For each student:

Completed sentence strip and illustrated event from Day One

Copy of **Figure 5.3.1.** *Ratio Comparison*

One crayon, any color

Story and Mini-Lesson: Day One

1. **P**rior to reading the story, hold up the sealed envelope. Tell your students that you have made a prediction, which is sealed inside the envelope. You will reveal the prediction when the mini-lesson is over. Say that you are confident that the prediction you made is correct.

2. Be very mysterious and refuse to answer any questions about the prediction. Set the envelope aside.

3. **P**review the book by doing a "picture walk" through the pages. Encourage students to describe what they see and **p**redict what the story will be about.

4. **R**ead and enjoy the story with your students.

5. After you have read the story, call on students to identify the main idea. Listen to their answers and prompt and clarify as needed by saying, "Yes, you're right, the story was about what will *probably* happen if you gave a pig a pancake."

6. **R**e-read the story. As you do, emphasize the words *probably* and *chances are.*

7. Then ask, "Did you like this story?" Ask students to give it a "thumbs up" if they liked it or a "thumbs down" if they didn't. Count the votes.

8. Open the sealed envelope and ask a student to read your prediction out loud. Was your prediction correct? Discuss.

Group Lesson: Day One

1. Ask students what the words *probably* and *chances are* mean. Clarify if necessary. (*Probably* and *chances are* mean that something is likely to happen.)

    > Have a student be a reader and checker for the correct order of the story sequence.

2. List the events that happened in the story on a piece of chart paper. Encourage students to tell the events in sequence as each event is connected to the next one.

3. Your students will probably notice that the story ends up right where it started, with a pig and a pancake.

4. Tell students that the entire class will write and illustrate a story together. Give them the lead-in, for example, *If you give a bear a bicycle.* (Remember, the lead-in must be pre-selected, because your partner class must use the same lead-in and ending as your class.)

5. Write the lead-in on a sentence strip.

6. Write the class story together. Call on each student, one by one, to tell you an event that will happen if you give a bear a bicycle. You, or student volunteers, may number and write each event consecutively on one sentence strip at a time.

    > Be sure you number the events because later you will assign one event per child to illustrate. In addition, the numbers will help your students reassemble the story when they have completed the illustrations. Make sure you and your partner class have the same number of events for both stories. Adjust for a mismatch in the number of students by assigning some students to illustrate more than one story event.

7. Encourage students to use the words *chances are* and *probably* as they tell you the events of their story. When you come to the last two or three children, tell them that they must think of events that will help Bear remember his bicycle. The story must end up where it began.

Discovery: Day One

When students have finished the story, pass out one numbered and completed sentence strip to each child. Hand out one sheet of white paper to each student. Have each student draw a picture to illustrate the sentence strip he or she received.

Reflection: Day One

Gather students together to share their illustrated events. If time remains, re-read the newly illustrated class story. Do not staple or bind the story together; tomorrow you will spread your class story out in sequence above your partner teacher's class story.

Story and Mini-Lesson: Day Two

1. Review and admire the class story, *If you give a bear a bicycle.*

2. Ask students if they think all stories that begin with *If you give a bear a bicycle* will probably be the same. Answers will vary. Some students will notice that if you keep with the circular pattern, the bear will always want his bicycle again at the end. So the beginning and ending will be the same.

3. Tell students that _____'s (partner teacher's name) class also wrote a story entitled *If you give a bear a bicycle.* Ask students if they think it is probable that the two stories will be alike. Discuss.

4. Tell students they will make a mathematical prediction about the probability of the two stories being the same.

5. Begin with the number of students in your class. Let's say there are twenty students. Ask if there is anything they *know* will be the same about the two stories. Some students will remember that the beginning and ending will be the same because this is a circle story. Therefore, two events out of twenty will probably be the same.

6. Show students the fraction $\frac{2}{20}$ or the ratio 2:20 to symbolize that the two parts (events) out of the whole twenty (total number of events) are the same.

7. Ask if students think any of the other parts or events in the two stories will be the same. Discuss.

8. As a class, make a prediction that seems likely or probable, such as, "$\frac{3}{20}$ or 3:20 events of the two stories will be the same, because it is possible that one person in Mr. or Mrs. _____'s class thought up the same event as a person in our class."

9. Once you have made your prediction about the probability of the stories being the same, gather the two classes together.

Group Lesson with Two Classes: Day Two

1. Post the predicted ratios from each class on the chalkboard or on chart paper. For example, you may have the fraction $\frac{3}{20}$ and the ratio 3:20 posted. The partner teacher's class may have posted the fraction $\frac{2}{20}$ and the ratio 2:20.

2. Read and enjoy both classes' *If you give a bear a bicycle* stories by first having each member of one class read aloud his or her sentence strip and show his or her illustrated event in story sequence.

3. Then have each student from one class place his or her numbered sentence strip and illustrated event in sequence, in the large area provided.

4. Next have each student from the partner class place his or her numbered sentence strip and illustrated event in the correct sequence, just below the corresponding numbered sentence strips and illustrated events of the first class.

5. Compare the two stories. Are the beginnings and endings the same? Are any other parts of the two stories the same?

6. How do the results of the above comparison match up with the predictions? Discuss. For example, if the illustrated events were only the same for the beginnings and the endings, then the prediction of $\frac{2}{20}$ would be an accurate prediction. If there were more parts or illustrated events that were the same, such as $\frac{5}{20}$ or five parts of the total of twenty parts, then the predictions would not be as close, but the stories would be more similar.

7. Distribute copies of **Figure 5.3.1. *Ratio Comparison*** and crayons.

8. Use the **Figure 5.3.1.** transparency and the overhead projector to demonstrate how to complete this record sheet. First, have students count the total number of illustrated events from one class only or the total number of pairs of illustrated events from the two classes. For example, if there are twenty illustrations for one class or twenty pairs of illustrated events for both classes, then have students color in twenty boxes on the bottom row of the table in **Figure 5.3.1.**

9. Count the number of pairs of illustrated events that are the same for the two classes.

10. If the first and last illustrated events of the two stories are the same, have students color in the first and last boxes on the top row of the first table. If there are additional matching illustrated events from the two stories, have students color in one box on the top row of the table for each matching pair. Older students may assist younger students.

    Please note that the illustrations need not be exactly alike. But to count illustrated events as a match or pair, the event must be the same.

11. Show students how to write the ratio. Have students refer to the top row of the table. Count up the number of filled-in boxes in the top row. Write the total from the top row first. Then count the total from the bottom row and write that number second. In our example, the ratio was 2:20; your ratio may be different.

12. Have students compare their ratios. The ratios should be the same for all the students from both classes.

Reflection: Day Two

Ask students to draw conclusions. Were the stories the same? What made them similar? What made them different? Do you think the results would be the same or different if you did the same lesson and activity with another class?

Assessment: Day Two

Observe and make notes. Did each student place his or her sentence strip and illustrated event in the appropriate sequential order? Did each student correctly complete **Figure 5.3.1.** *Ratio Comparison?*

Special Needs Adaptations

Auditory disability: An interpreter should sign the story and assist with the lesson.

Motor disability: Students with motor impairments could imagine and then describe illustrations into a tape recorder. These descriptions could be played back when both classes share their completed stories.

Visual disability: Students with visual impairments could work with partners to build three-dimensional, clay, or shoebox models to represent sequences in the story, or they could do as suggested for students with motor disabilities above.

English Language Learners: Have these students partner with bilingual students or same-language speakers. Students could label their illustrated events in their native languages. See the bibliography for references to Numeroff's books and tapes that are translated into Spanish.

Extensions

- Have students read Laura Numeroff's books to other classes. Predict which will be the favorite book. Have listeners vote on their favorite. Record the data. Report the results.

- Use the data above to make a graph using *The Graph Club* by Tom Snyder Productions.

- Have each student write three to five sentences to predict what will happen during his or her day. At the end of the day have students check their predictions.

- Brainstorm different story starters. Have students write other chain-of-events stories.

- Draw a class story map or mural of any of Laura Numeroff's books or of your own class story. Divide the map or mural into sections and have groups of four to five students do each section.

- Teach a "Cause and Effect Lesson." Have students make up sentences that show they understand the words *if* and *then,* such as, "If I jump in the swimming pool, then I'll get wet."

- Make vocabulary cards of the following words: *probably, chances are, maybe, certainly, absolutely not.* Then have students select and use the vocabulary cards by making appropriate predictions, such as, "I will *probably* play with Darcy at recess," "I will *certainly* eat a tuna sandwich for lunch," "*Maybe* I will read *If You Give a Moose a Muffin,*" or "I will *absolutely not* give a pig a ride home from school."

Bibliography

Burns, Marilyn. *Math and Literature: (K–3) Book One.* Sausalito, CA: Marilyn Burns Education Association, 1993.

———. *Math by All Means: Probability, Grades 3–4.* Sausalito, CA: Marilyn Burns Education Association, 1997.

———. *Writing in Math Class: A Resource for Grades 2–8.* Sausalito, CA: Marilyn Burns Education Association, 1995.

Numeroff, Laura Joffe. *Dogs Don't Wear Sneakers.* New York: Simon & Schuster Children's Books, 1996.

———. *If You Give a Moose a Muffin.* New York: HarperCollins, 1991.

———. *If You Give a Mouse a Cookie.* New York: HarperCollins, 2000.

———. *Si Le Das Un Panecillo a un Alce.* Translated by Teresa Mlawler. New York: HarperCollins, 1995.

———. *Si Le Das Un Panqueque a una Cerdita.* Translated by Teresa Mlawler. New York: HarperCollins, 1999.

———. *Si Le Das Una Galletita a un raton.* Translated by Teresa Mlawler. New York: HarperCollins, 1995.

Software

Tom Snyder Productions. 1998. *The Graph Club.* Macintosh and Windows, www.tomsnyder.com. (Accessed February 2001).

Related Standards 2000

Standard 1: Number and Operations

Standard 2: Algebra

Standard 3: Geometry

Standard 4: Measurement

Standard 6: Problem Solving

Standard 8: Communication

Standard 9: Connections

Standard 10: Representation

Related Standards 1989

Standard 1: Mathematics as Problem Solving

Standard 2: Mathematics as Communication

Standard 3: Mathematics as Reasoning

Standard 4: Mathematical Connections

Standard 5: Estimation

Standard 6: Number Sense and Numeration

Standard 9: Geometry and Spatial Sense

Standard 10: Measurement

Standard 12: Fractions and Decimals

Standard 13: Patterns and Relationships

LESSON 4

Make Snowflakes, Then Collect, Record, and Analyze Data

Martin, Jacqueline Briggs. *Snowflake Bentley.* New York: Houghton Mifflin, 1998.

Mary Azarian won the 1999 Caldecott Award for her subtly colored wood-cut illustrations in this biography of Vermont farmer and snowflake enthusiast Wilson Bentley. Bentley, a self-educated scientist, dedicated his life to the study of snow crystals. He collected, observed, and documented information about snowflakes with a special camera that was "taller than a newborn calf" and "cost as much as his father's herd of ten cows." *Snowflake Bentley* is the story of a man who never gave up and so succeeded in sharing the beauty and wonder of icy snow crystals with all the world.

Time Frame

Day One: 50 minutes

Day Two: 50 minutes

Day Three: 50 minutes

Materials

➤ **Day One**

For the teacher:

Chart paper

Marking pens

For each student:

Math journal

➢ **Day Two**

For the teacher:

Figure 5.4.1. *How to Make a Snowflake*

Chart from Day One

Sample snowflake, made from **Figure 5.4.1.**

For each student:

Journals from Day One

Pre-cut circles of white paper for snowflakes (8 inches in diameter)

Scissors and pencil

➢ **Day Three**

For the teacher:

Chart paper observations and data from Day One

Overhead projector

Transparency of **Figure 5.4.2.** *Snowflake Observations*

Figure 5.4.3. *Assessment, Data Collection*

For each student:

Snowflake from Day Two

Copy of **Figure 5.4.2.** *Snowflake Observations*

Pencil and ruler

Story and Mini-Lesson: Day One

1. **P**review, **make p**redictions about, and **r**ead the book.

2. **R**eview. Ask students to tell what Snowflake Bentley did to learn about snowflakes.

3. Use chart paper to list students' examples, such as

   ✓ Bentley tried to draw snowflakes but they melted before he could finish.

   ✓ He got a special camera at age seventeen and took pictures of snowflakes. It took Bentley more than one winter to learn how to take pictures of snowflakes. Some winters he took only a dozen pictures, and during other winters he took 100 or more pictures.

4. Ask students what they know about the words *data* and *statistics*. Discuss and clarify. *Data* means information someone collects. *Statistics* are the numbers used by mathematicians to collect, organize, and understand data.

5. **C**onnect this vocabulary to the chart paper list above with the following example: Bentley collected data such as his photographs of snowflakes, and he kept statistics by organizing and keeping records of his photographs.

6. Encourage students to come up with their own examples of data and statistics.

Reflection: Day One

Conclude today's lesson by having students return to their seats and write or draw what they know about snowflakes based on Bentley's data. Journal entries could include but are not limited to the following examples:

- Snowflakes have six sides.
- Snowflakes have hexagonal shapes.
- Each side has several branches.
- No two snowflakes are alike.

Conclude Day One by having students share their work. Collect math journals. Review and return math journals before Day Two.

Story and Mini-Lesson: Day Two

1. Review *Snowflake Bentley*.

2. Share writing and illustrations from math journals used during the Day One activity.

Group Lesson: Day Two

1. Tell students they will:
   a. Make their own snowflakes and
   b. Collect and record data about the snowflakes.

2. Review the number of sides each child's snowflake should have (6).

3. Demonstrate how to make snowflakes by following the pattern illustrated in **Figure 5.4.1. *How to Make a Snowflake.***

Discovery: Day Two

Distribute materials. Students should use this time to fold and cut their snowflakes.

Reflection: Day Two

Ask students to bring their snowflakes and join you in your group gathering place. Have students share their snowflakes. Observe and discuss how the snowflakes are different. Have students keep their own snowflakes for tomorrow's lesson. Conclude today's lesson by telling students they have described data about their own snowflakes. Tomorrow, they will collect and organize data and prepare statistics on the snowflakes.

Group Lesson: Day Three

1. Post chart paper observations and data from Day One.

2. Use the overhead projector and transparency of **Figure 5.4.2. *Snowflake Observations*** to demonstrate how to fill out this data collection record.

3. Select a sample snowflake.

4. Demonstrate how to fill out the information using the sample snowflake to fill in the columns from **Figure 5.4.2.** that describe "Snowflake #1, My Own Snowflake."

5. Guide students as needed in filling out the information on their own individual snowflakes. Begin by counting the number of sides of the sample snowflake, then identify the shape, and so on as indicated by the columns in **Figure 5.4.2.** Encourage students who understand the process to help other students.

6. When children have completed the information about their own snowflakes, ask each student to pass his or her snowflake to the person sitting clockwise or to the left of him or her. Ask peer partners to check and support one another in doing this.

7. Have students record data about the new snowflake, Snowflake #2, that has just been passed to them.

8. Continue steps 6 and 7 three more times so students fill out the information for snowflakes #3, #4, and #5. (Omit this step for young students.)

9. Have the students return the snowflakes to their owners.

Reflection: Day Three

In your group gathering place, ask students to refer to their own completed data collection record sheet, **Figure 5.4.2.** Discuss the following:

■ Were any snowflakes *exactly* the same? Explain why or why not.

■ Were any snowflakes *similar?* Explain why or why not.

■ Were any snowflakes *different?* Explain why or why not.

Discuss conclusions:

■ Is it *probable* or *likely* that each student's snowflake is different from all the others? Explain why or why not.

■ Do you conclude that Wilson Bentley was correct when he said that no snowflake is exactly like another?

Assessment: Day Three

■ Have students turn in **Figure 5.4.2. *Snowflake Observations*** and their snowflakes.

■ Use **Figure 5.4.3. *Assessment, Data Collection*** to evaluate student comprehension of the project.

■ Post and admire snowflakes and data sheets.

Special Needs Adaptations

Auditory disability: An interpreter should sign the story and assist with the lesson. List key words on the chalkboard. Post the chart paper list generated on Day One. Display a pre-made snowflake sample from Day Two. Display a completed copy of **Figure 5.4.2. *Snowflake Observations*** from Day Three. (Remind students that data sheets will be different for each child).

Motor disability: Students with motor impairments will need assistance with folding and cutting snowflakes and recording data about snowflakes.

Visual disability: Check for understanding of the story. Record a copy of *Snowflake Bentley* for these students to review. Provide assistance as these students fold and cut snowflakes. Demonstrate how to make tactile observations and comparisons of the snowflakes. Students can record their observations into a tape recorder.

English Language Learners: Have these students partner with bilingual students or same-language speakers.

Extensions

Be prepared for a snowy day. Have snowflake collecting sheets ready for each student. Put pre-cut, laminated $5\frac{1}{2}$-by-$8\frac{1}{2}$-inch sheets of black paper in a plastic bag in the freezer. Keep hand lenses handy. When it snows, give each student his or her own collecting sheet and hand lens. Enjoy collecting snowflakes just as Bentley did. Share and compare snowflakes with one another. Have the students use the second hand on a watch to time how long it takes snowflakes to melt, then record these data.

- Make snowflake soap block prints. Invite parent volunteers to help carve snowflakes from soap blocks, then make designs on wrapping paper.

- Have students write word problems using facts and information from *Snowflake Bentley,* such as, "Bentley photographed 100 snow crystals each winter for three winters. How many snow crystals did he photograph?"

- Have a hexagon scavenger hunt.

- Have the class estimate, then count, the number of snowflakes on the side panels of the pages of *Snowflake Bentley.*

Bibliography

Murphy, Stuart. *The Best Vacation Ever.* New York: HarperCollins, 1997.

———. *Lemonade for Sale.* New York: HarperCollins, 1997.

Vorderman, Carol. *How Math Works.* New York: Putnam, 1999.

Related Standards 2000

Standard 1: Number and Operations

Standard 2: Algebra

Standard 3: Geometry

Standard 4: Measurement

Standard 6: Problem Solving

Standard 8: Communication

Standard 9: Connections

Standard 10: Representation

Related Standards 1989

Standard 1: Mathematics as Problem Solving

Standard 2: Mathematics as Communication

Standard 3: Mathematics as Reasoning

Standard 4: Mathematical Connections

Standard 5: Estimation

Standard 6: Number Sense and Numeration

Standard 7: Concepts of Whole Number Operations

Standard 8: Whole Number Computation

Standard 9: Geometry and Spatial Sense

Standard 10: Measurement

Standard 13: Patterns and Relationships

Dear Parents,

As part of a math lesson based on Robert Louis Stevenson's poem, *Where Go the Boats?* students will make and launch boats and predict and map where the boats will be found. As students participate in this lesson, they will learn about chance and probability. They'll ask and answer questions to determine whether the boats traveled and landed randomly, or if there are probable places where the boats might land.

On _____(date)_____ , our class will launch homemade boats from _____(place)_____ . Enclosed is a field trip permission form for you to complete and return by _____(date)_____ . Before the field trip and boat launching, please help your child make a boat. It must float, be no less than $4\frac{1}{2}$ inches and no longer than 12 inches in length, include the following identification number _____ , and include a sealed and watertight message like the following:

Dear Boat Rescuer,

I launched boat (number) *on* (date) *at* (launching place) *in* (town name). *Please call my school at* (phone number) *and tell the boat number, date, and place where you found it.*

Thanks, (first name or initials)

You and your child may use whatever materials you have on hand to make a boat. Your child's boat may be as simple as a sealed and clear plastic bottle or as intricate as a wooden sailing vessel. Keep in mind that there is a *chance* that your child's boat will neither be found nor returned.

Sincerely,

Figure 5.1.1. *Letter Home*

Where Go the Boats?

Dark brown is the river,

Golden is the sand.

It flows along for ever,

With trees on either hand.

Green leaves a-floating,

Castles of the foam,

Boats of mine a-boating-

Where will all come home?

On goes the river

And out past the mill,

Away down the valley,

Away down the hill.

Away down the river,

A hundred miles or more,

Other little children

Shall bring my boats ashore.

Figure 5.1.2. *Where Go the Boats?* Source: Robert Louis Stevenson, *A Child's Garden of Verses*. **New York:** Oxford University Press, 1947.

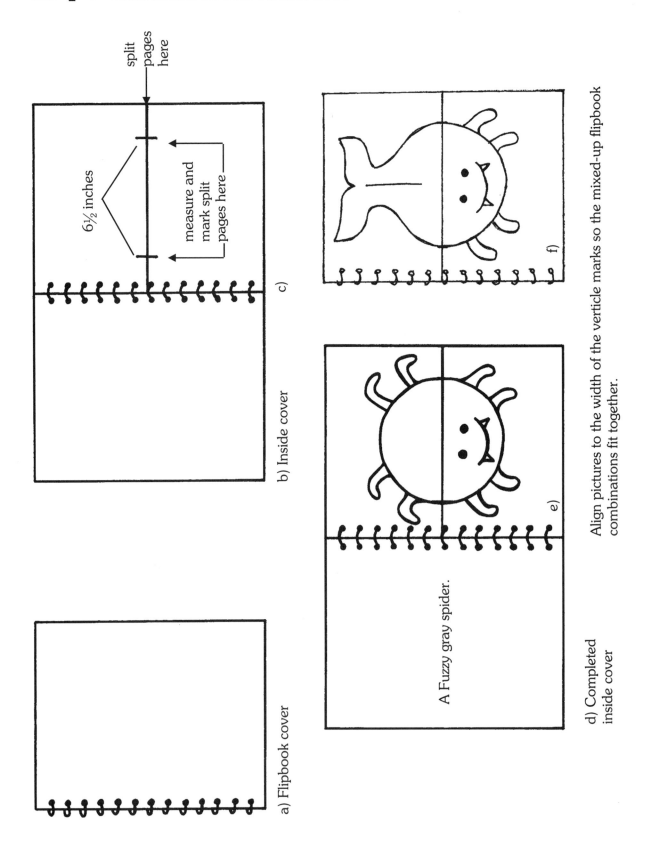

Figure 5.2.1. *Flipbook Model.* Illustration by Cherie Blackmore.

Before you teach Chapter 5, Lesson 2, instruct a parent volunteer or aide to construct one flipbook for each student. The flipbook should be 12 inches tall by 9 inches across and be bound with a plastic binder on the 12-inch left-hand side. There should be three pages plus a cover, with each page cut horizontally across the middle, 6½ inches from the top right-hand side.

For twenty students:

1. Cut forty sheets of 12-by-18-inch construction paper (any colors) in half, lengthwise so that each sheet measures 9 by 12 inches.

2. Mark measurements as done in item **c)** on a separate, white master copy.

3. Use a copy machine to print the measurements from the master copy onto the cut construction paper.

4. Separate the cut construction paper in groups of three pages plus cover page per flipbook.

5. Bind each flipbook on the left-hand 12-inch side with plastic binders.

6. Keep the binding intact. Measure 6½ inches down from the top right-hand 12-inch side of each book. Mark and cut through the three sheets of construction paper to the edge of the binding; see item **c**. Now the flipbooks are ready for students to make their own silly combination characters.

0–3	4–7	8–11	12–15
3 Alicia	6 Ramon 6 Charlie	10 Aimee 11 Kim	15 Laura 14 Jon
	6 Lily 5 Brent	10 Patrice 9 Erin	13 Annika
3 Tomas	10 Paul 6 Hermon	4 Rachel 9 Jacob	12 Leo 12 Suzuki

Reproduce this graph on chart paper.
Give one sticky note to each student.
Tell students to write their names and the number they estimate on their sticky notes.
Have each student place his or her sticky note on the chart paper graph in the appropriate box.

Figure 5.2.2. Sample—Prediction Graph

0–3	4–7	8–11	12–15

Reproduce this graph on chart paper.
Give one sticky note to each student.
Tell students to write their names and the number they estimate on their sticky notes.
Have each student place his or her sticky note on the chart paper graph in the appropriate box.

Figure 5.2.3. Prediction Graph

Use the following checklist and scoring system to assess student comprehension of the flipbook project:

Beginning: 0–4: Developing: 5–7; Proficient: 8–10

Name: _____ **Date:** _____

Student completed the flipbook. _____ (3)

Student matched pictures to pre-measured markings. _____ (3)

Student made a reasonable estimation (a number between three and fifteen) on the chart paper graph. _____ (1)

Student was able to recognize the most often and least often selected number on the chart paper graph. _____ (1)

Student used vocabulary words (*combinations, data, graph, estimation,* and *range*) appropriately in class discussions and in his or her math journal. _____ (1)

Student participated in problem-solving discussion on Day Three. _____ (1)

Total score: _____ (10)

Anecdotal notes:

_____

_____

Name: _____ **Date:** _____

Student completed the flipbook. _____ (3)

Student matched pictures to pre-measured markings. _____ (3)

Student made a reasonable estimation (a number between three and fifteen) on the chart paper graph. _____ (1)

Student was able to recognize the most often and least often selected number on the chart paper graph. _____ (1)

Student used vocabulary words (*combinations, data, graph, estimation,* and *range*) appropriately in class discussions and in his or her math journal. _____ (1)

Student participated in problem-solving discussion on Day Three. _____ (1)

Total score: _____ (10)

Anecdotal notes:

_____

_____

Figure 5.2.4. *Flipbook Assessment Checklist*

Name: _____ Date: _____

1. Count the total number of illustrated events for one class _____.

2. On the bottom row, color in one box for each illustrated event.

3. Count the number of pairs of illustrated events that were the same for two classes _____.

4. On the top row, fill in one box for each pair of illustrated events that were the same.

5. Now write the ratio. It will look like your boxes below.

Write the number of colored boxes from the top row first, then write the total number from the colored boxes on the bottom row next.

Ratio comparison is: _____ : _____.

Top																	
Bottom																	

Figure 5.3.1. *Ratio Comparison*

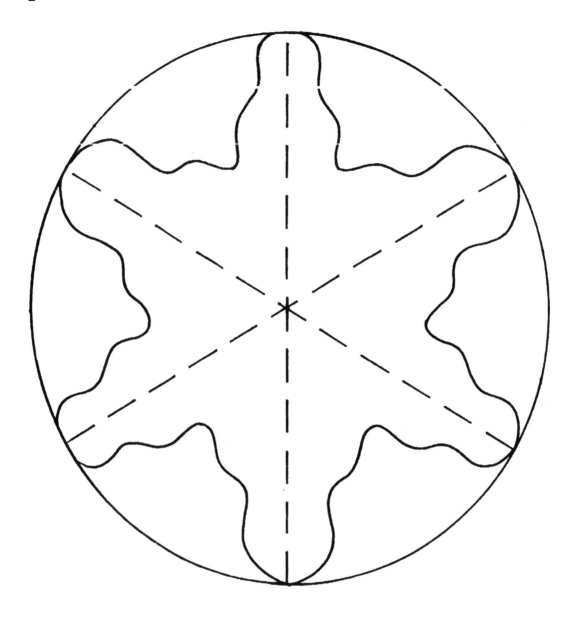

1. Cut the circle around the snowflake.

2. Fold the circle in half on one of the dotted lines.

3. First, fold one wedge on the dotted lines.

4. Next, fold the other wedge on the dotted lines.

5. Cut on the solid line through all layers.

6. Be creative. Cut triangles, squares, circles, and other designs through the folds.

7. Unfold your paper. Enjoy your snowflake.

Figure 5.4.1. *How to Make a Snowflake*

Name: _____ Date: _____

Snowflake Observations	Number of Sides	Shape	Number of Branches on One Side	Number of Shapes Inside the Snowflake	Measurement of One Snowflake Branch from End to End
Snowflake #1 (My Own Snowflake)					
Snowflake # 2					
Snowflake # 3					
Snowflake # 4					
Snowflake # 5					

Do you think there are any snowflakes in the world that are exactly alike? _____ Explain why or why not.

_____

Figure 5.4.2. Snowflake Observations

Use the following checklist and scoring system to assess student data collection for the snowflake project:

Beginning: 0–1; Developing: 2–3; Proficient: 4

Name: _____ **Date:** _____

The student knows a snowflake has six sides. _____ (1)

The student completed his or her data-recording sheet. _____ (1)

The student participated in the discussion. _____ (1)

The student articulated examples that made sense when supporting his or her conclusions about snowflakes. _____ (1)

Total score: _____ (4)

Anecdotal notes:

_____

_____

_____

_____

_____

Name: _____ **Date:** _____

The student knows a snowflake has six sides. _____ (1)

The student completed his or her data-recording sheet. _____ (1)

The student participated in the discussion. _____ (1)

The student articulated examples that made sense when supporting his or her conclusions about snowflakes. _____ (1)

Total score: _____ (4)

Anecdotal notes:

_____

_____

_____

_____

_____

Figure 5.4.3. Assessment, Data Collection

Chapter 6

Problem Solving

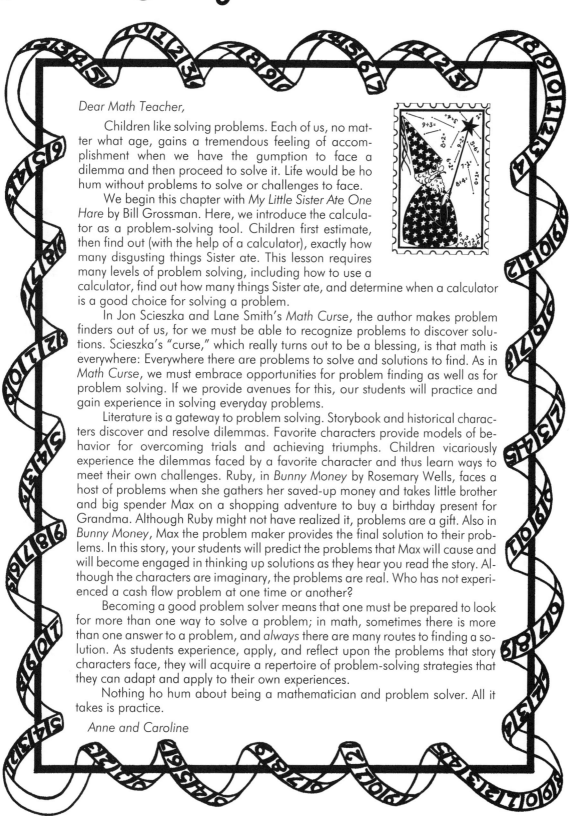

Dear Math Teacher,

Children like solving problems. Each of us, no matter what age, gains a tremendous feeling of accomplishment when we have the gumption to face a dilemma and then proceed to solve it. Life would be ho hum without problems to solve or challenges to face.

We begin this chapter with *My Little Sister Ate One Hare* by Bill Grossman. Here, we introduce the calculator as a problem-solving tool. Children first estimate, then find out (with the help of a calculator), exactly how many disgusting things Sister ate. This lesson requires many levels of problem solving, including how to use a calculator, find out how many things Sister ate, and determine when a calculator is a good choice for solving a problem.

In Jon Scieszka and Lane Smith's *Math Curse*, the author makes problem finders out of us, for we must be able to recognize problems to discover solutions. Scieszka's "curse," which really turns out to be a blessing, is that math is everywhere: Everywhere there are problems to solve and solutions to find. As in *Math Curse*, we must embrace opportunities for problem finding as well as for problem solving. If we provide avenues for this, our students will practice and gain experience in solving everyday problems.

Literature is a gateway to problem solving. Storybook and historical characters discover and resolve dilemmas. Favorite characters provide models of behavior for overcoming trials and achieving triumphs. Children vicariously experience the dilemmas faced by a favorite character and thus learn ways to meet their own challenges. Ruby, in *Bunny Money* by Rosemary Wells, faces a host of problems when she gathers her saved-up money and takes little brother and big spender Max on a shopping adventure to buy a birthday present for Grandma. Although Ruby might not have realized it, problems are a gift. Also in *Bunny Money*, Max the problem maker provides the final solution to their problems. In this story, your students will predict the problems that Max will cause and will become engaged in thinking up solutions as they hear you read the story. Although the characters are imaginary, the problems are real. Who has not experienced a cash flow problem at one time or another?

Becoming a good problem solver means that one must be prepared to look for more than one way to solve a problem; in math, sometimes there is more than one answer to a problem, and *always* there are many routes to finding a solution. As students experience, apply, and reflect upon the problems that story characters face, they will acquire a repertoire of problem-solving strategies that they can adapt and apply to their own experiences.

Nothing ho hum about being a mathematician and problem solver. All it takes is practice.

Anne and Caroline

LESSON 1

Use a Calculator to Solve a Big Addition Problem

Grossman, Bill. *My Little Sister Ate One Hare.* New York: Crown, 1996.

Addition has never been so fun and icky! In this book, the narrator's little sister has a knack for cumulatively adding interesting things to her stomach, that is, until the last healthy surprise! This is a hilarious story told in rhyme using a style similar to the folktale *There Was an Old Lady Who Swallowed a Fly*. Author Bill Grossman and illustrator Kevin Hawkes have created a book that appeals to children of all ages.

You may substitute the following books for this lesson:

Dorros, Arthur. *Ten Go Tango*. New York: HarperCollins, 2000.

Hutchins, Pat. *1 Hunter*. New York: Greenwillow, 1982.

Sloat, Teri. *There Was an Old Lady Who Swallowed a Trout*. New York: Henry Holt, 1998.

Taback, Simms. *There Was an Old Lady Who Swallowed a Fly*. New York: Viking Children's Books, 1997.

Time Frame

50 minutes

Materials

For the teacher:

Overhead projector and pen

Figure 6.1.1. *Prediction Graph,* transferred onto chart paper and placed in a prominent place in the classroom

Transparency of **Figure 6.1.2. *Calculator*** (You may also use an overhead calculator rather than this transparency.)

Figure 6.1.3. *Answers to Calculator Exercise*

For each student:

One small sticky note

Calculator

Figure 6.1.4. *Calculator Exercise*

Pencil

Figure 6.1.5. *Assessment, Calculator Exercise*

Story and Mini-Lesson

1. **P**review, make **p**redictions about, and **r**ead the story.

2. Invite students to **r**etell the story in sequence.

3. **R**eview the story by asking students, "Why did you like this story? Why was it funny?"

4. **C**onnect the story to the math lesson by asking, "How do you think this story relates to math? Did you notice a pattern in the story? What was it?" (This story has a pattern of increasing numbers. Sister keeps eating new, terrible things. First she eats one hare, then two snakes, then three ants, and so forth.)

5. Hand out one sticky note to each child. Instruct students to make a prediction about how many things Sister ate and write these predictions on their sticky notes along with their names.

6. Then have students place their predictions on the graph.

7. Discuss the results of **Figure 6.1.1. *Prediction Graph.*** Ask students to notice which column has the most predictions and which column has the least predictions. Tell students they will return to the graph at the end of the lesson to compare the correct answer with the predictions.

Group Lesson

1. Introduce calculators. Discuss what a calculator is and how it is used.

2. Display transparency of **Figure 6.1.2. *Calculator*** or an overhead calculator and discuss the calculator keys.

3. Have student volunteers come up to the overhead and find the [+], [–], [=], and [ON/C] keys on the transparency or calculator.

4. Hand out one calculator to each student; let students examine and explore the calculator freely for approximately five to ten minutes.

5. Compare how the student calculators are like or unlike the transparency or the overhead calculator.

6. Ask students for suggestions about how they could use their calculators to figure out how many things Sister ate. Discuss and support answers.

7. Give a copy of **Figure 6.1.4. *Calculator Exercise*** to each student.

8. Starting on page 1 of *My Little Sister Ate One Hare,* have students do each addition problem using their calculators. If this is the first time your students have used a calculator to solve a big problem, give the class direct instructions. For example: "Read page 1." Tell students to press [1] because Sister ate [1] thing. Then tell students to press the [+] button. Next, have students press the [0] button because Sister did not eat anything else. Now, have students press the [=] button. Ask, "What answer did you get?" Then say, "The answer is [1]." Have students record the answer on their copies of **Figure 6.1.4.** Then have students press [ON/C] to clear the answer.

9. Continue with this method: press the first number, press plus, press the other number, press equals, see answer, record answer, press clear. Do this for each page of the book, making sure that all students are following along.

10. Stop at page 15 of the story (when Sister eats nine lizards). Tell students that on this page and the next page they will figure out how many things Sister ate.

> It is important to go slowly and make sure all students are with you. Once students get lost, it is very hard for them to catch up.

11. Have students figure out problem number 9 while you read the page. At this point, tell the students. "Do **not** press CLEAR!" (If a student does make a mistake and presses CLEAR, it's not a problem: Just tell him or her to press the keys for the number 45.)

12. Leave the answer from problem number 9 on the calculator, then have students add problem 10 after reading page 17 of the book (when Sister eats the peas). You may need to repeat this process several times to support students.

13. Ask, "Who can tell me how many things Sister ate" (55)?

14. Compare the correct answer with the prediction graph generated during the Mini-Lesson.

Discovery

Have students compare the predictions on the graph with the correct answer. Use these questions as a guide: How many students predicted below 55? How many students predicted above 55? What was the closest prediction?

Reflection

Have students answer in their math journals, or discuss orally, *some* of the following questions:

- Could we solve the problem of how many things Sister ate without using a calculator? One student might suggest counting all the creatures and things Sister ate on each page until the end of the book. Another might suggest using cubes or tiles to represent each set of animals Sister ate, then adding them together in groups of tens and fives. Someone else might suggest making tally marks for each thing Sister ate, then counting the tallies by fives.

- How did the students' predictions compare with the correct answer? An answer might be, "My prediction was way off! I predicted 10 and the answer was 55! I was surprised! I didn't notice that the numbers kept adding up. I just counted from one to ten."

- Ask students how they liked using a calculator and why they did or didn't. You might get a response like this, "I liked using the calculator because it helped me figure out a problem that had a lot of addition in it. It is a quick way to add up a big problem."

- Ask students why people use calculators. A student might respond, "Because they help us get the right answer." Discuss how this may or may not be true; for example, if the wrong information is keyed into the calculator, the calculator will calculate the right answer to the wrong information.

■ Ask students, "When should we use calculators? When should we not?" One student might say, "It's a quick way to get the answer to a big problem"; another might say, "We really don't need to use a calculator to do problems we can do in our heads, like, 4 + 4 = 8."

Assessment

Have students turn in **Figure 6.1.4. *Calculator Exercise.*** Review the answers using **Figure 6.1.3.** During free exploration and discovery, circulate through the classroom and use **Figure 6.1.5. *Assessment, Calculator Exercise*** to assess students on the following skills: Does the student know how to use the calculator to do a basic addition problem? Can the student show you where the [+], [–], [=], and [ON/C] buttons are on the calculator? Can the student explain why the calculator was useful for solving this problem?

Special Needs Adaptations

Auditory disability: An interpreter should sign the story and lesson.

Motor disability: Student buddies or aides may assist these students while they operate the calculator and record answers.

Visual disability: Replace the calculator with an abacus or auditory calculator. A vision specialist or aide should help these children calculate the problem.

English Language Learners: Bilingual buddies should partner with these students to make sure they understand the calculator activity instructions. Place a copy of *My Little Sister Ate One Hare* and a cassette tape of the story in a listening center for students to listen to during free time. If a cassette tape of the story is not available, have a student or volunteer record the story on a blank cassette tape.

Extensions

■ Ask students to respond to several of the questions posed in the Reflection section of this lesson.

■ Note and do some of the many fun and interesting activities suggested inside the front and back covers of *My Little Sister Ate One Hare.*

■ Have students use the calculator to do further investigations. For example, they might figure out how far from the true answer their predictions were, how near was the closest prediction, and how far away was the farthest prediction. To get these answers, students will need to determine which of the following formats to use:

(answer) – (prediction) = _____
    or
(prediction) – (answer) = _____

Bibliography

Adler, David. *Calculator Riddles.* New York: Holiday House, 1998.

Anno, Masaichiro, and Mitsumasa Anno. *Anno's Mysterious Multiplying Jar.* New York Putnam, 1999.

Anno, Mitsumasa. *Anno's Math Games.* New York: Putnam, 1997.

Related Standards 2000

Standard 1: Number and Operations

Standard 2: Algebra

Standard 5: Data Analysis and Probability

Standard 7: Reasoning and Proof

Standard 8: Communication

Standard 9: Connections

Standard 10: Representation

Related Standards 1989

Standard 1: Mathematics as Problem Solving

Standard 2: Mathematics as Communication

Standard 3: Mathematics as Reasoning

Standard 4: Mathematical Connections

Standard 5: Estimation

Standard 6: Number Sense and Numeration

Standard 7: Concepts of Whole Number Operations

Standard 13: Patterns and Relationships

LESSON 2

Discover Math Problems Everywhere

Scieszka, Jon, and Lane Smith. *Math Curse.* New York: Viking, 1995.

This story is about a little girl who goes to school one day and gets the "Math Curse" from her teacher. Instantly, she sees math problems everywhere she goes and in everything she does. She soon discovers math is all around her and she can use math to solve almost any problem. After reading this book, you too will have the math curse! This book makes math lovers of us all!

Time Frame

50 minutes

Materials

For the teacher:

One large bulletin board to display finished projects; title the display, "We have the math curse. We see math EVERYWHERE!"

Figure 6.2.1. *Sample—I Have the Math Curse!*

Figure 6.2.2. *Project Sample—I Have the Math Curse!* (print one copy on colored construction paper)

Figure 6.2.3. *Instructions for I Have the Math Curse! Project*

Construction paper (various colors)

Chalkboard or chart paper

Magician hat and wand (optional)

Figure 6.2.4. *Assessment, Finding Math Problems*

For each student:

Pencil, scissors, markers, and crayons

Figure 6.2.5. *I Have the Math Curse!* (Practice Sheet)

Story and Mini-Lesson

1. **P**review the book by showing the cover, title, and several pictures from the story. Ask students, "What is the math curse? What do you think it is like to have the math curse?"

2. Discuss students' **p**redictions about the math curse.

3. **R**ead the story. During this reading, do not stop to answer the math questions in the book.

4. **R**eview the story. Ask students to retell what happened. Discuss the retellings. Then ask, "Were your predictions correct? How do you think the main character felt about having the math curse? How would you feel if you had the math curse? Would you feel frantic, crazed, excited, or alert?"

5. **R**e-read the story; this time, as a group, answer questions and solve problems together that are appropriate to your students' comprehension level.

6. **C**onnect the book to the math lesson by telling students that you will now give them the "math curse."

Put on the magician hat and use the wand. Wave the wand around and pretend to put a spell on the class. Say, "Subtraction, Addition, Multiplication, Division. Hocus Pocus, math makes you focus. Math is EVERYWHERE!"

7. **A**fter you have given students the "curse," tell students they are going to take a short walk (five to ten minutes) outside or around the school to look for, and to ask, math questions.

8. **A**s you walk, encourage students to point out the math they see. For example, "How many cars are in the parking lot? How many classrooms are in the building? How many minutes do we have until lunchtime? Is there enough room for all that trash to fit in the dumpster? How many dumpsters of trash do we generate each day?"

9. **C**ome back to the classroom and discuss the many math problems you noticed or thought about during the walk.

10. **R**ecord the math questions students generated during the walk.

Group Lesson

1. **A**s a group, brainstorm new math questions that relate to students' lives. Encourage students to think of something that is familiar to them. For example, if a student likes football, he or she could ask, "How many minutes long is a football game?" Record the questions on the chalkboard or chart paper.

2. **T**ell students that each of them will create a math curse question for other students in the class to answer.

3. **R**eview with students how the main character in the story felt when she was cursed (frantic, crazed, excited). The final product they make must demonstrate some or all of these emotions.

4. **S**how students **Figure 6.2.1. *Sample—I Have the Math Curse!*.** Read the sentence, the questions, and the answers aloud. Take time to think aloud about the first sample answer. Ask, "Are there other ways to solve this problem?" Students might suggest drawing a picture of a clock with a dial, then counting the hours on the dial, beginning at the eight when they went to bed and counting on until they end up at the six, when they got up.

5. Have the students write about how they have the math curse. Hand out **Figure 6.2.5. I Have the Math Curse! (Practice Sheet).** Wave the wand about and tell students you are dusting them with powerful thinking magic.

6. When students complete their practice sheets, show them **Figure 6.2.2. Project Sample—I Have the Math Curse!**

7. Ask the students to notice how the sample shows emotions. Students will notice that the letters and numbers are printed in bold, the sides of the paper are jagged and sharp, and the pattern around the edge is sideways and crooked. Tell students that when they make their final math curse project they must also show emotion with their words, letters, illustrations, or patterns.

8. Read aloud, then post, **Figure 6.2.3. Instructions for I Have the Math Curse! Project.** Answer any questions students have about the project, then distribute construction paper so they may begin working.

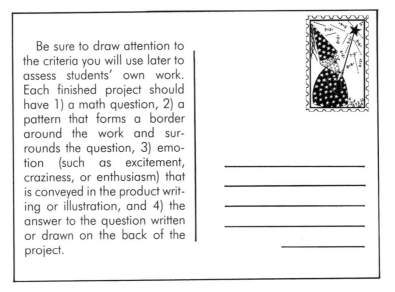

Be sure to draw attention to the criteria you will use later to assess students' own work. Each finished project should have 1) a math question, 2) a pattern that forms a border around the work and surrounds the question, 3) emotion (such as excitement, craziness, or enthusiasm) that is conveyed in the product writing or illustration, and 4) the answer to the question written or drawn on the back of the project.

9. Allow and encourage students to be creative in the way they design, write, and illustrate their projects.

Reflection

Gather as a group so students can share and present their final products with classmates. Encourage students to show emotion as they give their presentations. Encourage those who are listeners to try to solve the problem or answer the question posed by the presenter. Have each problem solver describe how he or she figured out the solution to the question. Students should celebrate each other's great thinking. Display all the projects on the classroom bulletin board underneath the title, "We have the Math Curse. We see math EVERYWHERE!"

Assessment

Use **Figure 6.2.4. Assessment, Finding Math Problems** to evaluate students' products.

Special Needs Adaptations

Auditory disability: An interpreter should sign the story and lesson.

Motor disability: These students may need assistance from an aide or a partner to complete the writing and cutting activity. Make sure your walk around the school is accessible to all children.

Visual disability: Instead of creating a written math curse project, have these students act out the project. Assign a small group of students to assist these students. Together they can act out math curse questions, answers, and emotions.

English Language Learners: When discussing the math curse emotions, have all students act out each emotion so that English Language Learners understand the feelings represented by the emotional expressions. Partner these students with others throughout the lesson. Check that these students understand the lesson and instructions.

Extensions

- Research math curse questions. When students find the answers to their questions, have them share these with the class.

- Carry over the curse to other subjects. Give students the science curse, reading curse, or social studies curse. Make a science curse book or another kind of curse book

- Wave the magic wand. Students may use the wand to point to math-related items or problems they notice in the classroom.

- Show off the bulletin board of students' math curse products to other classes.

Bibliography

Adler, David. *Easy Math Puzzles.* New York: Holiday House, 1997.

———. *The Many Troubles of Andy Russell.* New York: Harcourt Brace, 1998.

Anno, Mitsumasa. *Anno's Math Games II.* New York: Econo-Clad, 1999.

———. *Anno's Math Games III.* New York: Paper Star, 1997.

Burns, Marilyn. *The Book of Think, Or How to Solve a Problem Twice Your Size.* Boston: Little, Brown, 1976.

Clement, Rod. *Counting on Frank.* Milwaukee, WI: Gareth Stevens Children's Books, 1991.

Friedman, Aileen. *The King's Commissioners.* New York: Scholastic, 1995.

Kaye, Marilyn. *A Day with No Math.* New York: Harcourt Brace Jovanovich, 1996.

Neuschwander, Cindy. *Amanda Bean's Amazing Dream.* New York: Scholastic, 1998.

Rocklin, Joanne. *Three Smart Pals.* New York: Scholastic, 1994.

Tunnell, Michael O. *Mailing May.* New York: Greenwillow, 1997.

Software

Broderbund Software, Inc. *Carmen Sandiego Math Detective.* Macintosh and Windows 3.1, 95/98.

Related Standards 2000

Standard 1: Number and Operations

Standard 2: Algebra

Standard 3: Geometry

Standard 7: Reasoning and Proof

Standard 8: Communication

Standard 9: Connections

Standard 10: Representation

Related Standards 1989

Standard 1: Mathematics as Problem Solving

Standard 2: Mathematics as Communication

Standard 3: Mathematics as Reasoning

Standard 4: Mathematical Connections

Standard 5: Estimation

Standard 6: Number Sense and Numeration

Standard 7: Concepts of Whole Number Operations

Standard 13: Patterns and Relationships

LESSON 3

Solve Money Problems

Wells, Rosemary. ***Bunny Money.*** New York: Dial Books for Young Readers, 1997.

Ruby has saved a wallet full of money to buy a birthday present for Grandma. Come along on a trip to town with Ruby and little brother Max to buy Grandma's present. Author and illustrator Rosemary Wells includes two reproducible Bunny Money pages, so readers can count and spend money along with Wells's two main characters. But watch out for Max, because he just might spend all of Ruby's savings.

Time Frame

50 minutes

Materials

- Prior to the lesson, send parents **Figure 6.3.1. *Note Home.***

- Make Bunny Money: Follow the instructions on the last page of *Bunny Money*, "Making Money." Rather than glue the money as directed, copy it back-to-back on your choice of paper. Then have each student cut apart his or her own sheet of Bunny Money.

- Prepare wallets: You may skip this step if you prefer to use standard number 10 envelopes for students' wallets.

  1. Have students make a paper wallet similar to the one on the Bunny Money title page.

  2. Pre-cut a 12-by-$3\frac{1}{2}$-inch strip of red paper and an 8-by-3-inch strip of red paper for each student.

  3. Have students place the two strips of cut paper together so the left and bottom edges match.

  4. Then have students staple or stitch the left and bottom edges as shown in the title page illustration.

  5. Have students fold the longer strip of paper over the end of the shorter strip to close or "button" the wallet. They should first trim, then glue, the overlapping side down.

  6. Children may decorate their wallets. If you have a supply of buttons, have each student glue one button on top of the overlapping side so his or her wallet looks like Ruby's.

  7. For each student, provide a standard 9-by-13-inch envelope for safekeeping of the Bunny Money and wallet.

For the teacher:

Sample set of Bunny Money and wallet

Figure 6.3.2. *Signs* (to be stationed around the room)

Six envelopes (to be placed at each one of the signs)

Figure 6.3.3. *Cards and Tickets,* enough for each student. The cards and tickets should be cut, sorted, and placed in appropriate envelopes at corresponding signs; for example, the bus tickets should go in the envelope near the bus station sign.

Figure 6.3.4. *Assessment, Solving Money Problems*

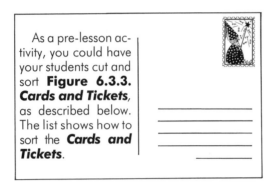

Bus Station: Bus Ticket to Town and Bus Ticket Home

Rosalinda's Gift Shop: Music Box with Skating Ballerinas, Bluebird Earrings, and Free Gift Wrap cards

Candi's Corner: Vampire Teeth and Glow in the Dark Vampire Teeth cards

Laundromat: Soap, Washer, and Dryer cards

Lunch: Peanut Butter and Jelly Sandwich, Coconut Cupcake, Banana Shake, and Lemonade cards

Telephone: Telephone Call cards

For each student:

One complete set of Bunny Money, twelve $1.00 bills, four $5.00 bills

One "lucky" quarter

One pre-made wallet

Story and Mini-Lesson

1. **P**review *Bunny Money.* Encourage students to describe and **p**redict what the book will be about.

2. As you **r**ead *Bunny Money* aloud, pause each time Ruby gives Max the wallet. Encourage students to predict what Max will do with the money. When you reach the seventeenth page (the pages are not numbered) where Rosalinda says, "You take care of this dollar young man!" stop and ask students how they think Max will take

care of the money. Is there enough money for the bus ride home? Will Max save the money or spend it all?

3. When you have finished reading the book, ask students to recall what the book was about. Your students will enjoy telling you all about the ways Max and Ruby spent Ruby's money. Have students describe why Max's 25 cents was a lucky quarter.

4. Tell students you will read the story again, but this time they are to act out how Max and Ruby spent the money. The Group Lesson describes how to do this.

Group Lesson

1. Instruct your students to take out their envelopes containing their Bunny Money, quarters, and wallets.

2. Have each student count the exact amount of Bunny Money that Ruby saved. This is shown on the title page ($15.00). Count the money together. Each student should have one $5.00 bill and ten $1.00 bills.

3. Tell students to put the remaining money back into their large envelopes and to put the envelopes away.

4. Divide the class into groups of three. In each group, one student will be Max, one will be Ruby, and one will be the Money Collector. The Money Collector will play the parts of the bus driver, Candi, the laundry machines, the lunch clerk, and Rosalinda.

5. Tell students that they may only use one wallet with the exact amount of money, $15.00, for each group of three. The person who is acting as Ruby will use his or her wallet. The person who is Max must have his or her lucky quarter handy. Instruct students to put their remaining money aside for later use.

6. Re-read *Bunny Money*. As you read about each money transaction, have the appropriate character in each group (Ruby or Max) place the money in the hands of the Money Collector.

7. You may wish to re-read the story more than once, as time and students' interest allow. Switch characters within each group for each re-reading of the story.

8. When you have finished re-reading *Bunny Money*, tell students you will put the book in an accessible spot where they may find it and act out the story.

Discovery

During this part of the lesson, students will get to go on a shopping adventure of their own. They will have $15.00 to spend, just like Ruby and Max, but now they can choose for themselves how to spend their money.

■ Show students the signs from **Figure 6.3.2.** *Signs* located around the classroom, such as Bus Station and Rosalinda's Gift Shop. Point out the card-filled envelopes at each station.

■ Model what students can do to spend their money. For example, say, "I will take my wallet and go to the bus. Now, I'll take a card from the envelope that says, 'Ticket to Town, $1.00,' and I'll pay for it with one Bunny Dollar that I'll put into the envelope.

Now, I'll imagine that I'm riding on the bus. When I get off, I think I'll go to Candi's Corner and buy two sets of Glow in the Dark Vampire Teeth, so I'll take two cards out of this envelope, and put two Bunny Dollars into the envelope."

■ Tell students they may visit any or all of the stations around the room until you give a signal. When you give the signal, they must return to the group meeting place with their cards and remaining money.

Reflection

Gather students in the group meeting place. Have students count up the value of their remaining money, then have them count up the value of the cards they purchased and add the two amounts together. Students can check each other's sums. Students should end up with the total value with which they began, $15.00. Get ready for another round of Bunny Money spending by having students exchange the cards they collected for Bunny Money.

Assessment

Use **Figure 6.3.4. *Assessment, Solving Money Problems*** to gather data and track students' money-changing skills. During the lesson and activities, write anecdotal notes regarding the strategies students used to count and exchange money.

Special Needs Adaptations

Auditory disability: An interpreter should sign the story and lesson.

Motor disability: Provide enough space for motor-impaired individuals to move around the classroom during the Discovery activity.

Visual disability: Orient these students to the locations of the different stations you have set up in your classroom. Attach Braille dots to Bunny Money to indicate dollar denominations and to the cards and tickets to indicate their value.

English Language Learners: Pair these students with English-speaking partners. Label stations, cards, and tickets in students' native languages.

Extensions

■ Have students research any of the sixteen famous people on the back cover of *Bunny Money*.

■ Have students make their own cards and tickets to buy.

■ Have students use different amounts of Bunny Money on other cards and tickets in the classroom.

■ Use different denominations to make $15.00, then have the students act out the story again.

■ Write a new Ruby and Max story. Begin with a different amount of money that Ruby has saved. Write about how Ruby and Max spend this new money.

■ Have students write word problems such as, "Max has two lucky quarters. How much money does he have now?"

Bibliography

Axelrod, Amy. *Pigs Will Be Pigs.* New York: Simon & Schuster, 1994.

Burns, Marilyn. *Math by All Means: Money, Grades 1–2.* Sausalito, CA: Math Solutions, 1997.

Caple, Kathy. *The Purse.* New York: Houghton Mifflin, 1992.

Glass, Julie. *A Dollar for Penny.* New York: Random House Books for Young Readers, 1998.

Godfrey, Neale S. *Kid's Money Book.* New York: Simon & Schuster Children's Books, 1998.

Hoban, Lillian. *Arthur's Funny Money.* New York: HarperCollins Children's Books, 1999.

Schwartz, David. *If You Made a Million.* New York: Lothrop, Lee & Shepard, 1994.

Slater, Teddy. *Max's Money.* New York: Scholastic, 1999.

Spann, Mary Beth. *25 Board Games: Instant Games That Teach Essential Math Skills.* New York: Scholastic, 1999.

Taback, Simms. *Joseph Had a Little Overcoat.* New York: Viking, 1999.

Software

Davidson. *Money Town.* Macintosh and Windows 3.1, 95/98.

IBM/Edmark. *Brain Bytes Money Math.* Macintosh and Windows 95/98.

Related Standards 2000

Standard 1: Number and Operations
Standard 2: Algebra
Standard 7: Reasoning and Proof
Standard 8: Communication
Standard 9: Connections
Standard 10: Representation

Related Standards 1989

Standard 1: Mathematics as Problem Solving
Standard 2: Mathematics as Communication
Standard 3: Mathematics as Reasoning
Standard 4: Mathematical Connections
Standard 6: Number Sense and Numeration
Standard 7: Whole Number Operations
Standard 8: Whole Number Computation
Standard 13: Patterns and Relationships

0–25	26–50	51–75	76–100

1. Reproduce this graph on chart paper.

2. Give one sticky note to each student.

3. Tell students to do the following:

   Write your name and the number you predict on your sticky note.

   Place your sticky note on the chart paper graph in the appropriate box.

Figure 6.1.1. Prediction Graph

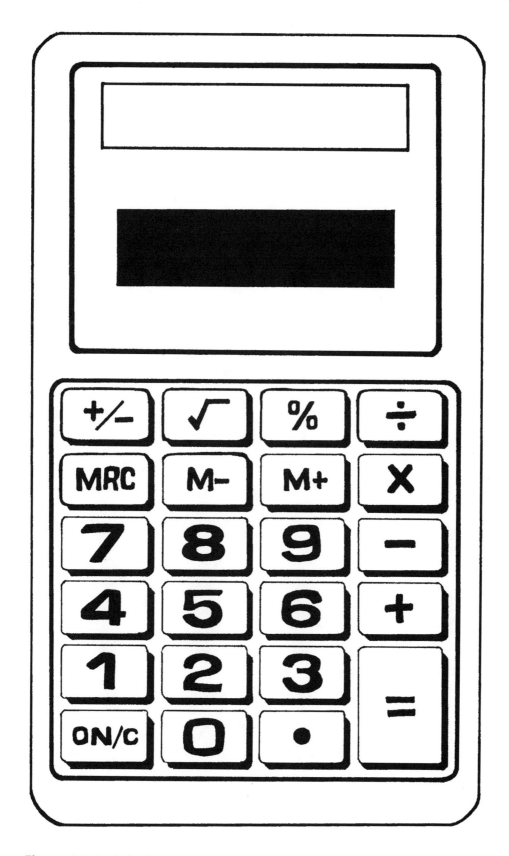

Figure 6.1.2. *Calculator.* Illustration by Cherie Blackmore.

Name: _____   **Date:** _____

1. $1 + 0 =$ **(1)**

2. $2 + 1 + 0 =$ **(3)**

3. $3 + 2 + 1 + 0 =$ **(6)**

4. $4 + 3 + 2 + 1 + 0 =$ **(10)**

5. $5 + 4 + 3 + 2 + 1 + 0 =$ **(15)**

6. $6 + 5 + 4 + 3 + 2 + 1 + 0 =$ **(21)**

7. $7 + 6 + 5 + 4 + 3 + 2 + 1 + 0 =$ **(28)**

8. $8 + 7 + 6 + 5 + 4 + 3 + 2 + 1 + 0 =$ **(36)**

9. $9 + 8 + 7 + 6 + 5 + 4 + 3 + 2 + 1 + 0 =$ **(45)**

10. Your answer from item 9 **(45)** $+ 10 =$ **(55)**

Sister ate (55) things!

When can a calculator be a good problem-solving tool? Explain.

Support students' answers, such as:

> Use a calculator for a big problem that a calculator can solve quickly.

> Use a calculator to add or subtract lists of numbers.

> Use a calculator to check your answers to a problem.

Figure 6.1.3. *Answers to Calculator Exercise*

Name: _____   **Date:** _____

1. $1 + 0 =$ _____

2. $2 + 1 + 0 =$ _____

3. $3 + 2 + 1 + 0 =$ _____

4. $4 + 3 + 2 + 1 + 0 =$ _____

5. $5 + 4 + 3 + 2 + 1 + 0 =$ _____

6. $6 + 5 + 4 + 3 + 2 + 1 + 0 =$ _____

7. $7 + 6 + 5 + 4 + 3 + 2 + 1 + 0 =$ _____

8. $8 + 7 + 6 + 5 + 4 + 3 + 2 + 1 + 0 =$ _____

9. $9 + 8 + 7 + 6 + 5 + 4 + 3 + 2 + 1 + 0 =$ _____

10. Your answer from item 9 _____ $+ 10 =$ _____

Sister ate _____ things!

When can a calculator be a good problem-solving tool? Explain.

Figure 6.1.4. *Calculator Exercise*

Name: _____   **Date:** _____

	Yes	No
Calculates addition facts on the calculator		
Recognizes [+]		
Recognizes [–]		
Recognizes [=]		
Recognizes [ON/C]		

Beginning: 0–2; Developing: 3–4; Proficient: 5

Anecdotal notes:

Name: _____   **Date:** _____

	Yes	No
Calculates addition facts on the calculator		
Recognizes [+]		
Recognizes [–]		
Recognizes [=]		
Recognizes [ON/C]		

Beginning: 0–2; Developing: 3–4; Proficient: 5

Anecdotal notes:

Figure 6.1.5. *Assessment, Calculator Exercise*

Name: _____   **Date:** _____

I see math when I <u>sleep .</u>

My question is:

<u>How many minutes of sleep do I get each night?</u>

<u>How many dreams do I have?</u>

My answer is:

<u>If I go to bed at 8:00 and I wake up at 6:00, I get 4 hours of sleep before mid-</u>
<u>night and I get 6 hours of sleep after midnight. So that is 4 + 6 = 10 hours of</u>
<u>sleep. I remember I had 2 dreams last night. I'll say, 2!</u>

Figure 6.2.1. *Sample—I Have the Math Curse!*

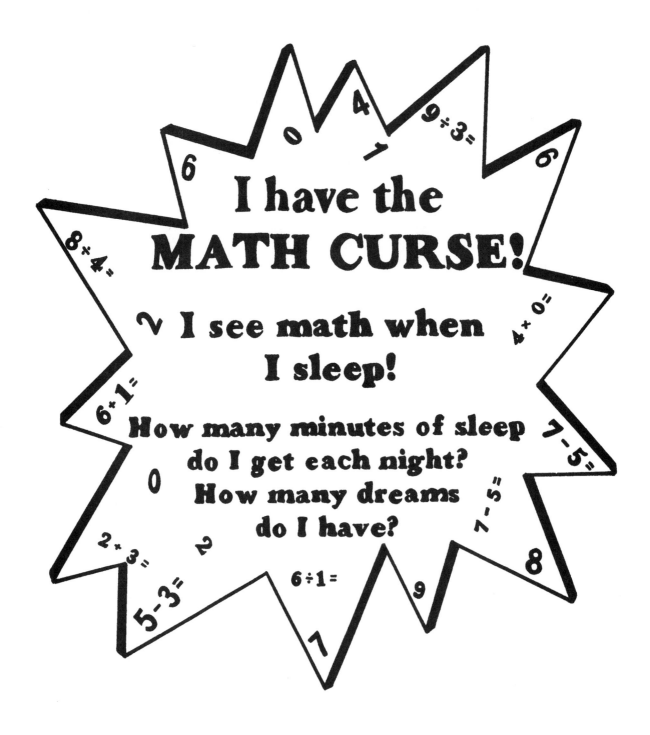

Figure 6.2.2. *Project Sample—I Have the Math Curse!* Illustration by Cherie Blackmore.

Use **Fig. 6.2.5.** to help you do the following:

- Write, "I see math . . ."

- Write your own math curse question.

    Give enough information so others can answer your question.

    Put the answer to the question on the back of your project so others can solve the problem on their own.

- Draw a pattern as a border around the entire construction paper product, as shown in **Figure 6.2.2. *Project Sample—I Have the Math Curse!***

Note: The pattern may contain math-related symbols or designs that relate to the student's question; for example, one could use numbers, football symbols, or shapes.

Figure 6.2.3. *Instructions for I Have the Math Curse! Project*

Name: _____   **Date:** _____

Did the student create a math question?   _____ (1)

Did the student answer his or her math curse question?   _____ (1)

Did the student draw a pattern that surrounds the entire work?   _____ (1)

Did the student convey emotion in his or her writing or illustration?   _____ (1)

Total score: _____ (4)

Beginning: 0–1; Developing: 2–3; Proficient: 4

Anecdotal notes:

Name: _____   **Date:** _____

Did the student create a math question?   _____ (1)

Did the student answer his or her math curse question?   _____ (1)

Did the student draw a pattern that surrounds the entire work?   _____ (1)

Did the student convey emotion in his or her writing or illustration?   _____ (1)

Total score: _____ (4)

Beginning: 0–1; Developing: 2–3; Proficient: 4

Anecdotal notes:

Figure 6.2.4. *Assessment, Finding Math Problems*

Name: _____   **Date:** _____

I see math when I _____

_____ .

My question is:

_____

_____

_____

_____

_____

My answer is:

_____

_____

_____

_____

_____

Figure 6.2.5. *I Have the Math Curse!* (Practice Sheet)

Dear Parents,

Students are currently learning to sort, count, add, and subtract money during math time. As part of a math lesson based on Rosemary Wells's book, *Bunny Money*, your child must bring a "lucky" quarter to class by (___date___). Just any quarter will do. In the story, a character by the name of Max always carries a "lucky" quarter with him. This turns out to be quite fortunate, because Max and his sister Ruby end up using the quarter to make an important phone call.

During this lesson, your child will make, count, and spend paper "Bunny Money" at school, in $1.00 and $5.00 denominations. He or she will also use the "lucky" quarter brought from home.

You may reinforce this study of money at home by collecting and counting money together. As you count bills or change, first have your child sort the money; next, arrange the money from larger to smaller denominations; then count the money beginning with the larger denominations. Count out loud so your child hears and repeats the counting patterns with you.

Also, you and your child may agree that having a "lucky" quarter may be just as good an idea for a kid as it is for Max.

Sincerely,

Figure 6.3.1. *Note Home*

Bus Station

Rosalinda's Gift Shop

Candi's Corner

Laundromat

Lunch

Telephone

Figure 6.3.2. *Signs*

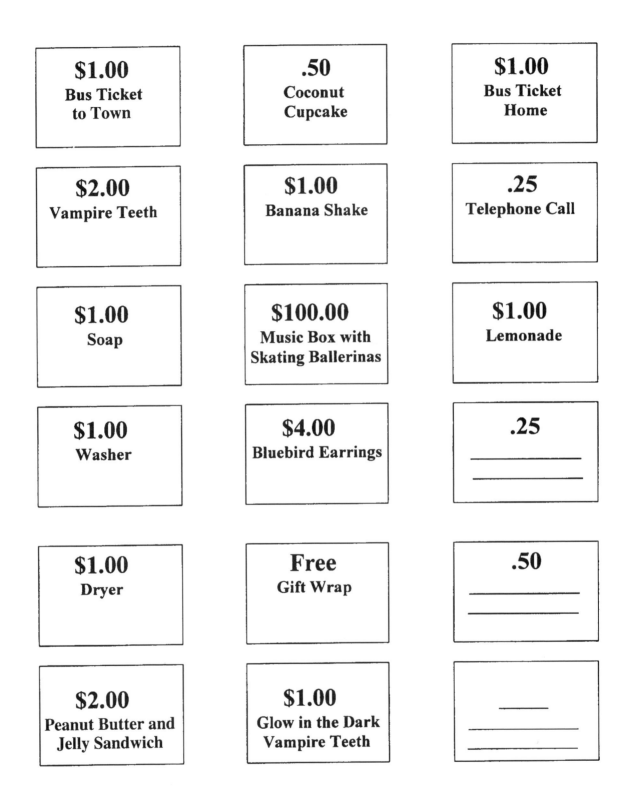

Figure 6.3.3. Cards and Tickets

Name: _____ **Date:** _____

The student predicted a problem that Max and Ruby might have. _____ (4)

The student used at least one strategy to correctly count out $15.00. _____ (4)

The student exchanged Bunny Money and cards of equal value. _____ (4)

At the end of the lesson, the student had cards and Bunny Money
totaling $15.00 value. _____ (4)

Total score: _____ (4)

Beginning: 0–1; Developing 2–3; Proficient: 4

Anecdotal notes:

Name: _____ **Date:** _____

The student predicted a problem that Max and Ruby might have. _____ (4)

The student used at least one strategy to correctly count out $15.00. _____ (4)

The student exchanged Bunny Money and cards of equal value. _____ (4)

At the end of the lesson, the student had cards and Bunny Money
totaling $15.00 value. _____ (4)

Total score: _____ (4)

Beginning: 0–1; Developing 2–3; Proficient: 4

Anecdotal notes:

Figure 6.3.4. *Assessment, Solving Money Problems*

Chapter 7

Reasoning and Proof

Dear Math Teacher,

Children learn that mathematics makes sense. They do this through repeated practice, such as when a child discovers that a group of five hippos is always five no matter whether she spreads them apart or crowds them together. Likewise, a child proves three hippos plus two hippos equals five, and always, two hippos plus three hippos equals the same. When children work with mathematics, they practice and acquire knowledge about mathematical rules.

Rules make sense to children. They are experts about rules on the playground and rules in games. A child's sense of fairness is betrayed when he sees a rule has been broken. But when a rule is upheld and proven again and again, it becomes something that can be relied upon and counted on. The rules of mathematics make sense to children.

Mathematical reasoning is an integral part of all the mathematics lessons included in this book. For example, in Chapter 4, Lesson 1, *Twelve Snails to One Lizard*, students reason, as does story character Milo Beaver, that the world is a very confusing place when we use different measuring tools to compare and measure objects. There must be rules for measuring, and there must be standard units of measurement. Students determine before the culmination of the lesson that the characters in the story must agree upon a standard unit of measurement to solve their measuring problems.

In the following three lessons, students will determine several mathematical truths. In the lesson accompanying *Arctic Fives Arrive* by Elinor Pinczes, students classify, sort, and skip count groups of five. They learn that whether one counts five whales or five pollywogs, the number is the same. If they group three groups of five together, no matter how they count the groups, the sum will always be fifteen. Here students have the opportunity to test and retest their solutions.

Demi, the author of *One Grain of Rice*, helps readers prove the power of doubling numbers. Who would have thought that by doubling one grain of rice every day for thirty days one would end up with an astronomical amount of rice? The awesome power of doubling will astound you and your students. All you have to do is begin with 1. Try it.

Loreen Leedy's character, Miss Prime, teaches several lessons in *Fraction Action*. Here students compare simple fractions such as $\frac{1}{2}$, $\frac{1}{3}$, and $\frac{1}{4}$. Together you and your students will pose the questions, "Which one is bigger? Which one is smaller? How can we test our answers? How do we prove we have a correct answer?" By creating fraction illustrations, students will identify and label fractions and will draw conclusions about the comparative size of each.

As students practice mathematics through children's literature and classroom lessons, they learn to generalize and apply their knowledge to the mathematics they discover in real life situations. Students discover that the rules of mathematics remain the same, that is, doubling a number always means adding the original number to itself; fractions are always parts of wholes; and no matter whether kids put five plastic pandas in three groups, or five purple pens in three groups, they will always count up a total of fifteen. Mathematics makes sense.

Caroline and Anne

LESSON 1

Classify, Sort, and Skip Count by Fives

Pinczes, Elinor J. *Arctic Fives Arrive.* New York: Scholastic, 1996.

First, a group of five snowy owls land on an iceberg to view the northern lights. Five polar bears join them, followed by groups of five ermine, walrus, arctic hares, and musk oxen. After viewing the northern lights, the animal groups leave the ice in reverse order. Elinor Pinczes tells this patterned story with rhythm and rhyme. Students pick up the beat and enjoy predicting the number and the group of animals that will next arrive or take off. Students will slap "high five" for this book.

Time Frame

50 minutes

Materials

For the teacher:

Transparency of **Figure 7.1.1. *100s Chart*** (set up prior to the lesson for reference)

Overhead projector

Chart paper or chalkboard

Three to five centers or tables set up with various objects for students to classify and sort into groups of five, such as animal figurines, Popsicle sticks, cards, beads, paper clips, pattern blocks, buttons, plastic links, or Legos

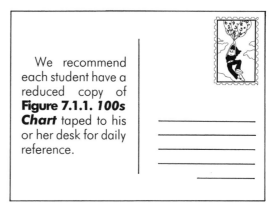

We recommend each student have a reduced copy of **Figure 7.1.1. *100s Chart*** taped to his or her desk for daily reference.

Figure 7.1.2. *Assessment, Counting by Fives*

For each group of five students:

One sheet of poster board or chart paper

For each student:

One sheet of white construction paper

Pencil, crayons, scissors, and glue

Story and Mini-Lesson

1. **P**review the story by taking a "picture walk" through the book.

2. Invite students to **p**redict what kind of a book this will be. Will it be a counting book? What will it be about?

3. **R**ead the story. As you read, invite students to join in as they pick up the story's pattern and rhythm. Students will quickly be able to predict the number in each group that gathers on the ice (five), and they'll enjoy predicting which species of animal will join the gathering next.

4. **R**e-read the story to reinforce skip counting by fives and to hear the rhyming patterns. This time, as you read the story aloud, have a student volunteer point to fives on the overhead transparency of **Figure 7.1.1. *100s Chart*** as you skip count and clap by fives to thirty and back down again.

5. Choose another student volunteer to use the 100s chart to point and count by fives up to thirty and beyond to 100. Encourage students to clap and count out loud with the leader.

6. Ask students to notice and share patterns they hear or see when they count by fives. For example, students hear a distinct rhythm when they count and clap by fives; they see that every other number ends in a five or a zero; or, when a student points to the 100s chart the pointer goes back and forth from the middle to the end of each consecutive row.

Group Lesson

1. **R**eview the story by asking students to name the animals (owls, polar bears, ermine, walrus, arctic hares, and musk oxen). Ask why the author may have chosen those animals. (The animals are arctic animals and the story took place in the Arctic.)

2. Discuss whether it would be silly to have lions and rhinoceroses leap onto the arctic ice. Where would one find lions and rhinoceroses? (They would be on an African savannah, steppe, or plain).

3. Ask students if there are particular animals that live in your neighborhood. (If you live in a city, you might have pigeons, peregrine falcons, squirrels, robins, cats, and dogs. If you live in the country, you might have prairie dogs, foxes, owls, badgers, and rabbits.)

4. Invite students to suggest the names of different habitats, which you will list on chart paper. These could include rain forests, meadows, deserts, plains, tide pools, and oceans. Then have students help you list five or more animals that live in each habitat. (For example, a rain forest habitat includes monkeys, parrots, boas, sloths, toucans, and frogs. A meadow habitat includes crickets, turtles, birds, frogs, and bees.)

5. Tell students to arrange themselves into groups of five. Don't worry if you have "remainders." Congratulate the remainders, group them together, and tell them they are a special group. You will name them the group of four, three, two, or one.

6. Reinforce skip counting by fives by counting groups of students, then adding the student(s) who are remainders.

7. Students should now stay with their groups. Refer to the chart paper list of habitats and animals. Each group must choose one habitat and choose the same number of animals for that habitat as there are students in the group. (A group of five would choose five different animals, and a remainder group of two would choose two different animals.)

8. Together, each group of students will make one habitat poster, as follows: First, each student in a group draws, colors, and cuts out five of one species of animal for the habitat; next, each student arranges and then pastes his or her group of five animals onto the poster; then, together, students in each group label the groups of animals by fives on their poster.

9. The finished product will be a poster with five groups of five different animals pasted onto chart paper or poster board. Next to each group of five animals, in sequential order, will be the number labels: 5, 10, 15, 20, and 25.

10. When students understand what they are to do, give one large sheet of poster board or chart paper to each group and one sheet of white construction paper to each student.

11. Students may begin working on their projects.

Discovery

As groups complete their projects, invite students to visit the classifying and sorting centers you have previously set up, where they will classify and sort objects into groups of five. Encourage students to sort three or more groups of five and then practice skip counting the groups by saying five, ten, fifteen, and so forth. Students should sort and resort several different classifications of objects.

Reflection

Gather the class together to share group posters. Invite students to tell about the habitat and animals selected. Ask, "What does three groups of five equal? Could three groups of five ever equal anything other than fifteen? If you counted three groups of five blue whales, would the number be any different than three groups of five wasps?" Encourage students to prove their answers by referring to their posters.

Assessment

Listen as students predict, skip count, and clap by fives. Watch as students classify and sort objects into groups. Use **Figure 7.1.2. Assessment, Counting by Fives** to record your observations.

Special Needs Adaptations:

Auditory disability: An interpreter should sign the story and lesson. List the Group Lesson directions from Group Lesson item 8 on the board or on chart paper as a visual reinforcement for these students.

Motor disability: Student buddies or aides may assist these students with drawing, coloring, cutting, and pasting.

Visual disability: Partners should assist these students throughout the lesson. Provide stuffed animals, puppets, or plastic or clay figurines of the six animals represented in *Arctic Fives Arrive*. The partner should say the name of each animal before offering it to the visually disabled student. Then the visually disabled student should be encouraged to feel, describe, and name each animal. During the Group Lesson project, these students should construct clay figures or sort animal figurines in groups of five to display and describe later to the rest of the class.

English Language Learners: Have a student helper or ELL teacher check that these students understand the lesson. Have these students skip count by fives in their native languages to share this knowledge with their English-speaking friends.

Extensions

- Act out *Arctic Fives Arrive*. Have students arrange themselves into groups of five, with each group representing an animal group from the story. Students who are "remainders" can read the story aloud as others act it out, then switch parts.

- Have the students cut out puppets or felt board figures of arctic animals. Use these to retell the story.

- Use "fives" as the inspiration to write a story, rap, or song.

■ Have students use a 100s chart to count by fives, then by twos, threes, and tens. Color fives blue, two yellow, threes orange, and tens green. Ask students, "Do you find any patterns? Do the patterns help you predict what the next number in a group will be?"

■ Make a book about groups of five. For example, students could rhyme, "Five pencils on a table/Five fractions you can label/Five posters on the wall/Five coats in the hall."

■ Have students brainstorm sets of five, such as flavors of ice cream, animals that start with the letter "B," types of fruit, or playground games.

■ Play store, telling the students they can use only nickels to buy things.

■ Use this lesson with a telling time activity. Provide Judy Clocks, or have students make paper plate clocks with paper hands attached to the plates with brass brads. Then count by fives around the clock.

Bibliography

Calmenson, Stephanie. *Dinner at the Panda Palace.* New York: HarperCollins, 1995.

Ehlert, Lois. *Fish Eyes: A Book You Can Count On.* New York: Harcourt, 1992.

McGrath, Barbara Barbieri. *M&M's Brand Chocolate Candies Counting Book.* New York: Charlesbridge, 1996.

Software

Encore Software. *Schoolhouse Rock Fun and Skills Pack: 1st and 2nd Grade.* Windows 95.

Related Standards 2000

Standard 1: Number and Operations

Standard 2: Algebra

Standard 6: Problem Solving

Standard 8: Communication

Standard 9: Connections

Standard 10: Representation

Related Standards 1989

Standard 1: Mathematics as Problem Solving

Standard 2: Mathematics as Communication

Standard 5: Estimation

Standard 8: Whole Number Computation

Standard 13: Patterns and Relationships

LESSON 2

Prove the Power of Doubling Numbers

Demi. *One Grain of Rice.* New York: Scholastic, 1997.

This legend from India tells the story of a greedy raja (ruler) who hordes rice and will not share it with his hungry people. When Rani, a young girl, discovers grains of rice trickling from a basket carried into the palace, she realizes she has a chance to teach the raja a lesson. She points out the lost rice to the raja, who decides to reward her for her scrutiny. Clever Rani asks for only one grain of rice, but the number of grains must be doubled *every* day for thirty days. The raja thinks this will be an easy deal for him, but Rani teaches the raja, and will teach your class, about the power of doubling numbers.

Time Frame

50 minutes

Materials

For the teacher:

A sticky note to mark page 13 (here Rani and the raja make a deal—mark this prior to reading the story)

Chalkboard or chart paper

Seven zipping storage bags

One sheet of poster board divided into eight sections, labeled as in **Figure 7.2.1. *How Many Grains of Rice?***

Figure 7.2.2. *Bulletin Board Label*

127 pieces of puffed rice, or several large handfuls of puffed rice cereal

Masking tape

One marker

Figure 7.2.3. *Doubling Practice, Rubric*

Yes, 127 pieces of puffed rice is the correct number to fill seven bags for seven days. You and your students could do an extension lesson to determine how you came up with that number.

_____

_____

_____

_____

For each group of four students:

One sheet of poster board divided into eight sections, labeled as illustrated in **Figure 7.2.1. How Many Grains of Rice?**

Seven zipping storage bags

Pencils and markers

Seven pieces of masking tape

127 pieces of puffed rice or several large handfuls of puffed rice cereal

One marker

For each student:

Figure 7.2.4. My Prediction—How Many Grains of Rice?

Figure 7.2.5. Doubling Practice

Story and Mini-Lesson

1. **P**review and make **p**redictions about the story. Show students the book cover. Ask, "What do you think this story will be about?" "What country do you think this story is from?"

2. **R**ead the story up to page 13 (where Rani and the raja make a deal), then stop. Do not finish the story. You will finish reading the book after the Group Lesson.

3. Hand out **Figure 7.2.4. My Prediction—How Many Grains of Rice?** to each student. Have students fill out only the top portion of the sheet with their predictions for the number of grains of rice Rani will receive at the end of thirty days. Collect these papers to use later.

4. Direct student's attention to your poster board, modeled after **Figure 7.2.1. How Many Grains of Rice?** Ask students to recall how many grains of rice Rani asked to receive on the first day (one).

5. Show students the puffed rice. Explain that you chose puffed rice because it is easier to see and handle than regular rice. Put one piece of puffed rice into a zipping storage bag to represent the grain of rice Rani received on Day One.

6. Tape the zipping storage bag to the poster board in the section labeled, "Day One."

7. Write the total amount of rice in the section labeled, "Day One."

8. At this time, introduce the concept of doubling. Remind the class that Rani made a deal with the raja that each day for thirty days, the raja would double the amount of rice from the day before. Explain that doubling means taking an original amount and adding that same amount. Ask students to tell you how to double the rice from Day One for the solution for Day Two. (As students give you instructions, hold up the one piece of puffed rice for Day One, match it with another piece for Day Two, and demonstrate to show $1 + 1 = 2$.)

9. Put two pieces of puffed rice into a zipping storage bag and tape it to the poster board in the section labeled "Day Two."

10. Write the total amount of rice in the section labeled "Day Two."

11. Continue to double the amount of rice Rani received from Day One to Day Seven and tape a zipping storage bag with the amount for each day on the poster board and label it. You and your students may use the formula below:

    Day One = one grain of rice

    Day Two = two grains of rice (1 + 1 = 2)

    Day Three = four grains of rice (2 + 2 = 4)

    Day Four = eight grains of rice (4 + 4 = 8)

    Day Five = sixteen grains of rice (8 + 8 = 16)

    Day Six = thirty-two grains of rice (16 + 16 = 32)

    Day Seven = sixty-four grains of rice (32 + 32 = 64)

12. Have several students assist you in counting out the rice. This is also a good time to reinforce counting by twos. As you put in two pieces of rice at a time, have the class count by twos until you reach the sum of each problem.

> Turn this into a problem-solving activity. Ask students if they have suggestions about how to solve the problem of doubling one grain of rice, then doubling the sum from the previous day on each consecutive day, every day for seven days. Have calculating tools such as puffed rice, 100s charts, or calculators available for students to solve this problem on their own.

13. **R**eview the amounts of rice for each day with the class. Ask, "Do you think Rani is going to get a lot of rice by the end of thirty days, or do you think the raja was right about thinking he made a good deal? (Discuss this, but don't give away the story ending.)

14. Hang the completed poster board as a reference in a prominent location.

Group Lesson

1. Tell students they will create a poster board chart just as you did.

2. Divide the class into groups of four.

3. Give each group a poster board marked with the same sections as the one you completed in the Mini-Lesson.

4. Give each group one zipping storage bag containing the tools and puffed rice from the materials list.

5. Instruct groups to work together to create a poster just like the one you made as a class.

6. Circulate through the room to assist students and take anecdotal records regarding students' comprehension of the concept of doubling.

7. When groups finish their posters, display these in the classroom.

Discovery

As groups complete their posters, direct students to complete **Figure 7.2.5. *Doubling Practice.*** Students may use the data on their posters and puffed rice or other counters to help them complete this practice sheet.

Reflection

- Gather students together to review and discuss **Figure 7.2.4. *My Prediction—How Many Grains of Rice?*** Explain that a prediction is a smart guess. Ask students to refer to their earlier predictions. Pose the question, "Now that you know more about doubling, do you think you will be able to come up with a more accurate prediction for how many grains of rice Rani will get at the end of thirty days?"

  Some students may reply, "Yes! Now we know that doubling can make numbers a lot bigger—fast." "After doubling for a total of thirty days, Rani might get a really, really huge amount of rice."

- Instruct students to record a new prediction on the bottom section of **Figure 7.2.4.** When they complete and turn in their predictions, finish reading *One Grain of Rice* out loud.

- Return to the adjusted predictions. Which prediction was the closest? Was any prediction anywhere near the amount of rice that Rani received?

- Conclude the lesson by asking students to respond to the story. "Did you like it? What did you like about it?"

Assessment

- Collect and review students' work from **Figure 7.2.1. *How Many Grains of Rice?*** (group poster); **Figure 7.2.4. *My Prediction—How Many Grains of Rice?;*** and **Figure 7.2.5. *Doubling Practice.***

- Check **Figure 7.2.4.** Did the student adjust his or her original prediction to a larger number after acquiring new knowledge during the Mini- and Group Lessons and the Discovery activity?

- Use **Figure 7.2.3. *Doubling Practice, Rubric*** to score students' individual work on **Figure 7.2.5. *Doubling Practice.***

Special Needs Adaptations:

Auditory disability: An interpreter should sign the lesson.

Motor disability: Student helpers should assist these students with putting the puffed rice into zipping storage bags. These students may calculate the doubling problems and then dictate these to a helper to record.

Visual disability: These students can be the rice counters. Have them count the correct amount of rice for each zipping storage bag. Encourage these students to feel and compare the baggies when the group posters are completed.

English Language Learners: Place the book in a listening center with an audio-tape of the story. If you do not have an audiotape, have a volunteer read and record the story.

Extensions

- Find doubles on a 100s chart, then mark them with transparent squares. Have the students look for patterns.

- Have students determine how many grains of rice there are in a teaspoon, tablespoon, and cup. They should then predict the number of grains of rice if you doubled each; that is, 2 t = _____ grains of rice; 2 T = _____ grains of rice; and 2 C = _____ grains of rice. Is there a way to check the students' predictions without counting? What tools could they use (calculator, weight scale, others)?

- As a class, make a list of "If . . . , then" statements, such as, "If my cat has two kittens this year, and each kitten has two kittens the next year, then I will have seven cats in two years."

- Ask students, "Does doubling work the same for anything you might double, such as Legos, marbles, Pokemon cards, or homework?" *Yes!* Prove it by using logic words such as *If* and *then* or *because*.

- Do a research project about rice. Have students find out one place it grows and learn why it grows there, then use reasoning to predict other places where rice grows. (For example, rice grows in wet flatlands in California; could it grow in wet flatlands in other places in the world?) Check the student's predictions.

- Read *How Much Is a Million?* by David M. Schwartz. Discuss what big numbers mean.

Bibliography

Birch, David. *The King's Chessboard.* New York: Econo-Clad, 1999.

McKissack, Pat. *A Million Fish . . . More or Less.* New York: Econo-Clad, 1999.

Schwartz, David M. *How Much Is a Million?* New York: William Morrow, 1994.

———. *If You Made a Million.* New York: William Morrow, 1994.

Wells, Robert. *Is a Blue Whale the Biggest Thing There Is?* New York: Whitman, 1993.

Related Standards 2000

Standard 1: Number and Operations

Standard 2: Algebra

Standard 6: Problem Solving

Standard 8: Communication

Standard 9: Connections

Standard 10: Representation

Related Standards 1989

Standard 1: Mathematics as Problem Solving

Standard 2: Mathematics as Communication

Standard 3: Mathematics as Reasoning

Standard 4: Mathematical Connections

Standard 5: Estimation

Standard 6: Number Sense and Numeration

Standard 7: Concepts of Whole Number Operations

Standard 13: Patterns and Relationships

LESSON 3

Compare Fractions

Leedy, Loreen. *Fraction Action.* New York: Holiday House, 1996.

Miss Prime, a zany hippo, loves fractions. She teaches her menagerie of students about halves, thirds, and fourths, and about sets, fair shares, and fractions in money. This entertaining series of five lessons in one story culminates with a test—a teacher test. The students test Miss Prime on what she knows about fractions.

Dear Math Teacher

Fraction Action lessons take little preparation time. Loreen Leedy has done all the work. Just read a chapter a day in *Fraction Action* to your students, provide paper and crayons, and join Miss Prime for some fraction fun.

_____
_____
_____
_____
_____

Time Frame

50 minutes

Materials

For the teacher:

Chalkboard, chart paper, or overhead with samples of fraction pictures, as shown on pages 4, 7, and 9, of the fractions $\frac{1}{2}$, $\frac{1}{3}$, and $\frac{1}{4}$

Figure 7.3.1. *Assessment, Drawing and Labeling Fractions*

For each student:

Construction paper

Crayons, colored pencils, or markers

Story and Mini-Lesson

1. **P**review *Fraction Action*. Discuss the title. Students will enjoy being able to give you an accurate **p**rediction about the book's contents.

2. **R**ead aloud the first lesson, "Fraction Action." As you read this lesson, interact with your students just as Miss Prime does. For instance, when Miss Prime says, "Now let's think of some fractions in real life. Use your imagination to make a picture in your mind of what I say," have students do as Miss Prime says. That is, imagine "A tuna sandwich cut in half," and so on. Proceed in this manner to page 10, and stop when you have finished reading the first two-thirds of that page.

3. Refer to the sample fractions on your chalkboard. Ask students to notice which fractions are bigger and which are smaller. Then ask students Miss Prime's question on the last one-third of page 10, "Which fraction is the smallest?"

4. Have students explain their answers; for example, some students might think that $\frac{1}{4}$ is bigger than $\frac{1}{2}$ because four is a larger number than two. To prove or disprove this, ask a student volunteer to draw two more lines in the picture that shows two halves, so it becomes a picture of four fourths. Then have the student look again and name what the fraction has become. Ask the student to use colored chalk to shade $\frac{1}{2}$ of the picture; then another color to shade $\frac{1}{4}$ of the picture. Ask again, "Which fraction is the biggest? Which fraction is the smallest?" Have the student refer to the pictures he or she has just shaded in to explain his or her new reasoning.

Group Lesson

1. Once again, refer to *Fraction Action*. **R**eview several of Leedy's fraction illustrations.

2. As a group, brainstorm and list on chart paper several real life fractions.

3. Tell students they will make drawings of real life fractions such as ice cream cones, sandwiches, cupcakes, and moons, just as in the story. They must make at least three different fraction drawings.

4. Instruct students *not* to label their fraction drawings because when they complete their work, each student will pass his or her work to a partner, who will identify and label the fractions for each drawing.

5. Tell students that they must 1) complete at least three drawings and 2) make drawings that clearly show fractions, as do the samples on page 5 of *Fraction Action*.

6. Pass out materials and send students to their seats to make at least three fraction drawings.

Discovery

- Instruct students to hold up and show their work for others to see. Tell students that it is time to identify and label each other's fraction drawings. Model how to do this; for example, if Amy drew watermelon halves, then Russell, her partner, would write the fraction $\frac{1}{2}$ below each half watermelon. Show students how to proceed in this manner until they have labeled their partners' fraction drawings accurately.

- Match students with partners and have partners exchange work.

Reflection

- When partners have completed labeling each other's work, have them return it and check each other's labels. Encourage students to discuss and explain drawings and labels to one another. Listen to students' conversations. Do students present logical arguments regarding their labels or pictures?

- Post student work on a bulletin board.

Assessment

Circulate throughout the room during the Discovery and Reflection activities. Check for understanding and clarify misunderstandings. Refer to **Figure 7.3.1. *Assessment, Drawing and Labeling Fractions.***

Special Needs Adaptations:

Auditory disability: An interpreter should sign the story and lesson.

Motor disability: An aide or student helper should assist with the drawing activity, or students with this disability may list examples of real life fractions for partner students to draw and label.

Visual disability: Students with this disability may list examples of real life fractions, as described for students with motor disabilities. In addition, provide several real life fractions for these students to touch, such as two wrapped halves of a peanut butter and jelly sandwich, two halves of a circle, three-thirds of a length of ribbon, and four sections of a paper plate.

English Language Learners: Pair these students with English-speaking partners. They may tell the class the fraction words *one-half, one-third,* and *one-fourth* in both English and other languages.

Extensions

- Do as Miss Prime does and teach one *Fraction Action* chapter per day. Instruct students to draw fractions in their journals, label them, and describe them.

- Have students give you the "Teacher Test," page 28. Then have students make up their own tests to give you and each other.

- Read *Give Me Half* by Stuart Murphy. Do the activities listed on pages 33 and 34. After reading *Give Me Half,* plan and do a pizza party. Divide the pizzas and drinks into fractions.

- Read *The Hershey's Milk Chocolate Bar Fractions Book* by Jerry Pallotta. Demonstrate the fraction activities with a Hershey's Milk Chocolate Bar. Then distribute Hershey's Milk Chocolate Bars (or fractions of chocolate bars) to your students and have them divide, sort, separate, stack, add, and eat fractions. Just before they pop fractions of chocolate bars into their mouths, the students should announce to partners what fraction(s) they are eating.

Bibliography

Hutchins, Pat. *The Doorbell Rang.* New York: William Morrow, 1994.

——. *Llaman a la Puerta (The Doorbell Rang).* New York: William Morrow, 1994.

McMillan, Bruce. *Eating Fractions.* New York: Scholastic, 1993.

Murphy, Stuart J. *A Fair Bear Share.* New York: HarperCollins, 1997.

——. *Give Me Half.* New York: Scholastic, 1996.

Pallotta, Jerry. *The Hershey's Milk Chocolate Bar Fractions Book.* New York: Scholastic, 1999.

Software

Knowledge Adventure. *Math Blaster, 1st Grade.* Macintosh and Windows 95/98.

Related Standards 2000

Standard 1: Number and Operations

Standard 2: Algebra

Standard 3: Geometry

Standard 4: Measurement

Standard 6: Problem Solving

Standard 8: Communication

Standard 9: Connections

Standard 10: Representation

Related Standards 1989

Standard 1: Mathematics as Problem Solving

Standard 2: Mathematics as Communication

Standard 3: Mathematics as Reasoning

Standard 4: Mathematical Connections

Standard 6: Number Sense and Numeration

Standard 7: Whole Number Operations

Standard 8: Whole Number Computation

Standard 9: Geometry and Spatial Sense

Standard 10: Measurement

Standard 13: Patterns and Relationships

Name: _____   Date: _____

1	2	3	4	5	6	7	8	9	10
11	12	13	14	15	16	17	18	19	20
21	22	23	24	25	26	27	28	29	30
31	32	33	34	35	36	37	38	39	40
41	42	43	44	45	46	47	48	49	50
51	52	53	54	55	56	57	58	59	60
61	62	63	64	65	66	67	68	69	70
71	72	73	74	75	76	77	78	79	80
81	82	83	84	85	86	87	88	89	90
91	92	93	94	95	96	97	98	99	100

Figure 7.1.1. *100s Chart*

Name: _____   **Date:** _____

Skip counts by fives from zero to thirty	_____ (1)
Skip counts by fives from 30 to 100	_____ (1)
Groups one set of five	_____ (1)
Groups three or more sets of five	_____ (1)
Is able to explain a problem such as, "Why are three groups of five whales equal to the same number as three groups of five wasps?"	_____ (2)
Total	_____ (6)

Beginning: 0–2; Developing: 3–4; Proficient:-5–6

Anecdotal notes:

Name: _____   **Date:** _____

Skip counts by fives from zero to thirty	_____ (1)
Skip counts by fives from 30 to 100	_____ (1)
Groups one set of five	_____ (1)
Groups three or more sets of five	_____ (1)
Is able to explain a problem such as, "Why are three groups of five whales equal to the same number as three groups of five wasps?"	_____ (2)
Total	_____ (6)

Beginning: 0–2; Developing: 3–4; Proficient:-5–6

Anecdotal notes:

Figure 7.1.2. Assessment, Counting by Fives

How many grains of rice?	Day One	Day Two	Day Three
	_____ grains of rice	_____ grains of rice	_____ grains of rice
Day Four	Day Five	Day Six	Day Seven
_____ grains of rice	_____ grains of rice	_____ grains of rice	_____ grains of rice

Figure 7.2.1. *How Many Grains of Rice?*

The Raja will give Rani one grain of rice, to be doubled every day for thirty days.

Use the charts to help you predict how many grains of rice Rani will get in thirty days.

To check your prediction READ THE BOOK *One Grain of Rice* by Demi

Figure 7.2.2. *Bulletin Board Label*

Name: _____ **Date:** _____

Directions: How many grains of rice did Rani receive from the raja? Fill in the missing numbers to answer the questions.

Day **(One)** = 1 grain of rice   (1)

Day Two: 1 + 1 = **(2)**   (1)

Day Three: 2 + **(2)** = 4   (1)

Day Four: **(4)** + 4 = 8   (1)

Day Five: **(8)** + **(8)** = 16   (2)

Day Six: 16 + **(16)** = 32   (1)

Day Seven: **(32)** + 32 = 64   (1)

How much rice do you think Rani received on Day 30? **(536,870,912) (no score)**

Draw a picture of Rani with her rice on Day 30.   **(2)**

Total   **(10)**

Beginning: 0–4; Developing: 5–7; Proficient: 8–10

Figure 7.2.3. *Doubling Practice, Rubric*

Name: _____ **Date:** _____

I predict that Rani will get _____ grains of rice because

_____

_____

_____

_____

_____

_____

_____

- -

Name: _____ **Date:** _____

I predict that Rani will get _____ grains of rice because

_____

_____

_____

_____

_____

_____

_____

Figure 7.2.4. My Prediction—How Many Grains of Rice?

Name: _____   **Date:** _____

Directions: How many grains of rice did Rani receive from the raja? Fill in the missing numbers to answer the questions.

Day _____ = 1 grain of rice

Day Two: $1 + 1 = $ _____

Day Three: $2 + $ _____ $= 4$

Day Four: _____ $+ 4 = 8$

Day Five: _____ $+$ _____ $= 16$

Day Six: $16 + $ _____ $= 32$

Day Seven: _____ $+ 32 = 64$

How much rice do you think Rani will have on Day 30? _____

Draw a picture of Rani with her rice on Day 30.

Figure 7.2.5. *Doubling Practice*

Name: _____   **Date:** _____

Student completed at least three drawings.   ___(3)

Student made drawings that clearly showed fractions as in the samples
on page 5 of *Fraction Action*.   ___(3)

Together, partners labeled and made corrections for labels of fractions drawings.   ___(3)

Total: ___(9)

Beginning: 0–5; Developing: 6–8; Proficient: 9

Anecdotal notes:

Name: _____   **Date:** _____

Student completed at least three drawings.   ___(3)

Student made drawings that clearly showed fractions as in the samples
on page 5 of *Fraction Action*.   ___(3)

Together, partners labeled and made corrections for labels of fractions drawings.   ___(3)

Total: ___(9)

Beginning: 0–5; Developing: 6–8; Proficient: 9

Anecdotal notes:

Figure 7.3.1. *Assessment, Drawing and Labeling Fractions*

Chapter 8

Communication

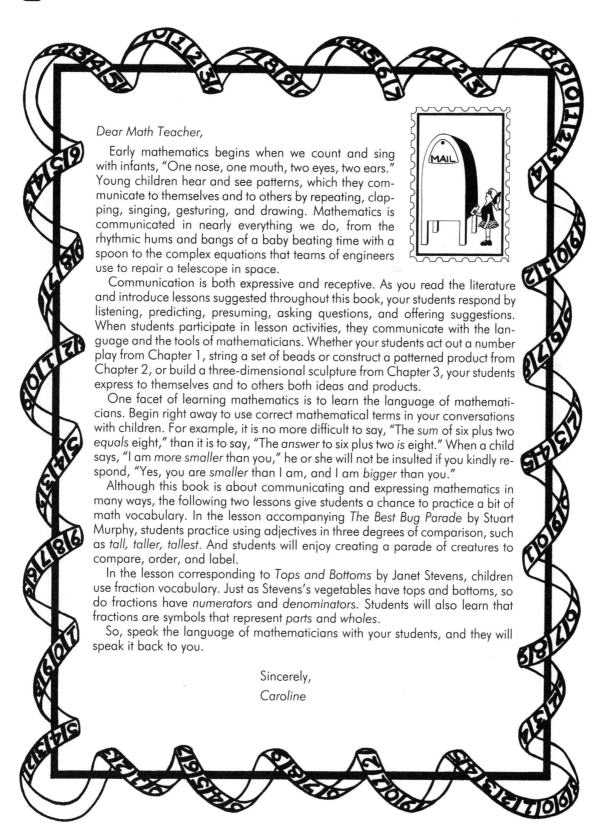

Dear Math Teacher,

Early mathematics begins when we count and sing with infants, "One nose, one mouth, two eyes, two ears." Young children hear and see patterns, which they communicate to themselves and to others by repeating, clapping, singing, gesturing, and drawing. Mathematics is communicated in nearly everything we do, from the rhythmic hums and bangs of a baby beating time with a spoon to the complex equations that teams of engineers use to repair a telescope in space.

Communication is both expressive and receptive. As you read the literature and introduce lessons suggested throughout this book, your students respond by listening, predicting, presuming, asking questions, and offering suggestions. When students participate in lesson activities, they communicate with the language and the tools of mathematicians. Whether your students act out a number play from Chapter 1, string a set of beads or construct a patterned product from Chapter 2, or build a three-dimensional sculpture from Chapter 3, your students express to themselves and to others both ideas and products.

One facet of learning mathematics is to learn the language of mathematicians. Begin right away to use correct mathematical terms in your conversations with children. For example, it is no more difficult to say, "The *sum* of six plus two *equals* eight," than it is to say, "The *answer* to six plus two *is* eight." When a child says, "I am *more smaller* than you," he or she will not be insulted if you kindly respond, "Yes, you are *smaller* than I am, and I am *bigger* than you."

Although this book is about communicating and expressing mathematics in many ways, the following two lessons give students a chance to practice a bit of math vocabulary. In the lesson accompanying *The Best Bug Parade* by Stuart Murphy, students practice using adjectives in three degrees of comparison, such as *tall, taller, tallest*. And students will enjoy creating a parade of creatures to compare, order, and label.

In the lesson corresponding to *Tops and Bottoms* by Janet Stevens, children use fraction vocabulary. Just as Stevens's vegetables have tops and bottoms, so do fractions have *numerators* and *denominators*. Students will also learn that fractions are symbols that represent *parts* and *wholes*.

So, speak the language of mathematicians with your students, and they will speak it back to you.

Sincerely,

Caroline

LESSON 1

Compare Sizes and Organize a Parade of Animals

Murphy, Stuart. *The Best Bug Parade.* New York: Harper-Collins, 1999.

This easy-to-read book is "good, better, best!" Follow this parade of bugs as they compare sizes with one another. Your students will enjoy the colorful illustrations and will become familiar with words we often use for size comparisons. Although the bugs in the book, just like your students, come in big, small, short, and tall sizes, altogether they make the "best bug parade" of all!

Time Frame

50 minutes

Materials

Use Stuart Murphy's *Just Enough Carrots* to teach a lesson using adjectives to compare amounts, or Bruce McMillan's *Super Super Superwords* to compare all kinds of things.

For the teacher:

Chalk and chalkboard, or overhead projector, or chart paper and marker

Several sheets of construction paper cut in half, in various colors

For each student:

One large piece of white construction paper

Pencil

Scissors

Glue

Story and Mini-Lesson

1. Slowly flip through the pages of the book so that children get a chance to **p**review it.

2. Ask students what they noticed about the book. Invite students to **p**redict what this book will be about.

3. **R**ead the story and allow students to describe what they see.

4. Discuss the comparison vocabulary: *big, bigger, biggest*; *small, smaller, smallest*; *long, longer, longest*; *good, better, best*. Ask students to give examples of ways they use these words, such as, "My dog is smaller than yours."

5. Ask students to arrange themselves in groups of three.

6. Tell students that each group must agree on a body part to compare, such as arms, legs, noses, or feet. Students should determine how to compare themselves and how to describe that comparison. Ask a volunteer group to act out the following comparison as a model: The group decides they will compare arms to see whose is the longest. Once they have compared arms, the group arranges themselves in order. One child holds out her arm and says, "Long"; the next child holds up his arm and says, "Longer"; and the last child holds up her arm and says, "Longest."

7. Invite all groups to participate. Allow approximately five or ten minutes for this activity. Encourage students to share comparative vocabulary with one another.

Group Lesson

1. Invite students to brainstorm size comparison words such as *long, longer, longest*; *thin, thinner, thinnest*; and *tall, taller, tallest*. Record students' suggestions on the chalkboard or on chart paper.

2. When you and your students are satisfied with your list of size comparison words, tell students they will refer to these during the upcoming project.

3. Now they will create their own parades of animals. Following are instructions for the project:

✓ First, choose one animal and three size comparison words from the list generated in item 1.

✓ Next, draw and decorate three pictures of the animal on colored construction paper.

✓ Then cut out and arrange the pictures in order by size from left to right on white construction paper.

✓ After that, glue the cut-out pictures on the white construction paper.

✓ Finally, write the appropriate size comparison word beneath each cut-out picture.

4. For example, one student's project might look like the following: Ramon chose an alligator for his animal and the size comparison words *long, longer, longest* from the list of words in Group Lesson item 1. He drew three different-sized alligators on green construction paper and decorated them with scraps of colored paper from other kids' projects. Then he cut out the alligators and arranged them in order from long to longest on his sheet of large white construction paper. He glued one long alligator on the left side of the paper, a longer alligator in the middle, and the longest alligator on the right side of the paper. Finally, Ramon wrote *long* under the first alligator, *longer* under the second alligator, and *longest* under the third and last alligator.

Have helpers pass out one sheet of white construction paper to each student, then put a tray of colored paper and scraps near each team or group of desks.

5. Distribute materials for students to begin their projects.

Discovery

Set up a center with several buckets filled with various-sized plastic figurines, rocks, or blocks. Include sets of three bowls, labeled in sequence, "big," "bigger," "biggest." At this station, students sort objects into a set of three labeled bowls. For example, one student might sort a group of three rocks. She would then arrange them in the bowls in order from big, to bigger, and finally to biggest.

For more discovery and practice activities, take a look at Stuart Murphy's list of suggestions on pages 32 and 33.

Reflection

When students have finished their projects, ask them to share and describe their work. Display the projects on a bulletin board or bind them together to make a book.

Assessment

Use **Figure 1.1.4. Anecdotal Record** (see Chapter 1) to make notes regarding students' understanding of comparative sizes and comparative vocabulary. Use **Figure 1.1.3. Sample—Anecdotal Record** (see Chapter 1) as a model for writing anecdotal notes.

Special Needs Adaptations

Auditory disability: An interpreter should sign the story and lesson. Post the following abbreviated project directions so these students can refer to them easily:

1. Choose an animal.

2. Select comparative vocabulary.

3. Draw, decorate, cut, arrange, and paste three of the same animal on your paper.

4. Label each animal with the appropriate comparative vocabulary word.

Motor disability: These students may need assistance from a student buddy or aide with cutting and pasting.

Visual disability: Invite these students to create a parade with play dough figures, plastic figurines, or blocks. Instruct students to arrange their parade of objects in order from least to greatest, or from largest to smallest.

English Language Learners: Have these students teach the class the comparative vocabulary in their native languages. Post these words on the chalkboard or bulletin board.

Extensions

- Laminate and bind students' work into a book modeled after *The Best Bug Parade*.

- Integrate this lesson with a unit on insects. Use the comparative vocabulary to compare sizes of several different species of insects.

- Read aloud one of the many versions of *Goldilocks and the Three Bears*, then have students retell or act out the story. Encourage students to use comparative vocabulary words such as *big, medium,* and *small*.

- Take students on a nature walk to locate objects that represent "same, fewer, and more," or "big, bigger, or biggest."

- For other words that describe size, see **Figure 2.3.2. Sample—Words That Describe Size** (see Chapter 2, Lesson 3), which is related to Stephanie Calmenson's *The Teeny Tiny Teacher*.

- Have students make up their own stories about an animal or object using comparative vocabulary.

- Hunt for items that are " bigger than" or "smaller than" a demonstration object held in one's hand, such as a piece of chalk, a globe, a pen, or a piece of paper. Students can choose partners and take turns comparing and hunting for objects.

- Have each student make one set of cards with comparative vocabulary words from *The Best Bug Parade, Super Super Superwords,* and *Just Enough Carrots.* Then label another set of cards with number symbols and words from one to twenty. Provide buckets or containers with a variety of math manipulatives. Have students choose one set of three comparative words and three number cards to match with manipulatives. These they will arrange in comparative order.

- Run Tom Snyder's *The Graph Club* software to collect, organize, and describe data. Use this software to construct quantitative comparisons with bar, picture, circle, table, and line graphs.

Bibliography

Brett, Jan. *Goldilocks and the Three Bears.* New York: G. P. Putnam's Sons, 1996.

Galdone, Paul. *The Three Bears.* NewYork: Clarion, Houghton Mifflin, 1985.

Murphy, Stuart. *Just Enough Carrots.* New York: HarperCollins Juvenile Books, 1997.

McMillan, Bruce. *Super Super Superwords.* New York: Lothrop, Lee & Shepard, 1989.

Nathan, Cheryl, and Lisa McCourt. *The Long and Short of It.* New York: Bridgewater Books, 1998.

Walton, Rick. *Pig Pigger Piggest.* New York: Scholastic, 1997.

Software

Tom Snyder Productions. 1998. *The Graph Club.* Macintosh and Windows, www.tomsnyder.com. (Accessed February 2001).

Related Standards 2000

Standard 1: Number and Operations

Standard 4: Measurement

Standard 6: Problem Solving

Standard 7: Reasoning and Proof

Standard 9: Connections

Standard 10: Representation

Related Standards 1989

Standard 1: Mathematics as Problem Solving

Standard 2: Mathematics as Communication

Standard 3: Mathematics as Reasoning

Standard 4: Patterns and Relationships

Standard 10: Measurement

LESSON 2

Match Fractions with Fraction Symbols

Stevens, Janet. *Tops and Bottoms.* San Diego: Harcourt Brace, 1995.

Caldecott Award winner Janet Stevens entertains readers in this traditional fable about a trickster hare who outwits a lazy but likeable bear. Hare tricks Bear into a business deal that is profitable for Hare but not for Bear. You may use the following lesson to help students learn and remember fraction vocabulary. *Tops and Bottoms* will help students remember that fractions, like vegetables, have tops (numerators) and bottoms (denominators).

You may read *Tops and Bottoms* and use this lesson in conjunction with Chapter 1, Lesson 6, to discuss and determine what is a *fair share.* You may also use this lesson to complement Chapter 1, Lesson 7, Identify and Build Fraction Models, and Chapter 7, Lesson 3, Compare Fractions, in which students learn how to represent and build fractions.

Time Frame

50 minutes

Materials

For the teacher:

Chart paper or chalkboard

Poster sample of **Figure 8.2.1. *Numerators and Denominators***

One copy of **Figure 8.2.2. *Vegetable Fractions*** (cut apart) to use as a demonstration sample

Copy of **Figure 8.2.3. *Vegetable Wholes***

For each student:

Figure 8.2.2. *Vegetable Fractions*

Figure 8.2.3. *Vegetable Wholes*

Figure 8.2.4. *Numerator and Denominator Labels*

Story and Mini-Lesson

1. **P**review *Tops and Bottoms*. Ask students what they notice about the way the book opens. (They will notice that this book opens from bottom to top, rather than from right to left, as do most books.) Discuss why the author used this format.

2. Ask students to **p**redict what the story will be about after you have previewed the book.

3. Before you read the book, prepare students to listen carefully by asking them to be on the lookout for objects with tops and bottoms.

3. **R**ead *Tops and Bottoms*.

4. Ask students to **r**ecall what the book was about. Discuss.

5. **R**eview your discussion about the book format (see item 1). Ask, "Does the format make you notice the book's top and bottom? What has tops and bottoms in the story?" Students will reply, "The vegetables."

Group Lesson

1. Ask students to help you brainstorm a list of things that have tops and bottoms. Use chart paper or the chalkboard to list students' ideas.

    Your list might look like this:

Carrots	Clothing
Radishes	Houses
Beets	Bookcases
Corn	Ice cream cones
Lettuce	Shoes
Broccoli	Refrigerator
Celery	

2. **C**onnect the book to the lesson by telling students that the mathematical symbols for fractions come in tops and bottoms too.

3. Write on the chalkboard the symbols $\frac{1}{2}$, $\frac{1}{3}$, and $\frac{1}{4}$.

4. Tell students that the name for the top part of a fraction is the *numerator* and the name for the bottom part is the *denominator*. The numerator represents a part of something, and the denominator represents the entire whole.

5. Show students the carrot cards in **Figure 8.2.2. *Vegetable Fractions.***

6. Ask, "If I have one whole carrot and I cut it into two equal parts, what do I have?" Students might answer, "You get two halves." Demonstrate this with a sample carrot card from **Figure 8.2.2.**

7. Give a half-carrot card to one student and keep the other half-carrot card.

8. Say, "I have ½ carrot and so do you. You have one part of a whole carrot and so do I. The number one in ½ is the 'top' number or the numerator. The number two is the 'bottom' number or the denominator. The denominator shows that when the carrot is cut in half, it needs two parts to make it be equal to one whole again. When we put the two carrot cards back together we get one whole carrot."

9. Demonstrate this procedure with the sample lettuce cards (⅓) and with the corn cards (¼) from **Figure 8.2.2.**

10. Tell students that during the Discovery activity, they will cut and then paste their vegetable fractions and labels onto **Figure 8.2.3. *Vegetable Wholes.***

11. Students must match the fraction vegetables with the corresponding fraction symbols. That is, if they have two parts of a carrot that make one whole carrot, they must match the "½" symbols with the carrot.

Discovery

1. Distribute materials.

2. Direct students to cut and divide the cards from **Figures 8.2.2.** and **8.2.4.** into separate parts. Allow time for students to sort and arrange the cards as they wish.

3. After five to seven minutes, instruct students to sort and arrange the cards to make complete wholes.

4. Students must then match the vegetable fractions to the corresponding vegetable wholes in **Figure 8.2.3.**

5. Have students paste the vegetable fractions onto **Figure 8.2.3.**

6. Finally, instruct students to paste the labels "numerator" and "denominator" next to the corresponding fraction symbols.

7. Post students' work on a bulletin board labeled, "Tops and Bottoms—Numerators and Denominators."

Assessment

Refer to **Figure 8.2.5. *Assessment, Vegetable Fractions.*** Review and construct fractions with Chapter 1, Lesson 7, and Chapter 7, Lesson 3.

Special Needs Adaptations

Auditory disability: An interpreter should sign the story and lesson. Check for understanding and clarify any misunderstandings. On the chalkboard, write abbreviated instructions from Discovery activity items 2 through 6, so these students will have a visual reminder of what they are supposed to do with their materials. Attach samples of **Figures 8.2.2.** and **8.2.4.** and a completed "Tops and Bottoms, Numerators and Denominators" sample poster, **Figure 8.2.1.,** beside the listed instructions.

Motor disability: Partners may assist students with motor impairments with the cutting and pasting activity.

Visual disability: Provide manipulatives for these students to sort and match by halves, such as pattern blocks and Cuisinaire rods. Provide cut felt shapes of the carrot tops and bottoms from **Figures 8.2.2.** through **8.2.4.**

English Language Learners: Partner these students with English-speaking buddies. List abbreviated instructions in native languages on the chalkboard, as described for students with auditory disabilities.

Extensions

- Re-read *Tops and Bottoms*. Have children listen for word patterns and invite them to chime in as you read patterns such as, "So Bear went back to sleep and Hare and his family went to work"

- Ask students to hunt for and describe picture patterns in the story. They might say, "Look, Hare planted rows of crops!" or "Do you see the rows of shutters on Bear's windows?"

- Discuss, draw, or write fraction problems inspired by Janet Stevens's story, such as "Bear wore $\frac{2}{2}$ shoes; Bear slept during $\frac{3}{4}$ planting seasons but worked during $\frac{1}{4}$ planting seasons; Hare's family worked during $\frac{4}{4}$ planting seasons."

- Make a list of jobs for Bear and Hare to do. Then have students make a chart or table that shows how Bear and Hare should divide the work equally.

- Students can cut out flannel *Tops and Bottoms* fraction symbols and vegetables using **Figures 8.2.2.** through **8.2.4.** They may sort, combine and match, take apart, and resort these at centers or activity tables.

Bibliography

Brunetto, Carolyn Ford. *Math Art*. New York: Scholastic, 1997.

King, Andrew. *Making Fractions*. Brookfield, CT: Millbrook Press, 1998.

Leedy, Loreen. *Fraction Action*. New York: Holiday House, 1994.

Murphy, Stuart J. *Give Me Half!* New York: HarperCollins Children's Books, 1996.

Silverstein, Shel. *A Giraffe and a Half*. New York: HarperCollins, 1964, 1993.

Related Standards 2000

Standard 1: Number and Operations

Standard 6: Problem Solving

Standard 7: Reasoning and Proof

Standard 9: Connections

Standard 10: Representation

Related Standards 1989

Standard 1: Mathematics as Problem Solving

Standard 2: Mathematics as Communication

Standard 3: Mathematics as Reasoning

Standard 4: Mathematical Connections

Standard 6: Number Sense and Numeration

Standard 12: Fractions and Decimals

Standard 13: Patterns and Relationships

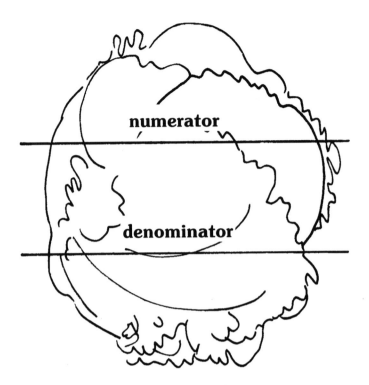

Figure 8.2.1. *Numerators and Denominators*

²⁄₂ = 1 whole carrot

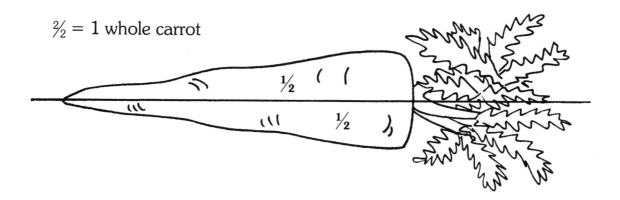

³⁄₃ = 1 whole lettuce

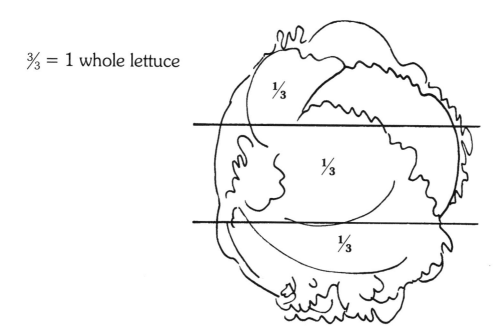

⁴⁄₄ = 1 whole corn

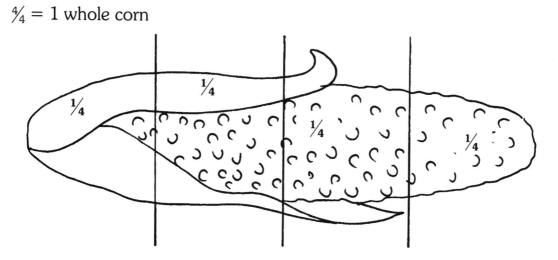

Figure 8.2.2. Vegetable Fractions

Figure 8.2.3. Vegetable Wholes

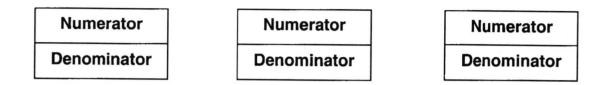

Figure 8.2.4. *Numerator and Denominator Labels*

Name: _____   **Date:** _____

The student matched the one-half carrot pieces to the ½ fraction symbols.   _____ (1)

The student matched the one-third slices of lettuce to the ⅓ fraction symbols.   _____ (1)

The student matched the one-fourth corn sections to the ¼ fraction symbols.   _____ (1)

The student matched and labeled numerators and denominators to the corresponding fraction symbols.   _____ (1)

Total score: _____ (4)

Beginning: 0–1: Developing: 2-3; Proficient: 4

Anecdotal notes:

Name: _____   **Date:** _____

The student matched the one-half carrot pieces to the ½ fraction symbols.   _____ (1)

The student matched the one-third slices of lettuce to the ⅓ fraction symbols.   _____ (1)

The student matched the one-fourth corn sections to the ¼ fraction symbols.   _____ (1)

The student matched and labeled numerators and denominators to the corresponding fraction symbols.   _____ (1)

Total score: _____ (4)

Beginning: 0–1: Developing: 2-3; Proficient: 4

Anecdotal notes:

Figure 8.2.5. Assessment, Vegetable Fractions

Chapter 9

Connections

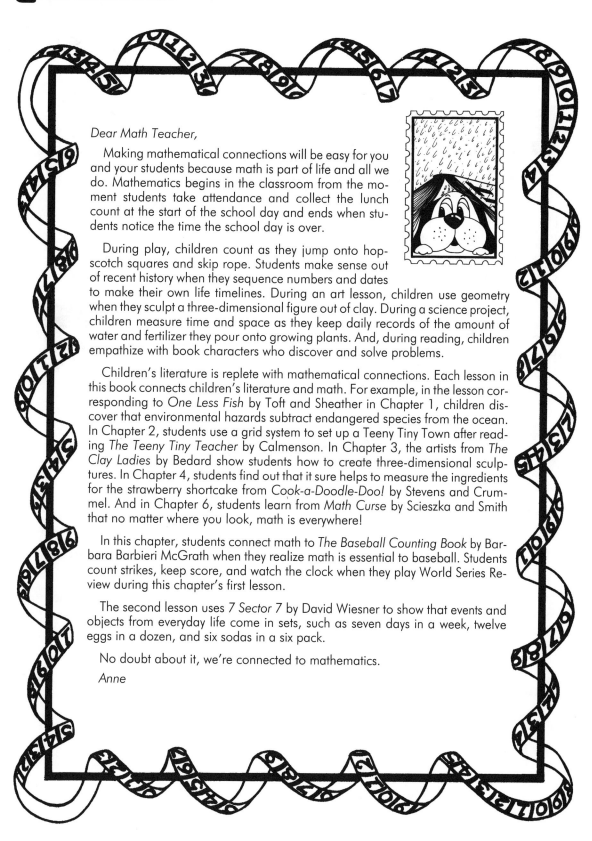

Dear Math Teacher,

Making mathematical connections will be easy for you and your students because math is part of life and all we do. Mathematics begins in the classroom from the moment students take attendance and collect the lunch count at the start of the school day and ends when students notice the time the school day is over.

During play, children count as they jump onto hopscotch squares and skip rope. Students make sense out of recent history when they sequence numbers and dates to make their own life timelines. During an art lesson, children use geometry when they sculpt a three-dimensional figure out of clay. During a science project, children measure time and space as they keep daily records of the amount of water and fertilizer they pour onto growing plants. And, during reading, children empathize with book characters who discover and solve problems.

Children's literature is replete with mathematical connections. Each lesson in this book connects children's literature and math. For example, in the lesson corresponding to *One Less Fish* by Toft and Sheather in Chapter 1, children discover that environmental hazards subtract endangered species from the ocean. In Chapter 2, students use a grid system to set up a Teeny Tiny Town after reading *The Teeny Tiny Teacher* by Calmenson. In Chapter 3, the artists from *The Clay Ladies* by Bedard show students how to create three-dimensional sculptures. In Chapter 4, students find out that it sure helps to measure the ingredients for the strawberry shortcake from *Cook-a-Doodle-Doo!* by Stevens and Crummel. And in Chapter 6, students learn from *Math Curse* by Scieszka and Smith that no matter where you look, math is everywhere!

In this chapter, students connect math to *The Baseball Counting Book* by Barbara Barbieri McGrath when they realize math is essential to baseball. Students count strikes, keep score, and watch the clock when they play World Series Review during this chapter's first lesson.

The second lesson uses *7 Sector 7* by David Wiesner to show that events and objects from everyday life come in sets, such as seven days in a week, twelve eggs in a dozen, and six sodas in a six pack.

No doubt about it, we're connected to mathematics.

Anne

LESSON 1

Discover Mathematics in Baseball

McGrath, Barbara Barbieri. *The Baseball Counting Book.* Watertown, MA: Charlesbridge, 1999.

Introduce your students to baseball! On each page, starting with zero and ending with twenty, children discover how each number corresponds to baseball. Children learn important concepts of the game, and that math is an integral part of baseball. Now, play ball!

Time Frame

Day One: 50 minutes

Day Two: 50 minutes

Day Three: 50 minutes

Prior to the lesson: Use one package of index cards. Write out math review questions on each card. Choose to review one of the following math concepts, such as addition facts, subtraction facts, story problems, telling time, or counting money.

Materials

➤ Day One

For the teacher:

Chart paper and pen to record baseball vocabulary

➤ Day Two

Prior to the lesson: Mark the chalkboard like a scoreboard for baseball; refer to **Figure 9.1.1. *World Series Review.***

For the teacher:

Chart paper with baseball vocabulary from Day One

Masking tape

Clock with a second hand, or a stopwatch

Math manipulatives such as flashcards, clocks, or play money

Four handkerchiefs

➤ Day Three

For each pair of students:

A pair of dice (students may share with a partner)

Figure 9.1.2. *Baseball Math*

Figure 9.1.3. *Baseball Math Record Sheet*

Pencil

Story and Mini-Lesson: Day One

1. **P**redict. Show students *The Baseball Counting Book* cover. Ask, "What do you think the book will be about?"

2. Develop background knowledge by asking students to share what they know about baseball.

3. **P**review the story by taking a "picture walk" through the book. Ask students, "What kind of a book do you think this is?" Many will chime in, "It's a counting book." Ask students to tell about other counting books they have read. Discuss. Tell students that after you read the story, you will ask them to share something they learned about baseball.

4. **R**ead *The Baseball Counting Book.*

5. **C**onnect the story to the math lesson by asking students to share what they learned about baseball. A student response may be, "I learned that you get three strikes and you're out!"

Group Lesson: Day One

1. **R**eview the following baseball terms with your students. As you discuss each term, write it and its definition on chart paper.

   Strikes: When the batter misses the baseball.

   Outs: Three strikes equal an out. Re-read page 5 (the page about the number 3). There are three outs for each team.

   Innings: There are nine innings during a game. During an inning each team gets three outs.

2. **R**eview team players and positions:

   Teams: Ask the students to recall from the book how many teams play during a baseball game (2). Re-read page 4 (the page about the number 2).

   Players: Ask, "How many players are on each team (9)? The jobs for each team player are as follows:

   ✓ *The batter* tries to hit the baseball when it is pitched. If the batter gets a hit, he or she runs to first base, second base, third, then home.

   ✓ *The pitcher* pitches or throws the ball to the batter.

   ✓ *The catcher* retrieves the ball if the batter misses and guards home plate.

   ✓ *The first, second, and third basemen* protect the bases. They also try to get the ball when it is hit.

   ✓ *The shortstop, right field, center, and left field outfielders* get ready to catch the ball when the batter gets a hit.

   ✓ *The umpire* stands at home plate and calls the strikes. Refer to page 5 (the page about the number 3).

   ✓ *Positions:* Ask, "What are the positions?" Refer to pages 13 and 14 (the pages about the number 9).

3. Save the chart paper list of baseball terms to use during Day Two and Day Three.

Reflection: Day One

Review baseball math. Instruct students to answer the following questions in their math journals: What position do you want to play? What math do you use when you play this position? For example, one student might write, "I want to be the pitcher for a baseball team. If I were the pitcher, I would count how many strikes I threw to the batter."

Story and Mini-Lesson: Day Two

1. Post the chart paper list of baseball terms from Day One. Together, discuss and **r**eview baseball terms.

2. Say to students, "Today we'll play a new type of baseball called, World Series Review." Ask, "Does anyone know what the World Series is?" Discuss. (At the end of baseball season, the top two North American teams play each other in The World Series to see which is the best team.)

3. Explain, "We'll play World Series Review to go over math concepts we learned this year."

4. Tell students, "Now, we'll set up teams."

5. Divide the class into two teams and direct students to name their teams. Write the team names on the scoreboard from **Figure 9.1.1. *World Series Review.*** Demonstrate how to write the score on the board.

6. Set up the classroom like a baseball diamond. Ask students, "How many bases are on a baseball field (4)?" "What shape is a baseball field?" (It's a rhombus that is called a baseball diamond.)

7. Next, set up the bases. Choose four students to decide where to place the bases. Use a handkerchief to represent each base.

8. Assign one team to play infield, the other team to play outfield. If you have more than nine students in the outfield, assign one team member to be the scorekeeper. The scorekeeper records points earned on the scoreboard. Any extra players can help in the outfield.

9. Announce that you will be the umpire.

10. Direct the other team to sit in a row against a wall behind home plate. This is the *dugout.* Show students the math manipulatives (see Materials). Instruct students to use the math manipulatives to practice math skills while they wait their turn. Students may use the flashcards to quiz each other on addition or subtraction facts, practice reading the clock, or practice counting money.

11. Following are the rules for the game:

    ✓ *The pitcher* pitches a math review question to the batter.

    ✓ *The batter* must answer a math review question in thirty seconds. (Show students the math review cards made prior to the lesson.)

    ✓ Each team member in the outfield gets a review card and a chance to score a point for the team.

    ✓ Remind students that the batter gets three strikes before he or she is out.

    ✓ Each team gets three outs before switching sides. When both teams get three outs, that is the end of the inning.

    ✓ *Stealing bases:* Often in a real baseball game, runners on base try to *steal* the next base by running there before the next pitch. This is a race between the pitcher and the runner. The pitcher can throw the ball to the baseman to get the player out. Tell students that in World Series Review stealing bases is different. In this game, the pitcher tries to catch a base runner off guard by pitching a question to him or her. If the runner gets the answer right, he or she advances to the next base; otherwise the runner is out. Students must be ready at any moment to answer a question.

Group Lesson: Day Two

1. Ask students if they have any questions before the game begins. Answer all questions, then shout, "Play ball!"

2. Play World Series Review.

3. You, as the umpire, will referee the game, decide which answers are correct, and call strikes and outs.

4. Play ball until time is up.

Story and Mini-Lesson: Day Three

1. Re-read *The Baseball Counting Book*. Encourage students to join in as you read.

2. Review baseball vocabulary terms from Day One.

3. Connect baseball to math by asking students to recall how they used math when they played World Series Review on Day Two.

Group Lesson: Day Three

1. Tell students they will play another type of baseball today called Baseball Math.

2. Direct students to partner up.

3. Distribute **Figure 9.1.2. *Baseball Math*** and **Figure 9.1.3. *Baseball Math Record Sheet*** to each pair of students. Together, read the directions on top of **Figure 9.1.2.**

4. Invite a student volunteer to help you demonstrate how to play the game. Pretend you are player one, and the student volunteer is player two. Demonstrate each step of the directions for the game. Play two rounds so that the class can see how each player plays the game.

5. Students will record the points on **Figure 9.1.3.** just as the scorekeeper recorded the score for the World Series Review on Day Two. When partners finish the ninth inning, they must add up the score to see who wins.

Discovery: Day Three

Play Baseball Math. If there is time, partners may play more than one game.

Reflection: Day Three

Together, review ways to use math and numbers in baseball. Record students' responses on the chalkboard. Direct students to write in their math journals three different ways people use math in baseball.

Assessment: Day Three

Check students' journals. Use the following checklist to assess student journals:

One written example   _____ (1)

Two written examples   _____ (2)

Three written examples   _____ (3)

Beginning: 0–1; Developing: 2; Proficient: 3

A student journal may look like this:

One way to use math in baseball is to count the strikes. (1)

Another way to use math in baseball is to keep track of the score. (1)

You also use math in baseball when you count the players on each team. (1)

Special Needs Adaptations

Auditory disability: An interpreter should sign the story and the lesson.

Motor disability: Provide ample space for these students to move about during World Series Review. A student helper or an aide may assist these students in moving around the bases. Partners may help roll the dice and record answers during Baseball Math.

Visual disability: Assign student buddies to assist these students in maneuvering around the baseball diamond. Assign student buddies to assist while playing Baseball Math by reading the dots on the dice. Provide a tape recorder for students to record answers to the math journal questions.

English Language Learners: Post all baseball vocabulary terms for students' reference. A bilingual buddy or ELL teacher may explain in students' native languages the rules and procedures for the World Series Review and Baseball Math.

Extensions

- Take a field trip to a baseball game. Print out scorecards for each student to keep score.
- Invite a baseball player to talk to your class.
- Pick another sport and discover the math in that sport.
- Invite students to write new question cards for the next time you play World Series Review.

Bibliography

Axelrod, Amy. *Pigs on the Ball: Fun with Math and Sports.* New York: Scholastic, 1998.

Fraser, Don. *Sports Math.* New York: Dale Seymour, 1987.

———. *Stats: Math Made Fun! (NHL Hockey).* New York: Somerville House, 1999.

Golenbock, Peter. *Teammates.* San Diego: Harcourt Brace, 1992.

Mochizuki, Ken. *Baseball Saved Us.* New York: Lee & Low, 1995.

Thayer, Ernest Lawrence. *Casey at the Bat.* Boston: Godine, 2000.

Related Standards 2000

Standard 1: Number and Operations

Standard 3: Geometry

Standard 6: Problem Solving

Standard 7: Reasoning and Proof

Standard 8: Communication

Standard 10: Representation

Related Standards 1989

Standard 1: Mathematics as Problem Solving

Standard 2: Mathematics as Communication

Standard 3: Mathematics as Reasoning

Standard 4: Mathematical Connections

Standard 6: Number Sense and Numeration

Standard 8: Whole Number Computation

Standard 13: Patterns and Relationships

LESSON 2

Recognize That Everyday Objects Come in Sets

Wiesner, David. *7 Sector 7.* New York: Clarion Books, 1999.

David Wiesner has done it again! Just as in *Tuesday* and *June 29, 1999,* David Wiesner focuses on the sky. In this book, a creative student discovers *7 Sector 7* during a foggy day field trip to the Empire State building. His imagination and drawing skills take him on an adventure beyond the confines of the field trip to a cloud factory. This story has no words, but says a lot with pictures. Your students will want ample time to study the mysterious and inviting illustrations, and so will you!

Time Frame

Day One: 50 minutes

Day Two: 50 minutes

Materials

Prior to the lesson: Use **Figure 9.2.1. *Set Collage*** to make a sample for the class to refer to later.

➢ Day One

For the teacher:

Seven pieces of white scrap paper

Seven pieces of white construction paper

Chart paper and markers, or chalkboard and chalk

For each student:

Pencils, crayons, markers, or colored pencils

One piece of construction paper

➢ Day Two

Lists of sets from Day One

Sample set collage from **Figure 9.2.1.** (made prior to the lesson)

Glue

Old magazines

Story and Mini-Lesson: Day One

1. **P**review the book. Show the cover of *7 Sector 7* and read the title. Ask, "What could this book be about?"

2. Invite students to make **p**redictions and to share them with each other.

3. Ask students to tell what their partners said. (*Note:* This promotes listening skills because students must not say their own predictions but rather what their friends predicted.)

4. Show students the page before the title page. Ask students, "Does this picture change your prediction?" Have students discuss this with a neighbor.

5. **R**ead *7 Sector 7*. Once again, allow ample time for the students to examine and enjoy each picture.

6. **R**eview the story. Instruct students to talk to one another about the story. Choose several students to present their interpretations of the story.

7. **C**onnect the story to students' experiences. Ask, "Have you seen pictures in the clouds?" Select a few students to share what they have seen.

8. Take a break and go outside for five minutes or so to look at the clouds. Discuss what you see. Return to the classroom.

9. Ask, "Why do you think the book is called, *7 Sector 7?*" Take several suggestions.

10. Ask students to notice the number seven as you **re**-read the story. Instruct students to share what they noticed.

11. Tell students that you noticed several things in the story that are in groups of seven, such as seven windows in the "Cloud Dispatch Center" and seven departure times at the train station.

12. Introduce the concept of sets. Encourage students to think about things that are arranged, sorted, or packaged in sets, such as two shoes, six pop cans, four tires on a car, ten fingers, or seven days of the week.

13. Write the number 1 on chart paper or on the chalkboard.

14. Invite students to name sets of one. For example: one nose, one mouth, or one carton of milk. Record students' suggestions on the chart paper or chalkboard.

15. Write the number 2 on the chart paper or chalkboard.

16. Encourage students to name sets of two. For example: two eyes, two ears, two shoes, or two lenses in a pair of glasses. Record these suggestions.

17. Continue recording suggestions of sets for the numbers 3, 4, 5, 6, and 7. Following are examples:

    Three: three tennis balls in a container, three blind mice, three little pigs

    Four: four-leaf clover, four corners on a square, four weeks in a month

    Five: five fingers on a hand, five toes on a foot, five days in a school week

Six: six-pack of soda, six points for a touchdown, six legs on an insect

Seven: seven days in a week, seven brides for seven brothers

Have students make a counting book based on the sets they just brainstormed. The book should have seven pages.

Group Lesson: Day One

1. Divide students into seven groups.

2. Assign numbers to each group so that one group is number one, and so on through seven.

3. Instruct each group to make a picture that represents sets that correspond to their number. They may refer to the chart paper or chalkboard list. For example, the group that has the number 5 may draw five-fingered hands, five-toed feet, five days of the school week, and five members of a basketball team.

4. Encourage groups to be creative and announce that each group will share completed illustrations with the class during the Reflection activity.

5. Distribute one sheet of scrap paper to each group. Tell students they must write their group number on the top center of the paper and sketch a plan for their set illustrations.

6. When groups complete the sketches, they may take one piece of white construction paper to complete their final illustrations. Once again, have groups record group numbers on the top center of their paper.

Reflection: Day One

Gather students together. Have groups share their illustrations. Challenge groups to find and name the sets they see. Collect all the illustrations afterwards and bind them in a book.

Story and Mini-Lesson: Day Two

1. **R**eview *7 Sector 7.*

2. **R**e-read the story. Have different students than on Day One share what they think the story is about.

3. **R**eview the chart paper list from Day One.

4. Ask students if there are any new sets they would like to add.

Discovery: Day Two

- Show students the set collage you made previously from **Figure 9.2.1.** Discuss the set collage.

- Call on students to describe what is in each box. Post your sample where students can refer to it easily. Tell students that today they will make their own set collages. Distribute one piece of construction paper to each student.

■ Direct students to label the first box with the words, "These things come in sets." Next, label the top of the following boxes "Sets of One," "Sets of Two," and so forth. Place the magazines in an easily accessible location. Instruct students to look through the magazines and find items that represent sets of each number. Students should then glue the items into the appropriate boxes.

Demonstrate how to fold paper into eight boxes. Fold the paper in half once. Then, with the paper still folded, fold it in half again. While the paper is still folded, fold it one more time. Unfold the paper; it should have eight boxes.

Some sets may be hard to find in magazines. Tell students that if this is the case, they may draw sets, rather than paste pictures, in the boxes.

Reflection: Day Two

Instruct students to write in their journals, "These things come in sets." Next have students write one set for each number, one through seven. A sample journal looks like this:

These things come in sets.

1 = nose

2 = eyes

3 = three blind mice

4 = four-leaf clover

5 = fingers

6 = pop cans

7 = days in a week

Assessment

Score students' journals as follows:

■ One example per set equals one point.

■ Beginning: 0–2; Developing: 3-5; Proficient: 6-7

Special Needs Adaptations

Auditory disability: An interpreter should sign the lesson. No other modifications are needed because this is a visual lesson.

Motor disability: Students may need assistance with drawing, coloring, cutting, and gluing. Assign a student buddy or aide to assist these students.

Visual disability: Use pattern blocks. Assign an aide or a student buddy to work with the student to examine and feel shapes and to count sides. Next, instruct the student to represent each shape on a geoboard. Assign a student buddy to describe the details of *7 Sector 7* into a tape recorder. Provide this tape in a listening center for the visually disabled student.

English Language Learners: As you list sets of items on the chart paper or chalkboard, draw pictures to represent those items. Ask English Language Learners to tell the class how to say the words in their primary languages.

Extensions

- Take a field trip to a local grocery store and look for items that come in sets.

- Have students work with pattern blocks and geoboards to make shapes with different numbers of sides.

- Study clouds. Have the students research how they are formed, what types there are, and how they move.

- Discuss multiplication and how it relates to sets.

- Create books inspired by *7 Sector 7*. Have students choose three numbers in order (for example, 10, 11, 12), then illustrate one number on each page (for example, 10 fish in a lake, 11 frogs on lily pads, and 12 birds in the sky).

- Use *The Graph Club* to graph sets from students' math journals.

Bibliography

Hoberman, Mary Ann. *The Seven Silly Eaters.* New York: Harcourt, 2000.

Kaye, Marilyn. *A Day with No Math.* New York: Harcourt Brace Jovanovich, 1992.

Shaw, Charles G. *It Looked Like Spilt Milk.* New York: Harper Trophy, 1998.

Wiesner, David. *June 29, 1999.* New York: Clarion Books, 1995.

———. *Tuesday.* New York: Clarion Books, 1997.

Software

Tom Snyder Productions. 1998. *The Graph Club.* Macintosh and Windows, www.tomsnyder.com. (Accessed February 2001).

Related Standards 2000

Standard 1: Numbers and Operations

Standard 6: Problem Solving

Standard 7: Reasoning and Proof

Standard 8: Communication

Standard 10: Representation

Related Standards 1989

Standard 1: Mathematics as Problem Solving

Standard 2: Mathematics as Communication

Standard 3: Mathematics as Reasoning

Standard 4: Mathematical Connections

Standard 6: Number Sense and Numeration

Standard 13: Patterns and Relationships

Inning	1	2	3	4	5	6	7	8	9	Total Score
Team 1 ___										
Team 2 ___										

Figure 9.1.1. *World Series Review*

Directions:

1. Choose a partner.

2. Decide who will go first.

3. Players record their names on the record sheet under Player 1 and Player 2.

4. Player 1 rolls the dice and adds up the total number shown on the dice.

5. Player 1 then refers to the numbers below to determine his or her score.

6. Player 1 then records the score on the scorecard under Inning 1.

7. Player 1 continues to play until he or she gets three outs.

8. Now it is Player 2's turn, and he or she will do the same.

9. Continue to record scores until the ninth inning.

10. Total up all the scores to see who is the winner!

Numbers shown on dice:

2 = Solo home run, one point

3 = Ball hit to pitcher, one out

4 = Ground ball to second and double play, two outs

5 = Pop out, one out

6 = Homer over the left wall, two points

7 = Strike out, one out

8 = Foul pop out, one out

9 = Double off the wall, one point

10 = Outfielder drops a pop hit, one point

11 = Line drive to a diving shortstop, one out

12 = Grand slam home run, four points

Figure 9.1.2. *Baseball Math*

Inning	1	2	3	4	5	6	7	8	9	Total Score
Player 1 _____										
Player 2 _____										

Figure 9.1.3. Baseball Math Record Sheet

These things come in sets.	Sets of One	Sets of Two	Sets of Three
Sets of Four	Sets of Five	Sets of Six	Sets of Seven

Figure 9.2.1. Set Collage

Chapter 10

Representation

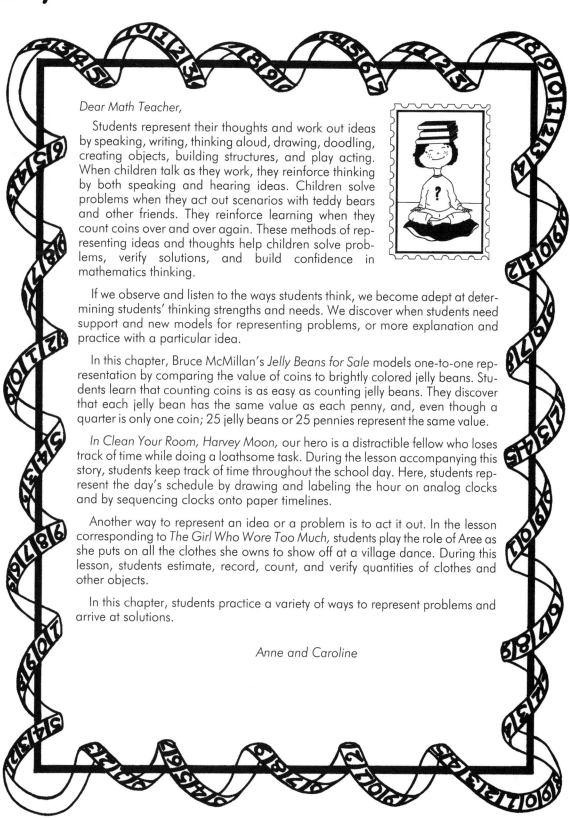

Dear Math Teacher,

Students represent their thoughts and work out ideas by speaking, writing, thinking aloud, drawing, doodling, creating objects, building structures, and play acting. When children talk as they work, they reinforce thinking by both speaking and hearing ideas. Children solve problems when they act out scenarios with teddy bears and other friends. They reinforce learning when they count coins over and over again. These methods of representing ideas and thoughts help children solve problems, verify solutions, and build confidence in mathematics thinking.

If we observe and listen to the ways students think, we become adept at determining students' thinking strengths and needs. We discover when students need support and new models for representing problems, or more explanation and practice with a particular idea.

In this chapter, Bruce McMillan's *Jelly Beans for Sale* models one-to-one representation by comparing the value of coins to brightly colored jelly beans. Students learn that counting coins is as easy as counting jelly beans. They discover that each jelly bean has the same value as each penny, and, even though a quarter is only one coin; 25 jelly beans or 25 pennies represent the same value.

In *Clean Your Room, Harvey Moon*, our hero is a distractible fellow who loses track of time while doing a loathsome task. During the lesson accompanying this story, students keep track of time throughout the school day. Here, students represent the day's schedule by drawing and labeling the hour on analog clocks and by sequencing clocks onto paper timelines.

Another way to represent an idea or a problem is to act it out. In the lesson corresponding to *The Girl Who Wore Too Much*, students play the role of Aree as she puts on all the clothes she owns to show off at a village dance. During this lesson, students estimate, record, count, and verify quantities of clothes and other objects.

In this chapter, students practice a variety of ways to represent problems and arrive at solutions.

Anne and Caroline

LESSON 1

Use Jelly Beans to Represent the Value of Coins

McMillan, Bruce. *Jelly Beans for Sale.* New York: Scholastic, 1996.

This mouth-watering book introduces the value of coins with colorful photographs of children counting coins and jelly beans. *Jelly Beans for Sale* introduces pennies, nickels, dimes, and quarters and the value of each; that is, each cent is worth one jelly bean! Author Bruce McMillan represents several different amounts of money with many combinations of coins. Your students will enjoy counting money along with the children photographed in this book. Do you have a penny? Then you can purchase one jelly bean. Delicious!

Time Frame

Day One: 50 minutes

Day Two: 50 minutes

Materials

Prior to the lesson: Send **Figure 10.1.1. *Garage Sale*** to parents and community volunteers to invite them to the garage sale. They won't want to miss it! Send a copy of this lesson to a partner teacher and his or her students and ask them to join you for this activity.

Make an index card for each student in your class. Use **Figure 10.1.2. *Combinations of 25 Cents for Various Class Sizes*** to determine which coins you'll need to correspond with the number of students in your class. Draw, stamp, or attach the appropriate coins on index cards. For example, if you have twenty students you will make five penny cards, nine nickel cards, five dime cards, and one quarter card. This will make five combinations of 25 cents.

For the teacher:

Figure 10.1.1. *Garage Sale*

Figure 10.1.2. *Combinations of 25 Cents for Various Class Sizes*

➤ **Day One**

For the teacher:

One bag of jelly beans (approximately five jelly beans per student)

Chalkboard, chart paper, or overhead projector

For each student:

Five to seven items of "junk" from home that students don't want anymore (see **Figure 10.1.1.**)

Five to seven small sticky notes

Crayons and construction paper

Figure 10.1.3. *Assessment, Ways to Represent 25 Cents*

Figure 10.1.4. *Scoring Rubric, Ways to Represent 25 Cents*

➤ **Day Two**

For the teacher:

Minute-timer with a bell

Figure 10.1.5. *Assessment, Counting and Adding Coins*

For each student:

A plastic bag containing the following plastic or real coins: twenty pennies, eight nickels, four dimes, and one quarter

Story and Mini-Lesson: Day One

1. **P**review *Jelly Beans for Sale.* Ask, "How many colors of jelly beans do you see on the cover?"

2. Take a "picture walk" through the book by flipping through the pages, but don't read the story yet. Ask students to comment about what they notice and to make **p**redictions about the story as you flip through the pages.

3. **R**ead *Jelly Beans for Sale.*

4. **R**eview the story. Ask students to compare their **p**redictions with what they learned from listening to the story. Were the predictions correct? Discuss.

5. **C**onnect the story to the math lesson by telling students that today they will earn jelly beans. When they earn jelly beans, they'll get to eat them.

6. Give each student a coin card. (See materials list above.) Challenge students to find others with value cards that combine to make 25 cents. Following is an example: *Patrice has a 10 cent card; she finds Sam who has another 10 cent card. Together, they look for someone who has a 5 cent card, or five other students who each have a 1 cent card.*

7. When students think they have 25 cents, they must check the total value with each other.

8. Mix up the cards and repeat step 6 for five to ten minutes. During the last round of play, instruct students to keep their money cards.

9. Students may use their cards to buy jelly beans. Each student may purchase five jelly beans.

10. Gather once again, and ask students to share the many ways they know how to represent 25 cents. Write these coin combinations on the chalkboard, chart paper, or an overhead.

11. Pass out **Figure 10.1.3. *Assessment, Ways to Represent 25 Cents.*** Instruct students to draw or write four different ways to represent 25 cents on their papers.

12. Collect the remaining coin cards and place them in a center where students can use them again.

Group Lesson: Day One

1. Prepare for tomorrow's Garage Sale.

2. Direct students to put a sticky note price tag on each junk item with any of the following prices: 1 cent, 5 cents, 10 cents, or 25 cents. Encourage peers to discuss "fair" prices with each other.

Discovery: Day One

When students finish pricing "junk," invite them to design advertisements to sell their "junk." Distribute crayons and construction paper for this project. Students who finish early may team up with others to combine coin cards from Mini-Lesson item 12 above.

Group Lesson: Day Two, Garage Sale

1. Take ten or fifteen minutes to set up "junk" at tables or desks, then get ready to sell.

2. Garage Sale instructions:

   ✓ Assign a "banker" to distribute the plastic bags filled with money.

   ✓ Divide the class into four groups.

   ✓ Three groups sell while one group buys.

   ✓ Rotate group assignments every five to seven minutes so that everyone gets a chance to buy and sell.

   ✓ Use a minute timer to notify students when to rotate.

   ✓ Have fun buying and selling junk!

Discovery: Day Two, Garage Sale

During slow selling or buying times, instruct students to:

Separate and sort coins;

Put piles of coins in order from greatest to least in value; and

Count the money, beginning with the pile of greatest value.

If you have invited another class to join in the Garage Sale, instruct older students to assist younger ones with sorting and counting money.

Reflection: Day Two, Garage Sale

When the Garage Sale is over, invite students to return to the group meeting place. Ask, "Did you sell all your junk? What did you notice or learn when you counted coins to pay for an item? Did you make change when you sold items? Did you figure out how to make change? What strategies did you use? What junk sold well, what did not? If we do this again, what should we do differently?"

Instruct students to choose one of these questions to write about in their journals.

Assessment

■ Provide many opportunities for students to sort and count coins. Record students' progress on **Figure 10.1.5. *Assessment, Counting and Adding Coins.***

■ Review student responses using **Figure 10.1.3. *Assessment, Ways to Represent 25 Cents.***

■ Use **Figure 10.1.4. *Scoring Rubric, Ways to Represent 25 Cents*** to evaluate students' understanding of the lesson.

Special Needs Adaptations

Auditory disability: An interpreter should sign the story, lesson, and the Garage Sale instructions and activities.

Motor disability: Partner these students with buddies. Remove obstructions from the room so these students have access to buying and selling stations during the Garage Sale. Buddies may help these students write and record answers during the assessment. You may also provide tape players to record these students' answers.

Visual disability: Partner these students with buddies and make similar adjustments as for students with motor disabilities. Provide time for these students to explore the Garage Sale layout before the sale begins. Allow these students to answer assessment questions by arranging and counting out real coins or by describing arrangements of coins into a tape player.

English Language Learners: Partner these students with buddies. Invite these students to teach others the numbers from one to twenty-five in their primary languages.

Extensions

- Ask a local bank to donate empty money rolls for pennies, nickels, dimes, and quarters.
- Set up a center for students to sort and count coins.
- Have students write story problems, such as, "Enrique had thirty jelly beans; he ate five. How many jelly beans does he have now?"
- Have students write or draw addition or subtraction problems to make 25, such as $5 + 5 + 5 + 5 + 5 = 25$, or $45 - 20 = 25$.
- Have students create piggy banks, purses, or wallets. They should save and count money to put into these money holders.
- Encourage students to design and make money, such as a 35 cent coin to use in a pay phone.
- Display money from around the world.
- Invite students to display coins from other countries. Make a chart to describe similarities and differences between United States coins and coins from other countries.
- As a class, visit a mint, local bank, or store. Ask employees to demonstrate how they use money in their work.

Bibliography

Axelrod, Amy. *Pigs Will Be Pigs: Fun with Math and Money.* New York: Simon & Schuster, 1997.

Caple, Kathy. *The Purse.* Portland, OR: Sandpiper, 1992.

Godfrey, Neale. *Neale S. Godfrey's Ultimate Kids' Money Book.* New York: Simon & Schuster, 1998.

Schwartz, David M. *If You Made a Million.* New York: Lothrop, Lee & Shepard, 1999.

Viorst, Judith. *Alexander Who Used to Be Rich Last Sunday.* New York: Aladdin, 1999.

Wells, Rosemary. *Bunny Money.* New York: Dial Books for Young Readers, 1997.

Williams, Vera. *A Chair for My Mother.* New York: Greenwillow, 1999.

Related Standards 2000

Standard 1: Number and Operations

Standard 4: Measurement

Standard 6: Problem Solving

Standard 7: Reasoning and Proof

Standard 8: Communication

Standard 9: Connections

Related Standards 1989

Standard 1: Mathematics as Problem Solving

Standard 2: Mathematics as Communication

Standard 3: Mathematics as Reasoning

Standard 4: Mathematics as Connections

Standard 5: Estimation

Standard 6: Number Sense and Numeration

Standard 8: Whole Number Computation

Standard 12: Fractions and Decimals

LESSON 2

Draw Clocks and Create Timelines

Cummings, Pat. *Clean Your Room, Harvey Moon.* Boston: Houghton Mifflin, 1996.

Harvey Moon wants to watch cartoons, but not until he cleans his room! Time passes quickly as forgotten toys, rotten food, and smelly clothes distract Harvey. Will he manage to clean this bedroom disaster in time for his favorite TV show? Read this book to your students to find out.

Time Frame

➤ Day One

Story and mini-lesson, 30 minutes

Every hour, 10 minutes of each hour from the first to the last hour of the day

Reflection, 20 minutes at the end of the day

➤ Day Two

50 minutes

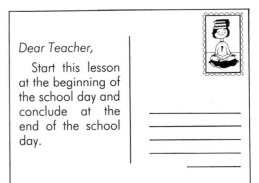

Dear Teacher,

Start this lesson at the beginning of the school day and conclude at the end of the school day.

Materials

➤ Day One

For the teacher:

One manual clock, such as a Judy Clock

One classroom analog clock

Chart paper entitled *Predictions: Our School Day Schedule*

Figure 1.1.4. Anecdotal Record (see Chapter 1)

For each student:

Two pieces of standard construction paper (18 by 12 inches) to make one 36-by-6-inch timeline

Five or six clock cards from **Figure 10.2.1. Clock Cards**

Prior to the lesson, ask a parent or community volunteer to cut and prepare the paper for the timelines. First, cut one piece of 18-by-12-inch construction paper in half, lengthwise, then tape together the two construction paper strips to make one 36-by-6-inch paper timeline. Make one timeline for each student.

> ## Day Two

For the teacher:

Prior to the lesson: Set up centers with one manual analog clock for each pair of students. Post a list of analog and digital times at each. Pairs of students manipulate the hands of manual clocks to match the posted times. Students also quiz each other about telling time. Prepare for student interviews. Refer to **Figure 10.2.2.** *Time Representation Interview*. Prepare a quiet place for you and one student at a time to meet. You'll need pencils, one manual clock, scratch paper, and one copy of **Figure 10.2.2.** for each student.

Figure 10.2.3. *Time Representation Interview (Teacher)*

Story and Mini-Lesson: Day One

1. **P**review *Clean Your Room, Harvey Moon.* Take a "picture walk" by turning through the pages slowly.

2. Ask students to **p**redict what will happen in the story.

3. **R**ead and enjoy the story.

4. **C**onnect the story to the math lesson by asking the following questions, "Do you like to clean your room? What does Harvey Moon think about cleaning his room? Explain how he feels. How long does it take you to clean your room? How long does it take Harvey to clean his?"

5. **R**e-read and **r**eview *Clean Your Room, Harvey Moon.* As you read, instruct a student volunteer to use the manual clock to track the amount of time it takes Harvey to clean his room.

6. Repeat step 5 for one or two more readings if you wish.

7. **C**onnect the story to the upcoming group lesson by asking students to **p**redict what time they think classroom activities occur. For example, ask, "What time are math time, lunchtime, and recess?"

8. Record these predictions on the chart paper entitled *Predictions: Our School Day Schedule.* Set this aside to use later.

Group Lesson: Day One

During this part of the lesson, have students make a school day timeline.

1. First, enlist students' interest by asking them to notice the time they do different activities throughout the day. You'll alert them to stop on the hour to record these times and activities.

2. Distribute one construction paper timeline to each student.

3. At 9:00 A.M., or at the first hour after you begin this portion of the lesson, pass one clock card to each student. Demonstrate how to draw hands on the clock card to match the time on the classroom analog clock. Ask a student volunteer to write the digital time on the chalkboard for others to copy and write on their own clock cards. Then ask a student volunteer to tell what the class does at 9:00 A.M. An answer might be, "We begin handwriting." Write this sentence on the chalkboard for students to copy onto their clock cards. Finally, instruct students to paste completed clock cards onto the left side of their construction paper timelines.

4. Continue to pass out cards, on the hour, for students to add to their school day timelines. Direct students to record both analog and digital times and to write a sentence about their class schedule on each new clock card. Then instruct students to paste the new card just to the right of the last card.

If you are unable to be in your classroom on the hour, adjust the lesson to fit your schedule.

Reflection: Day One

At the end of the day, invite students to share timelines with one another. Refer to the chart *Predictions: Our School Day Schedule* and compare these times with the actual times at which class activities occurred. Host a discussion, or invite students to answer the following questions in their math journals: Were our predictions accurate? Explain why or why not. Which times of day went by quickly? Which times of day went slowly?

Set aside students' timelines at the end of the lesson to use again during the next day's lesson.

Assessment: Day One

Refer to **Figure 1.1.4.** *Anecdotal Record* (see Chapter 1). Make notes throughout the day regarding students' understanding of the lesson. Evaluate students' timelines. Did students label and place clocks in sequential order? Did students' analog and digital times match? Did students write accurate activity labels to correspond with each clock card?

Group Lesson: Day Two

1. Review and re-read *Clean Your Room, Harvey Moon*, then ask students to retell the story to a nearby partner.

2. Announce to students that today they will demonstrate what they know about time. You will interview each student for a few minutes while the rest participate in the Discovery activity.

3. Return timelines to students; they will refer to them during the interviews.

Discovery: Day Two

■ Introduce the clock centers. First, model how to "think aloud" as you demonstrate how to turn the dials on a manual clock and recall which hand is the hour hand and which is the minute hand. Next, review how to tell time by matching the time on the manual clock to one of the posted analog or digital times. Then call on a student volunteer to use the manual clock to quiz you on telling time. Switch roles and repeat. Finally, invite students to partner up and go to centers to practice these time-telling skills.

■ While students work at centers, call on one student at a time to participate in the ***Time Representation Interview*** (see **Figure 10.2.2**). Remind students to bring their timelines when they join you for interviews.

■ Students who finish working at centers before you complete the interviews may do one of the following extension activities:

> ✓ Write or draw a schedule for an ideal day.
>
> ✓ Make a poster of a daily schedule. Include an analog clock, the digital time, and the corresponding activity on the poster.

Assessment

Plan three to five minutes for each interview. Invite students to use the tools (pencil, paper, manual clock, timeline) to work out answers to the questions. Record students' answers on **Figure 10.2.2.** ***Time Representation Interview.*** Refer to **Figure 10.2.3.** ***Time Representation Interview (Teacher)*** to view sample answers. Use the grading scale on the bottom of **Figure 10.2.2.**

Special Needs Adaptations

Auditory disability: An interpreter should sign the story and lesson. This lesson is user-friendly to students with auditory disabilities because it includes visual aides and manipulatives.

Motor disability: Modify this lesson for students who have difficulty writing. These students do not need to write or draw on each clock card; rather, provide pre-made analog cards and digital labels for these students to match and arrange in sequential order. These students may also use pre-cut magazine pictures to illustrate their timelines.

Visual disability: Have these students make a "talking clock." As other students work at centers, instruct a volunteer to work with visually disabled students. Provide a tape player for these students to record each hour of the school day and to announce the activity for each hour. Encourage these students to be creative and to improvise coo-coo clock or other interesting noises to represent each hour and activity.

English Language Learners: Partner these students with buddies. Post time-telling phrases in these students' primary languages for others to learn.

Extensions

- Have students make a paper plate clock. They should draw a clock face on a paper plate, write the numbers from 1 to 12 on the face, cut a minute and second hand from scratch paper, then insert brass brads to attach the hands to the clock.

- Create a class timeline of weekend or vacation activities.

- Play "clock concentration" by matching analog and digital clock cards.

- Have students write a story about what happened one day. Use Eric Carle's *The Grouchy Ladybug* as a story model.

Bibliography

Anastasio, Dina. *It's About Time.* New York: Grosset & Dunlap, 1993.

Carle, Eric. *The Grouchy Ladybug.* New York: HarperFestival, 1999.

Hutchins, Pat. *Clocks and More Clocks.* New York: Simon & Schuster, 1994.

Kaye, Marilyn. *A Day with No Math.* New York: Harcourt Brace Jovanovich, 1992.

Verdet, Andre. *All About Time.* New York: Cartwheel Books, 1995.

Related Standards 2000

Standard 1: Number and Operations

Standard 4: Measurement

Standard 5: Data Analysis and Probability

Standard 6: Problem Solving

Standard 7: Reasoning and Proof

Standard 8: Communication

Standard 9: Connections

Related Standards 1989

Standard 1: Mathematics as Problem Solving

Standard 2: Mathematics as Communication

Standard 3: Mathematics as Reasoning

Standard 4: Mathematical Connections

Standard 5: Estimation

Standard 6: Number Sense and Numeration

Standard 9: Geometry and Spatial Sense

LESSON 3

Estimate, Record, and Count Clothing and Other Objects

Read, Margaret MacDonald. ***The Girl Who Wore Too Much: A Folktale from Thailand.*** Little Rock, AR: August House, 1998.

> Aree loves jewelry and clothing. When she learns about a big dance in the next village, she can't decide what to wear. Finally, she comes up with a solution: She'll wear all her clothes! This folktale from Thailand teaches children that material possessions don't always bring joy, and keeping friends is more important than impressing them. In the lesson corresponding to this story, students re-enact Aree's role by putting on as many clothes as they can, but first each student must estimate how many clothes he or she can wear.

Time Frame

50 minutes

■ Prior to the lesson: One week before the lesson, send home **Figure 10.3.1. *Letter to Parents.***

■ On the morning of the lesson, set up four stations where students will dress up as Aree did, and set up four estimation centers where students will practice estimating skills.

■ To set up the four stations, distribute the clothing (see **Figure 10.3.1. *Letter to Parents***) into four bags, then place the bags in four different areas in the classroom. Count and record the number of items in each bag on sticky notes. Keep the sticky notes to refer to during the reflection activity.

■ To set up the four estimation centers, place the following materials at each center:

> One zipping storage bag containing an item to estimate. (For example, place a zipping storage bag of beans at the first center, buttons at the second center, blocks at the third, and cereal at the fourth. At each center, students estimate the number of items the zipping storage bag contains.)
>
> One set of sticky notes and several pencils for students to record estimates
>
> One coffee can or container in which students can deposit sticky note estimations
>
> One envelope to hold the answer for the number of items contained in the zipping storage bag

Decide the number of items to put in each zipping storage bag according to students' levels of understanding. For example, if your students are learning number sense for the numbers 1 to 20, do not put more than twenty items in each zipping storage bag, but if your class has a good grasp of these numbers, increase the amounts in the zipping storage bags. Also, vary the amount in each zipping storage bag, and record those amounts in the sealed envelopes. Place each envelope underneath the coffee can at each estimation center. You will open the envelopes and reveal the answers at the end of this lesson.

Materials

For the teacher:
(See materials listed above for setting up centers and stations.)

Chart paper or chalkboard

Stickers or prizes for "smart guesses"

Figure 10.3.2. *Assessment, Estimation (Teacher)*

For each student:

Clothing items from home (See **Figure 10.3.1.** *Letter to Parents*)

Figure 10.3.3. *Estimating Clothes*

Pencil

Math journal

Figure 10.3.4. *Assessment, Estimating Clothes*

Story and Mini-Lesson

1. **P**review the story by showing the cover and reading the title. Take a "picture walk" through the book by showing the pictures, but don't read the text.

2. Encourage students to **p**redict what they think the story will be about. Ask students to share predictions with each other.

3. **R**ead *The Girl Who Wore Too Much: A Folktale from Thailand.*

4. Invite students to discuss with neighbors how their predictions about the story held up.

5. **R**eview the story's message. Encourage children to give examples of times when they tried to *impress* a friend by showing off new shoes, a computer game, jewelry, or toys. Pose the question, "Do you think your friend liked you better because you had a new toy?"

6. Discuss why Aree decided to wear all her clothes. (She couldn't decide what to wear and she wanted to impress her friends with the clothes she owned.)

7. Introduce *estimation*. Explain that estimation is a way to make a smart guess. Often it is all right not to know the exact number. Parents often estimate how many minutes it takes to drive to work, how many people will come to a party, or how much money to budget for a vacation.

8. Practice estimating. Ask, "How many shirts do you think Aree wore in the story?" Write students' predictions on chart paper or the chalkboard.

9. Discuss a "smart guess" for the number of shirts Aree wore (5). Contrast this with an example of a "far off guess" (1,000,000).

10. Have students practice estimating other items such as desks in the room, pencils on a desk, and books on a bookshelf.

11. Now for the estimation challenge! Divide students into four groups. Instruct each group of students to go to one of the four stations containing the bags of clothing. Challenge students to estimate how many items of clothing are in the bag at their station. Instruct students to write their names and estimations on pieces of scrap paper. Collect the estimations and announce the closest estimators. Allow these estimators to explain how they determined their estimations. Give "smart guess" stickers to these students.

Group Lesson

Students will act out Aree's role in the story.

1. Direct students to return to their stations. Instruct students to pull clothes out of the bags and sort them into the following categories: coats, hats or caps, socks, and pants.

2. When student have sorted the clothes, distribute **Figure 10.3.3. *Estimating Clothes*** to students.

3. Gather all students at one of the four stations. Choose a student volunteer to help demonstrate how to do the activity.

   ✓ For example, Joe looks at the pile of hats and caps at his group's station and estimates he can wear seven hats without them falling off. He uses **Figure 10.3.3.** to record this estimate. First, he writes the word *hats* in the box under the column entitled "Type of Clothing." Then he writes the number 7 in the box under the column entitled "Estimated Amount."

   ✓ Next Joe pretends he is Aree. He tries to put on as many of the items as he can. Joe successfully gets five caps on is head. Oops, a hat fell off. Now he's got four. Joe writes the number *4* on **Figure 10.3.3. *Estimating Clothes*** in the first box under the column headed "Actual Amount."

   ✓ When Joe finishes with the pile of hats, he moves on to another pile of clothes at his group's station and begins the process again.

   Thank Joe for his help. It's nearly time for all students to begin the activity.

4. Discuss the following rules: 1) Students must put on all clothes without help from others and 2) at each station, students must be able to:

   Button or zip coats

   Balance hats on their heads without the hats falling off

   Put socks on first, then shoes

   Button or zip pants

5. Direct students to return with their groups to their assigned stations and begin the activity.

6. You may have groups rotate to other piles of clothing and continue the activity, as time permits.

   Do not allow students to stop at certain numbers just because that is what they guessed. If it looks like they can continue putting on clothes, they must.

Discovery

As students finish the above activity, direct them to work at estimation centers. Instruct students to first, observe the items in the zipping storage bag; second, estimate the number of items; third, record that amount and the estimator's name on the sticky note; fourth, place the sticky note in the coffee can; and finally, move to the next estimation center. When students complete the estimation center activities, they return to their groups.

Reflection

Lead a class discussion by asking the following questions: "What items did you estimate at the centers? Was it easy or hard to estimate these items? Why or why not?"

Distribute **Figure 10.3.4. *Assessment, Estimating Clothes*** to each student. Instruct students to work independently on this assessment. While students work, review the estimations from the centers, and check for "smart guesses." When students complete

Figure 10.3.4. open the envelopes from the estimation centers and tell students the correct numbers of items in the zipping storage bags. Award "smart guess" stickers to students who had the closest estimations.

Assessment

Collect **Figure 10.3.3.** *Estimating Clothes* from students. Read and review these papers. Note students whose estimations were unreasonable. Plan to support these students and to prepare activities so these students will have more opportunities to practice estimating. Collect **Figure 10.3.4.** *Assessment, Estimating Clothes* from students. Use **Figure 10.3.2.** *Assessment, Estimation (Teacher)* to view sample answers.

Special Needs Adaptations

Auditory disability: An interpreter should sign the lesson.

Motor disability: An adult or student volunteer will assist students in putting on clothing and recording estimations. Provide a tape recorder for students to use to dictate answers to the assessment.

Visual disability: Provide these students with time to locate and examine each pile of clothing prior to the activity. A peer partner can assist these students during the lesson and activities. These students may record their estimations into a tape recorder. Provide a tape recorder for assessment, as done for students with motor disabilities. Blindfold all students in the class prior to teaching this so other students can better understand students with visual disabilities.

English Language Learners: Assign a bilingual partner to help these students understand the instructions. English Language Learners can teach the class the names for the clothing used in the activity above.

Extensions

- Assign an "Estimation Student of the Day or Week." Each day, this student brings in an item to estimate such as a bag of cereal, matchbox cars, cards, buttons, beans, or toys.

- Have the students walk around the school and notice things to estimate such as chairs in a room, people in a group, trees in a park, forks in a basket, or books on a shelf.

- Assign homework activities such as estimating how many windows or chairs there are in a home or the number of times a family uses estimation.

- Make an estimation book. Have students write about and illustrate a time they used estimation.

- Create an estimation box. Have students write on a piece of paper suggestions for things to estimate.

- As a class, go to the Lost and Found and estimate the number of clothes there. Count the clothes and then sort them as a good deed for the school custodian.

Bibliography

Falda, Dominique. *The Treasure Chest.* New York: North South Books, 1999.

Hanford, Martin. *Where's Waldo?* New York: Candlewick Press, 1997.

Murphy, Stuart. *Just Enough Carrots.* New York: HarperCollins Juvenile Books, 1997.

Rogers, Paul. *What Can You See?* New York: Doubleday, 1998.

Ryder, Joanne. *Earthdance.* New York: Henry Holt, 1996.

Slobodkina, Esphyr. *Caps for Sale.* New York: W. R. Scott, 1999.

Related Standards 2000

Standard   1: Number and Operations

Standard   5: Data Analysis and Probability

Standard   6: Problem Solving

Standard   7: Reasoning and Proof

Standard   8: Communication

Standard   9: Connections

Related Standards 1989

Standard   1: Mathematics as Problem Solving

Standard   2: Mathematics as Communication

Standard   3: Mathematics as Reasoning

Standard   4: Mathematical Connections

Standard 11: Statistics and Probability

Dear Parents,

To better understand the concept of money, our class will host a mock garage sale. Please help your child choose five to seven items of "junk" (small things your child doesn't want anymore). Make sure your child understands that this "junk" may not be returned, and he or she must be willing to part with it.

Send the items to school with your child by _____.

If junk is hard to come by, you and your child can make cookies, punch, or anything else he or she wants to sell. You are welcome to come and help!

When:_____

What time:_____

Where: _____

Sincerely,

Figure 10.1.1. *Garage Sale*

Number of Students in Class	Pennies	Nickels	Dimes	Quarters
15	5	6	4	0
16	5	6	4	1
17	5	6	4	2
18	5	7	6	0
19	5	7	6	1
20	5	9	5	1
21	5	9	5	2
22	5	10	7	0
23	5	10	7	0
24	5	12	6	1
25	5	12	6	2
26	5	13	8	0
27	10	9	7	1
28	10	9	7	2
29	10	10	9	0
30	10	10	9	1

Figure 10.1.2. Combinations of 25 Cents for Various Class Sizes

Name: _____ **Date:** _____

Write or draw four different ways to represent 25 cents. Be ready to talk about your answers.

Figure 10.1.3. *Assessment, Ways to Represent 25 Cents*

Name: _____   **Date:** _____

Beginning 0–1	Developing 2–3	Proficient 4
Student represents 25 cents in one way or less.	Student represents 25 cents in two to three different ways.	Student represents 25 cents in four different ways.

Name: _____   **Date:** _____

Beginning 0–1	Developing 2–3	Proficient 4
Student represents 25 cents in one way or less.	Student represents 25 cents in two to three different ways.	Student represents 25 cents in four different ways.

Name: _____   **Date:** _____

Beginning 0–1	Developing 2–3	Proficient 4
Student represents 25 cents in one way or less.	Student represents 25 cents in two to three different ways.	Student represents 25 cents in four different ways.

Name: _____   **Date:** _____

Beginning 0–1	Developing 2–3	Proficient 4
Student represents 25 cents in one way or less.	Student represents 25 cents in two to three different ways.	Student represents 25 cents in four different ways.

Figure 10.1.4. *Scoring Rubric, Ways to Represent 25 cents*

Name: _____   **Date:** _____

1. Student identifies and states the value of a penny. _____ (2)

2. Student identifies and states the value of a nickel. _____ (2)

3. Student identifies and states the value of a dime. _____ (2)

4. Student identifies and states the value of a quarter. _____ (2)

5. Student adds five pennies or more. _____ (3)

6. Student adds five nickels or more. _____ (3)

7. Student adds five dimes or more. _____ (3)

8. Student adds a penny, nickel, and dime together _____ (3)

Total: _____ (20)

Beginning: 0–10; Developing: 11–19; Proficient: 20

Anecdotal notes:

Name: _____   **Date:** _____

1. Student identifies and states the value of a penny. _____ (2)

2. Student identifies and states the value of a nickel. _____ (2)

3. Student identifies and states the value of a dime. _____ (2)

4. Student identifies and states the value of a quarter. _____ (2)

5. Student adds five pennies or more. _____ (3)

6. Student adds five nickels or more. _____ (3)

7. Student adds five dimes or more. _____ (3)

8. Student adds a penny, nickel, and dime together _____ (3)

Total: _____ (20)

Beginning: 0–10; Developing: 11–19; Proficient: 20

Anecdotal notes:

Figure 10.1.5. Assessment, Counting and Adding Coins

Figure 10.2.1. *Clock Cards*

Name: _____   **Date:** _____

1. Does it take you six hours to eat lunch at school? Why or why not?   (2)

   _____

   _____

   _____

2. About how long is recess? How do you know?   (2)

   _____

   _____

   _____

3. If you get to school at 8:00 A.M. and you go to lunch at 12:00 P.M.,
   how long is it from the time you get to school until lunch? How do you know?   (2)

   _____

   _____

   _____

4. Referring to your timeline, write down two things you do at school and
   when you do them.   (2)

   _____

   _____

   _____

5. What time do we _____? How do you know?   (2)

   _____

   _____

   _____

Total: _____ (10)

Beginning: 0–4; Developing: 5–8; Proficient: 9–10

Anecdotal notes:

Figure 10.2.2. *Time Representation Interview*

Name: _____   **Date:** _____

1. Does it take you six hours to eat lunch at school? Why or why not?   (2)

    no. (1)

    I looked at my timeline yesterday.
    I know it takes me less than an hour to eat. (1)

2. About how long is recess? How do you know?   (2)

    20 minutes. (1)

    I know it is 20 minutes because I timed it on my watch.

3. If you get to school at 8:00 A.M. and you go to lunch at 12:00 P.M., how long is it from the time you get to school until lunch? How do you know?   (2)

    4 hours (1)

    I know because I used the clock and I counted the hours from 8 to 12.

4. Referring to your timeline, write two things you do at school and when you do them.   (2)

    I go to PE at 9:00. (1)

    I read at 1:00. (1)

5. What time do we _____? How do you know?   (2)

    We eat lunch at 12:00. (1)

    I know we eat lunch at 12:00 because I wrote it on my timeline. (1)

Total: _____ (10)

Beginning: 0–4; Developing: 5–8; Proficient: 9–10

Anecdotal notes:

Figure 10.2.3. *Time Representation Interview (Teacher)*

Dear Parents,

Next week we will be reading *The Girl Who Wore Too Much* by Margaret MacDonald Read. This story is a folktale from Thailand about a girl named Aree. Aree loves jewelry and clothes and when she finds out there will be a big dance in the next village is very excited to go. She can't decide what to wear, so she wears it all! This story teaches children that excess material possessions don't always bring joy, and that keeping friends is better than impressing them.

We will be doing a math lesson to go along with this story. In our lesson students will be making estimations about the number of clothing items they can wear. Therefore, we need to collect any extra hats, socks, pants, or coats your child may have. All clothing items will be sorted and placed in plastic bags for our estimation game, then returned to the owner after the completion of the lesson. To assure that the clothing will be safely returned to you, please be sure to label each item of clothing sent in.

Thank you for your support in this learning experience.

Sincerely,

Figure 10.3.1. *Letter to Parents*

Name: _____   **Date:** _____

Read the question and circle the number that is most correct for the problem. Explain why you chose the answer on the lines below each problem.

1. Aree wanted to wear all her hats to the dance. How many do you think she could wear without any falling off? (1)

    1   4   30

    Explain your answer (2):

    Today, I found I could wear 4 hats.

2. After dancing many dances, Aree was thirsty. How many glasses of juice do you think she drank?

    3   15   50

    Explain your answer:

    I think she drank 3 glasses because I drink about that many when I am really thirsty.

3. About how old do you think Aree is?

    1   9   62

    Explain your answer:

    I think she is 9 because 1 is too young to dance and 62 is my grandma's age.

_____

Figure 10.3.2. *Assessment, Estimating Clothes (Teacher)*

Type of Clothing	Estimated Number of Items	Actual Number of Items

Figure 10.3.3. *Estimating Clothes*

Name: _____   **Date:** _____

Read the question and circle the number that is most correct for the problem. Explain why you chose the answer on the lines below each problem.

1. Aree wanted to wear all her hats to the dance. How many do you think she could wear without any falling off?

    1   4   30

    Explain your answer: _____

    _____

2. After dancing many dances, Aree was thirsty. How many glasses of juice do you think she drank?

    3   15   50

    Explain your answer: _____

    _____

3. About how old do you think Aree is?

    1   9   62

    Explain your answer: _____

    _____

Figure 10.3.4. Assessment, Estimating Clothes

Author/Title Index

Adler, David
  Calculator Riddles, 183
  Easy Math Puzzles, 187
  Fraction Fun, 31
  How Tall, How Short, How Faraway?, 114
  The Many Troubles of Andy Russell, 187
  Shape Up! Fun with Triangles and Other
      Polygons, 89
Aker, Suzanne, What Comes in 2's, 3's, & 4's?,
      12, 25
Alexander Who Used to Be Rich Last Sunday, 273
All About Time, 278
Amanda Bean's Amazing Dream, 25, 187
Anastasio, Dina, It's about Time, 278
Animals on Board, 16
Anno, Masaichiro, Anno's Mysterious Multiplying
      Jar, 25, 183
Anno, Mitsumasa
  Anno's Counting Book, 6, 12
  Anno's Math Games, 183
  Anno's Math Games II, 187
  Anno's Math Games III, 103, 187
  Anno's Mysterious Multiplying Jar, 25, 183
Anno's Counting Book, 6, 12
Anno's Math Games, 183
Anno's Math Games II, 187
Anno's Math Games III, 103, 187
Anno's Mysterious Multiplying Jar, 25, 183
Another Important Book, 52
Arctic Fives Arrive, 209, 210
Arthur's Funny Money, 193
Axelrod, Amy
  Pigs on the Ball: Fun with Math and Sports, 98,
      255
  Pigs Will Be Pigs: Fun with Math and Money,
      193, 272

Bad Case of Stripes, 69
Baker, Keith
  Big Fat Hen, 6
  Quack and Count, 13
Barn Cat, a Counting Book, 2, 12
Bartch, Marian R., Math Stories, 52
Baseball Counting Book, 249, 250
Baseball Saved Us, 257
Bear in a Square, 85, 90

Bedard, Michael, The Clay Ladies, 85, 99, 249
Beep Beep, Vroom Vroom!, 58
Beil, Karen Magnuson, A Cake All for Me!, 33, 129
Best Bug Parade, 233, 234
Best Vacation Ever, 146, 151, 165
Big Fat Hen, 6
Biggest Pumpkin Ever, 119
Birch, David, The King's Chessboard, 219
Bird Talk, 58
Blackstone, Stella, Bear in a Square, 85, 90
Blake, William, The Tyger, 102, 103
Book of Think, Or How to Solve a Problem Twice
      Your Size, 187
Bourde, Linda, Eye Count: A Book of Counting
      Puzzles, 123
Brain Bytes Money Math, 193
Brett, Jan
  Goldilocks and the Three Bears, 12, 238
  The Mitten, 123
Briggs, Raymond, Jim and the Beanstalk, 114
Brink, Carol, Goody O' Grumpity, 129
Broderbund Software, Inc.
  Carmen Sandiego Math Detective, 188
  Kid Pix Deluxe, 52, 89, 90, 94
Brooks, Alan, Frogs Jump: A Counting Book, 8
Brown, Margaret Wise
  Another Important Book, 52
  The Little Scarecrow Boy, 50
Brown, Ron, Math Concepts I, 25
Browning, Dave, Marvin Measures Up, 114
Brunetto, Carolyn Ford, Math Art, 69, 242
Buckley, Richard, The Foolish Tortoise, 58
Bunny Money, 177, 189, 273
Burns, Marilyn
  The Book of Think, Or How to Solve a Problem
      Twice Your Size, 187
  The Greedy Triangle, 89
  Math and Literature: (K–3) Book One, 159
  Math by All Means: Money, Grades 1–2, 193
  Math by All Means: Probability, Grades 3–4,
      159
  Spaghetti and Meatballs for All: A Mathematical
      Story, 85, 95
  Three Pigs, One Wolf, and Seven Magic Shapes,
      94
  Writing in Math Class: A Resource for Grades
      2–8, 159

Cake All for Me!, 33, 129
Calculator Riddles, 183
Calmenson, Stephanie
   Dinner at the Panda Palace, 214
   The Teeny Tiny Teacher, 59, 98, 237, 249
Caple, Kathy, *The Purse,* 193, 272
Caps for Sale, 284
Carle, Eric
   The Grouchy Ladybug, 278
   Pancakes, Pancakes, 58
   The Secret Birthday Message, 98
Carmen Sandiego Math Detective, 188
Casey at the Bat, 256
Chair for My Mother, 273
Cheerios Counting Book, 7, 69
Cheese and Tomato Spider, 141, 147
Cherrill, Paul, *Ten Tiny Turtles, a Crazy Counting Book,* 2, 12
Children's Beading Book, 69
Chouinard, Mariko, *One Magic Box,* 123
Chouinard, Roger, *One Magic Box,* 123
Christelow, Eileen, *Five Little Monkeys Jumping on the Bed,* 21
City, 103
Clay Ladies, 85, 99, 249
Clean Your Room, Harvey Moon, 267, 274
Clement, Rod, *Counting on Frank,* 187
Clocks and More Clocks, 278
Close, Closer, Closest, 89
Conner, Wendy Simpson, *The Children's Beading Book,* 69
Cook-a-Doodle-Doo!, 124, 249
Counting on Frank, 187
Crayon Counting Book, 69
Crews, Donald, *Ten Black Dots,* 7, 12
Crummel, Susan Stevens, *Cook-a-Doodle-Doo!,* 124, 249
Cucumber Soup, 130
Cummings, Pat, *Clean Your Room, Harvey Moon,* 267, 274
Cuyler, Margery, *100th Day Worries,* 7

Davidson, *Money Town,* 193
Day with No Math, 187, 261, 278
Demi
   Demi's Count the Animals 1 2 3, 2
   One Grain of Rice, 209, 215
Demi's Count the Animals 1 2 3, 2
Dewan, Ted, *The Sorcerer's Apprentice,* 98
Dinner at the Panda Palace, 214
Divide and Ride, 30
Dixon, Ann, *Trick-or-Treat,* 25
Dogs Don't Wear Sneakers, 159
Dollar for Penny, 193

Doorbell Rang, 29–30, 224
Dorros, Arthur, *Ten Go Tango,* 179
Dotlich, Rebecca Kai, *What Is a Square?,* 89
Dr. Seuss. *See* Geisel, Theodor
Dunbar, Joyce, *Ten Little Mice,* 21

Each Orange Had 8 Slices, 25
Earthdance, 284
Easy Math Puzzles, 187
Eating Fractions, 33, 224
Edwards, Pamela Duncan, *Roar! A Noisy Counting Book,* 2
Ehlert, Lois, *Fish Eyes: A Book You Can Count On,* 21, 214
Elffers, Joost, *One Lonely Sea Horse,* 12
Emily's First 100 Days of School, 7
Encore Software, *Schoolhouse Rock Fun and Skills Pack: 1st and 2nd Grade,* 214
Eye Count: A Book of Counting Puzzles, 123

Fair Bear Share, 224
Falda, Dominique, *The Treasure Chest,* 284
Fattest, Tallest, Biggest Snowman Ever, 114
Fish Eyes: A Book You Can Count On, 21, 214
500 Hats of Bartholomew Cubbins, 12
Five Little Monkeys Jumping on the Bed, 21
Foolish Tortoise, 58
Fraction Action, 33, 209, 221, 242
Fraction Fun, 31
Fractions Jump, 33
Fraser, Don
   Sports Math, 255
   Stats: Math Made Fun! (NHL Hockey), 255
Friedman, Aileen, *The King's Commissioners,* 187
Frogs Jump: A Counting Book, 8
From One to One Hundred, 7

Gag, Wanda, *Millions of Cats,* 12
Galdone, Paul
   The Teeny Tiny Woman, a Ghost Story, 59
   The Three Bears, 238
Geisel, Theodor (Dr. Seuss)
   The 500 Hats of Bartholomew Cubbins, 12
   One Fish Two Fish, Red Fish Blue Fish, 7
   The Shape of Me and Other Stuff, 94, 103
Geisert, Arthur, *Roman Numerals I to MM,* 7
Geometry for Every Kid, 98
Giant Carrot, 115
Gibbons, Gail, *Tool Book,* 69
Giganti, Paul, Jr., *Each Orange Had 8 Slices,* 25
Gigantic Turnip, 119
Giraffe and a Half, 242

Girl Who Wore Too Much: A Folktale from Thailand, 267, 279
Give Me Half, 33, 223, 224, 242
Glass, Julie, *A Dollar for Penny,* 193
Godfrey, Neale S.
  Kid's Money Book, 193
  Neale S. Godfrey's Ultimate Kids' Money Book, 272
Goldilocks and the Three Bears, 238
Golenbock, Peter, *Teammates,* 256
Goody O' Grumpity, 129
Grandfather Tang's Story, 94
Graph Club, 16, 93, 94, 159, 238, 261
Greedy Triangle, 89
Greene, Rhonda Gowler, *When a Line Bends . . . A Shape Begins,* 85, 86
Grossman, Bill, *My Little Sister Ate One Hare,* 177, 178
Grossman, Virginia, *Ten Little Rabbits,* 2, 6, 7
Grouchy Ladybug, 278

Hanford, Martin, *Where's Waldo?,* 284
Hershey's Milk Chocolate Bar Fractions Book, 33, 223, 224
Hewitt, Sally
  Making Fractions, 33
  Shapes, 89
Hightower, Susan, *Twelve Snails to One Lizard, a Tale of Mischief and Measurement,* 112, 209
Hoban, Lillian, *Arthur's Funny Money,* 193
Hoban, Tana, *So Many Circles, So Many Squares,* 94
Hoberman, Mary Ann
  One of Each, 26
  The Seven Silly Eaters, 261
Holling, Holling C., *Paddle to the Sea,* 146
Hong, Lily Toy, *Two of Everything,* 25
House I'll Build for the Wrens, 98
Houses and Homes, 98
How Math Works, 146, 151, 165
How Much Is a Million?, 219
How Tall, How Short, How Faraway?, 114
Hulme, Joy N., *Sea Sums,* 21
Hutchins, Pat
  Clocks and More Clocks, 278
  The Doorbell Rang, 29–30, 224
  Llaman a la Puerta (The Doorbell Rang), 224
  1 Hunter, 179

I Spy Two Eyes, 7
IBM/Edmark, *Brain Bytes Money Math,* 193

If You Give a Moose a Muffin, 159
If You Give a Mouse a Cookie, 159
If You Give a Pig a Pancake, 141, 153
If You Made a Million, 193, 219, 273
Interactive Math Journey, 112, 129, 130
Is a Blue Whale the Biggest Thing There Is?, 219
It Looked Like Spilt Milk, 261
It's About Time, 278

Jelly Beans for Sale, 267, 268
Jim and the Beanstalk, 114
Jonas, Ann, *Bird Talk,* 58
Joseph Had a Little Overcoat, 193
Jumanji, 16
June 29, 1999, 261
Just Enough Carrots, 235, 284

Kaye, Marilyn, *A Day with No Math,* 187, 261, 278
Keenan, Sheila, *What Time Is It? A Book of Math Riddles,* 123
Kid Pix Deluxe, 52, 89, 90, 94
Kid's Money Book, 193
King, Andrew, *Making Fractions,* 242
King's Chessboard, 219
King's Commissioners, 187
Kirk, David, *Miss Spider's Tea Party,* 2
Kitchen, Bert, *Animal Numbers,* 7
Knowledge Adventure, *Math Blaster, 1st Grade,* 224
Kroll, Steven, *The Biggest Pumpkin Ever,* 119
Krudwig, Vickie Leigh, *Cucumber Soup,* 130

Lane Smith, *Math Curse,* 184, 249
Learning Company
  Interactive Math Journey, 112, 129, 130
  Reader Rabbit Personalized Math, 123
Leedy, Loreen
  Fraction Action, 33, 209, 221, 242
  Measuring Penny, 114
  Mission: Addition, 16
  2x2 = BOO! A Set of Multiplication Stories, 22
Lego Chess, 98
Lego Media International, Inc., *Lego Chess,* 98
Lemonade for Sale, 165
Let's Investigate Number Patterns, 52
Like, Likes, Like, 25, 58
Ling, Bettina, *The Fattest, Tallest, Biggest Snowman Ever,* 114
Little Scarecrow Boy, 50
Llaman a la Puerta (The Doorbell Rang), 224
Lobel, Anita, *One Lighthouse One Moon,* 2, 12
London, Jonathan, *The Village Basket Weaver,* 52

Long, Sylvia, *Ten Little Rabbits*, 2, 6, 7
Long and Short of It, 238

M & M's Chocolate Candies Counting Book
      (1994), 7
M&M's Brand Chocolate Candies Counting Book
      (1996), 69, 214
Macaulay, David
   City, 103
   Pyramid, 98
Maccarone, Grace
   The Silly Story of Goldie Locks and the Three
         Squares, 94
   Three Pigs, One Wolf, and Seven Magic Shapes,
         94
MacDonald, Sharon, *Squish, Sort, Paint and Build*,
      69
Mailing May, 187
Making Fractions, 33, 242
Many Troubles of Andy Russell, 187
Martin, Bill, Jr., *Polar Bear, Polar Bear*, 58
Martin, Jacqueline Briggs, *Snowflake Bentley*,
      141, 160
Marvin Measures Up, 114
Math and Literature: (K–3) Book One, 159
Math Art, 69, 242
Math Blaster, 1st Grade, 224
Math by All Means: Money, Grades 1–2, 193
Math by All Means: Probability, Grades 3–4, 159
Math Concepts I, 25
Math Curse, 177, 184, 249
Math Stories, 52
Max's Money, 193
McCourt, Lisa, *The Long and Short of It*, 238
McGrath, Barbara Barbieri
   The Baseball Counting Book, 249, 250
   The Cheerios Counting Book, 7, 69
   The M & M's Chocolate Candies Counting Book
         (1994), 7
   M&M's Brand Chocolate Candies Counting
         Book (1996), 69, 214
McKissack, Pat, *A Million Fish . . . More or Less*,
      219
McMillan, Bruce
   Eating Fractions, 33, 224
   Jelly Beans for Sale, 267, 268
   Super Super Superwords, 235, 238
Measuring Penny, 114
Micklethwait, Lucy, *I Spy Two Eyes*, 7
Microsoft PowerPoint, 90, 94
Million Fish . . . More or Less, 219
Miranda, Anne, *To Market, To Market*, 130
Miss Bindergarten Celebrates the 100th Day of
      Kindergarten, 7

Miss Spider's Tea Party, 2
Mission: Addition, 16
Mitchell, Rhonda, *The Talking Cloth*, 53
Mitten, 123
Mochizuki, Ken, *Baseball Saved Us*, 257
Money Town, 193
More Than One, 25
Morris, Ann, *Houses and Homes*, 98
Mosel, Arlene
   Tikki Tikki Tembo, 52
   Tikki Tikki Tembo, Spanish ed., 52
Murphy, Stuart J.
   Animals on Board, 16
   Beep Beep, Vroom Vroom!, 58
   The Best Bug Parade, 233, 234
   The Best Vacation Ever, 146, 151, 165
   Divide and Ride, 30
   A Fair Bear Share, 224
   Fractions Jump, 33
   Give Me Half, 33, 223, 224, 242
   Just Enough Carrots, 235, 284
   Lemonade for Sale, 165
My Little Sister Ate One Hare, 177, 178

Nathan, Cheryl, *The Long and Short of It*, 238
Neale S. Godfrey's Ultimate Kids' Money Book,
      272
Neighborhood MapMachine, 63, 146
Neitzel, Shirley, *The House I'll Build for the Wrens*,
      98
Neuschwander, Cindy, *Amanda Bean's Amazing*
      Dream, 25, 187
Numeroff, Laura Joffe
   Dogs Don't Wear Sneakers, 159
   If You Give a Moose a Muffin, 159
   If You Give a Mouse a Cookie, 159
   If You Give a Pig a Pancake, 141, 153
   Si Le Das Un Panecillo a un Alce, 159
   Si Le Das Un Panqueque a una Cerdita, 159
   Si Le Das Una Galletita a un raton, 159

Old MacDonald, 58
Olivo, Richard, *Close, Closer, Closest*, 89
One Fish Two Fish, Red Fish Blue Fish, 7
One Grain of Rice, 209, 215
One Hundred Hungry Ants, 30
100th Day Worries, 7
1 Hunter, 179
1 Is One, 2
One Less Fish, 17, 249
One Lighthouse One Moon, 2, 12
One Lonely Sea Horse, 12
One Magic Box, 123

One More Bunny, 16
One of Each, 26
One Was Johnny: A Counting Book, 8

Paddle to the Sea, 146
Pallotta, Jerry
    *The Hershey's Milk Chocolate Bar Fractions
        Book,* 33, 223, 224
    Reese's Pieces Count by Fives, 7
Pancakes, Pancakes, 58
Peck, Jan, *The Giant Carrot,* 115
Pfister, Marcus, *The Rainbow Fish,* 30
Pig Pigger Piggest, 238
Pigs on the Ball: Fun with Math and Sports, 98,
    255
Pigs Will Be Pigs: Fun with Math and Money, 193,
    272
Pinczes, Elinor J.
    Arctic Fives Arrive, 209, 210
    One Hundred Hungry Ants, 30
    A Remainder of One, 30
Pluckrose, Henry Arthur, *Sorting,* 69
Polar Bear, Polar Bear, 58
Purse, 193, 272
Pyramid, 98

Quack and Count, 12

Rainbow Fish, 30
Raschka, Chris, *Like, Likes, Like,* 25, 58
Rathmann, Peggy, *Ten Minutes Till Bedtime,* 120
Read, Margaret MacDonald, *The Girl Who Wore
        Too Much: A Folktale from Thailand,* 267,
        279
Reader Rabbit Personalized Math, 123
Reese's Pieces Count by Fives, 7
Reid, Margarette S., *A String of Beads,* 64
Remainder of One, 30
Roar! A Noisy Counting Book, 2
Robins, Arthur, *The Teeny Tiny Woman: A Tradi-
        tional Tale,* 59
Rocklin, Joanne, *Three Smart Pals,* 187
Rogers, Paul, *What Can You See?,* 284
Roman Numerals I to MM, 7
Rotner, Shelley, *Close, Closer, Closest,* 89
Ryan, Pam Munoz, *The Crayon Counting Book,* 69
Ryder, Joanne, *Earthdance,* 284

Saul, Carol P., *Barn Cat, a Counting Book,* 2, 12
Saxton, Freyman, *One Lonely Sea Horse,* 12

Schlein, Miriam, *More Than One,* 25
Schnetzler, Pattie, *Ten Little Dinosaurs,* 12
*Schoolhouse Rock Fun and Skills Pack: 1st and
        2nd Grade,* 214
Schreiber, Anne, *Shoes, Shoes, Shoes,* 69
Schwartz, Amy, *Old MacDonald,* 58
Schwartz, David M.
    How Much Is a Million?, 219
    If You Made a Million, 219, 193, 273
Scieszka, Jon
    Math Curse, 177, 184, 249
    The True Story of the 3 Little Pigs, 12
Sea Sums, 21
Secret Birthday Message, 98
Sendak, Maurice, *One Was Johnny: A Counting
        Book,* 8
7 Sector 7, 249, 257
Seven Silly Eaters, 261
Shannon, David, *A Bad Case of Stripes,* 69
Shape of Me and Other Stuff, 94, 103
Shape Up! Fun with Triangles and Other Polygons,
        89
Shapes, 89
Sharratt, Nick, *A Cheese and Tomato Spider,* 141,
        147
Shaw, Charles G., *It Looked Like Spilt Milk,* 261
Sheather, Allan, *One Less Fish,* 17, 249
Shoes, 69
Shoes, Shoes, Shoes, 69
Si Le Das Un Panecillo a un Alce, 159
Si Le Das Un Panqueque a una Cerdita, 159
Si Le Das Una Galletita a un raton, 159
Silly Story of Goldie Locks and the Three Squares,
        94
Silverstein, Shel, *A Giraffe and a Half,* 242
Slate, Joseph, *Miss Bindergarten Celebrates the
        100th Day of Kindergarten,* 7
Slater, Teddy, *Max's Money,* 193
Sloat, Teri
    From One to One Hundred, 7
    There Was an Old Lady Who Swallowed a Trout,
        52, 63, 179
Slobodkina, Esphyr, *Caps for Sale,* 284
Smoothey, Marion, *Let's Investigate Number
        Patterns,* 52
Snowflake Bentley, 141, 160
Snowy, Flowy, Blowy, 52
So Many Circles, So Many Squares, 94
Sorcerer's Apprentice, 98
Sorting, 69
*Spaghetti and Meatballs for All: A Mathematical
        Story,* 85, 95
Spann, Mary Beth, *25 Board Games: Instant
        Games That Teach Essential Math Skills,*
        193

Sports Math, 255
Squish, Sort, Paint and Build, 69
Stats: Math Made Fun! (NHL Hockey), 255
Stevens, Janet
    Cook-a-Doodle-Doo!, 124, 249
    Tops and Bottoms, 30, 233, 239
Stevenson, Robert Louis, *Where Go the Boats?*,
    141, 142
Stickland, Paul, *Ten Terrible Dinosaurs*, 7
*Stop! The Watch: A Book of Everyday, Ordinary,
    Anybody Olympics*, 121, 123
String of Beads, 64
Super Super Superwords, 235, 238

Taback, Simms
    Joseph Had a Little Overcoat, 193
    There Was an Old Lady Who Swallowed a Fly,
        52, 63, 179
Tafuri, Nancy
    Snowy, Flowy, Blowy, 52
    Who's Counting, 7
Talking Cloth, 53
Tatler, Sarah, *We Can Share It!*, 30
Teammates, 256
Teeny Tiny Ghost, 59
Teeny Tiny Teacher, 59, 98, 237, 249
Teeny Tiny Woman, a Ghost Story, 59
Teeny Tiny Woman: A Traditional Tale, 59
Ten Black Dots, 7, 12
Ten Go Tango, 179
Ten Little Dinosaurs, 12
Ten Little Mice, 21
Ten Little Rabbits, 2, 6, 7
Ten Minutes Till Bedtime, 120
Ten Terrible Dinosaurs, 7
Ten Tiny Turtles, a Crazy Counting Book, 2, 12
Thayer, Ernest Lawrence, *Casey at the Bat*, 256
There Was an Old Lady Who Swallowed a Fly, 52,
    63, 179
There Was an Old Lady Who Swallowed a Trout,
    52, 63, 179
Three Bears, 238
Three Pigs, One Wolf, and Seven Magic Shapes,
    94
Three Smart Pals, 187
Tikki Tikki Tembo, 52
Tikki Tikki Tembo, Spanish ed., 52
To Market, To Market, 130
Toft, Kim Michelle, *One Less Fish*, 17, 249
Tolstoy, Alexei, *The Gigantic Turnip*, 119
Tom Snyder Productions
    The Graph Club, 16, 93, 94, 159, 238, 261
    Neighborhood MapMachine, 63, 146
Tompert, Ann, *Grandfather Tang's Story*, 94

Too Many Pumpkins, 119
Tool Book, 69
Tops and Bottoms, 30, 233
Treasure Chest, 284
True Story of the 3 Little Pigs, 12
Tudor, Tasha, *1 Is One*, 2
Tuesday, 261
Tunnell, Michael O., *Mailing May*, 187
*Twelve Snails to One Lizard, a Tale of Mischief and
    Measurement*, 112, 209
*25 Board Games: Instant Games That Teach Essen-
    tial Math Skills*, 193
2x2 = BOO! A Set of Multiplication Stories, 22
Two of Everything, 25
Tyger, 102, 103

Van Allsburg, Chris, *Jumanji*, 16
Van Cleave, Janice, *Geometry for Every Kid*, 98
Verdet, Andre, *All about Time*, 278
Village Basket Weaver, 52
Viorst, Judith, *Alexander Who Used to Be Rich Last
    Sunday*, 273
Vorderman, Carol, *How Math Works*, 146, 151,
    165

Walton, Rick
    One More Bunny, 16
    Pig Pigger Piggest, 238
We Can Share It!, 30
Wells, Robert, *Is a Blue Whale the Biggest Thing
    There Is?*, 219
Wells, Rosemary
    Bunny Money, 177, 189, 273
    Emily's First 100 Days of School, 7
What Can You See?, 284
What Comes in 2's, 3's, & 4's?, 12, 25
What Is a Square?, 89
What Time Is It? A Book of Math Riddles, 123
When a Line Bends . . . A Shape Begins, 85, 86
Where's Waldo?, 284
Where Go the Boats?, 141, 142
White, Linda, *Too Many Pumpkins*, 119
Who's Counting, 7
Wiesner, David
    June 29, 1999, 261
    7 Sector 7, 249, 257
    Tuesday, 261
Williams, Vera, *A Chair for My Mother*, 273
Winters, Kay, *The Teeny Tiny Ghost*, 59
Winthrop, Elizabeth, *Shoes*, 69
Writing in Math Class: A Resource for Grades 2–8,
    159

Subject Index

The boldface numbers are the pages on which the primary activities for each 2000 standard can be found.

Addend, 14–16
Addition, 9–16, 178–183
Algebra, activities related to, 2–7, 8–12, 13–16, 17–21, 22–25, 26–30, 31–34, **49–84,** 86–89, 90–94, 112–115, 115–119, 120–124, 124–130, 141–146, 147–152, 153–159, 160–165, 178–183, 184–188, 189–193, 210–214, 215–220, 221–224
Area, activities involving, 95–98
Auditory disability, adaptations for, 5, 11, 15, 20, 24, 29, 33, 51, 57, 63, 68, 88, 93, 97, 102, 114, 117, 122, 129, 145, 150, 158, 164, 182, 187, 192, 213, 219, 223, 237, 240, 255, 261, 272, 277, 283

Baseball, math in, 250–256
Build a town, using math to, 59–64

Calculator, activities using, 178–183
Capacity, measuring, 115–119, 124–130
Chance, activities involving, 153–160
Classifying, activities involving, 64–70, 210–214
Clocks, activities involving, 274–278
Collages, activities involving, 24, 259
Combinations, activities involving, 147–152
Communication, activities related to, 2–7, 8–12, 13–16, 17–21, 22–25, 26–30, 31–34, 50–53, 53–58, 59–64, 64–69, 99–103, 112–115, 115–119, 120–124, 124–130, 141–146, 147–152, 153–159, 160–165, 178–183, 184–188, 189–193, 210–214, 215–220, 221–224, **233–248**, 250–256, 257–262, 268–273, 274–278, 279–284
Comparison, activities involving
    fractions, 221–224
    sizes, 234–238
Concepts of whole number operations, activities related to, 13–16, 17–21, 22–26, 26–30, 141–146, 147–152, 160–165, 178–183, 184–188, 189–193, 215–220, 221–224

Connections, activities related to, 2–7, 8–12, 13–16, 17–21, 22–26, 26–30, 31–34, 50–53, 53–58, 59–64, 64–69, 86–89, 90–94, 95–98, 99–103, 112–115, 115–119, 120–124, 124–130, 141–146, 147–152, 153–159, 160–165, 178–183, 184–188, 189–193, 210–214, 215–220, 221–224, 234–238, 239–242, **249–266**, 268–273, 274–278, 279–284
Counting
    and adding, 9–16
    back, and subtracting, 17–22
    objects, 279–284
    one to ten, 2–7
    skip counting, 23, 210–214
    to twelve and back, 8–13

Data analysis and probability, activities related to, 50–53, 115–119, 120–124, **141–176**, 178–183, 274–278, 279–284
Data collection, activities involving, 160–165. *See also* data analysis and probability, activities related to
Denominator, 239–242
Design a town, using math to, 59–64
Division, 26–30
Doubling, 215–220

English Language Learners, adaptations for, 6, 11, 15, 21, 24, 29, 33, 51, 58, 63, 69, 88, 93, 97, 102, 114, 117, 123, 129, 145, 150, 158, 164, 182, 187, 192, 213, 219, 223, 237, 241, 255, 261, 272, 277, 283
Estimation, activities related to, 53–58, 59–64, 64–70, 86–89, 95–98, 99–103, 141–146, 147–152, 153–160, 160–165, 178–183, 184–188, 210–214, 215–220, 268–273, 274–278, 279–284

Flipbook, activities involving, 147–152
Fractions, activities related to, 26–30, 31–34, 115–119, 153–160, 239–243, 268–273
 comparing, 221–224
 and fraction symbols, 239–243

Geometry and spatial sense, activities related to, 50–53, 53–58, 59–64, 64–70, **85–109**, 112–115, 124–130, 141–146, 147–152, 153–160, 160–165, 184–188, 221–224, 250–256, 268–273, 274–278
Grids, activities involving, 61–62, 97
Group lessons, 4, 10, 13, 19, 23, 28, 32, 51, 56, 61, 66, 67, 87, 91, 92, 96, 100, 101, 113, 117, 121, 144, 149, 150, 155, 156, 162, 163, 180, 185, 191, 212, 217, 222, 235, 240, 252, 254, 259, 270, 271, 275, 281

Length, measuring, 112–119

Manipulatives, activities involving, 3, 5, 9, 16, 21, 25, 28, 60, 96, 211, 238, 251
Mathematical connections, activities related to, 2–7, 8–12, 13–16, 17–21, 22–26, 26–30, 31–34, 50–53, 53–58, 59–64, 64–70, 95–98, 99–103, 112–115, 124–130, 141–146, 147–152, 153–159, 160–165, 178–183, 184–188, 189–193, 215–220, 221–224, 234–238, 239–243, 250–256, 257–262, 268–273, 274–278, 279–284
Mathematics as communication, activities related to, 2–7, 8–12, 13–16, 17–21, 22–26, 26–30, 31–34, 50–53, 53–58, 59–64, 64–70, 86–89, 90–94, 95–98, 99–103, 112–115, 115–119, 120–124, 124–130, 141–146, 147–152, 153–159, 160–165, 178–183, 184–188, 189–193, 210–214, 215–220, 221–224, 234–238, 239–243, 250–256, 257–262, 268–273, 274–278, 279–284
Mathematics as problem solving, activities related to, 2–7, 17–21, 22–26, 26–30, 31–34, 50–53, 53–58, 59–64, 64–70, 90–94, 95–98, 99–103, 112–115, 115–119, 120–124, 124–130, 141–146, 147–152, 153–159, 160–165, 178–183, 184–188, 189–193, 210–214, 215–220, 221–224, 234–238, 239–243, 250–256, 257–262, 268–273, 274–278, 279–284

Mathematics as reasoning, activities related to, 2–7, 17–21, 22–26, 26–30, 31–34, 50–53, 53–58, 64–70, 95–98, 112–115, 115–119, 120–124, 124–130, 141–146, 147–152, 153–159, 160–165, 178–183, 184–188, 189–193, 215–220, 221–224, 234–238, 239–243, 250–256, 257–262, 268–273, 274–278, 279–284
Measurement, activities related to, 50–53, 59–63, 64–69, 95–98, 99–103, **111–140**, 141–146, 147–152, 153–159, 160–165, 221–224, 234–238, 274–278
 of capacity, 115–119, 124–130
 of length, using standard and nonstandard tools, 112–115, 115–119
 of time, 115–119, 120–124
 of weight, 115–119
Money calculations, activities involving, 189–193, 268–273
Motor disability, adaptations for, 5, 11, 15, 20, 24, 29, 33, 51, 57, 63, 68, 88, 93, 97, 102, 114, 117, 122, 129, 145, 150, 158, 164, 182, 187, 192, 213, 219, 223, 237, 241, 255, 261, 272, 277, 283
Multiplication, 22–26
Murals, activities involving, 10–11, 52

Number and operations, activities related to, **1–47,** 50–53, 53–58, 59–63, 64–69, 112–115, 115–119, 120–124, 124–130, 141–146, 147–152, 153–159, 160–165, 178–183, 184–188, 189–193, 210–214, 215–220, 221–224, 234–238, 239–242, 250–256, 257–262, 268–273, 274–278, 279–284
Number sense and numeration, activities related to, 2–7, 8–12, 13–16, 17–21, 22–26, 26–30, 31–34, 50–53, 53–58, 59–64, 64–70, 112–115, 124–130, 141–146, 147–152, 153–160, 160–165, 178–183, 184–188, 189–193, 215–220, 221–224, 239–243, 250–256, 257–262, 268–273, 274–278
Numerator, 239–242

Patterns and relationships, activities related to, 2–7, 8–12, 13–16, 17–21, 22–26, 26–30, 31–34, 86–89, 90–94, 99–103, 124–130, 141–146, 147–152, 153–160, 160–165, 178–183, 184–188, 189–193, 210–214, 215–220, 221–224, 239–243, 250–256, 257–262
 creating, 53–58
 repeating, 50–53

Perimeter, activities involving, 95–98

Picture walks, activities involving, 13, 32, 50, 67, 91, 95, 100, 112, 117, 127, 154, 211, 251, 275, 280

Probability, activities involving, 142–146, 153–160. *See also* Data analysis and probability, activities related to

Problem solving, activities related to, 17–21, 22–25, 26–30, 31–34, 50–53, 53–58, 59–64, 64–69, 90–94, 95–98, 112–115, 115–119, 120–124, 124–130, 141–146, 147–152, 153–159, 160–165, **177–207,** 210–214, 215–220, 221–224, 234–238, 239–242, 250–256, 257–262, 268–273, 274–278, 279–284

Proof, activities related to, 17–21, 22–25, 26–30, 31–34, 86–89, 90–94, 95–98, 99–103, 112–115, 115–119, 120–124, 124–130, 178–183, 184–188, 189–193, **209–232**, 234–238, 239–242, 250–256, 257–262, 268–273, 274–278, 279–284

Reasoning, activities related to, 17–21, 22–25, 26–30, 31–34, 86–89, 90–94, 95–98, 99–103, 112–115, 115–119, 120–124, 124–130, 178–183, 184–188, 189–193, **209–232**, 234–238, 239–242, 250–256, 257–262, 268–273, 274–278, 279–284

Representation, activities related to, 2–7, 8–12, 13–16, 17–21, 22–26, 26–30, 31–34, 50–53, 53–58, 59–64, 64–69, 86–89, 90–94, 95–98, 99–103, 112–115, 115–119, 120–124, 124–130, 141–146, 147–152, 153–159, 160–165, 178–183, 184–188, 189–193, 210–214, 215–220, 221–224, 234–238, 239–242, 250–256, 257–262, **267–296**

Sets, 22–26, 257–262

Shares, determining, 26–30

Sorting, activities involving, 64–70, 210–214

Special needs, adaptations for
  auditory, 5, 11, 15, 20, 24, 29, 33, 51, 57, 63, 68, 88, 93, 97, 102, 114, 117, 122, 129, 145, 150, 158, 164, 182, 187, 192, 213, 219, 223, 237, 240, 255, 261, 272, 277, 283
  ELL, 6, 11, 15, 21, 24, 29, 33, 51, 58, 63, 69, 88, 93, 97, 102, 114, 117, 123, 129, 145, 150, 158, 164, 182, 187, 192, 213, 219, 223, 237, 241, 255, 261, 272, 277, 283
  motor, 5, 11, 15, 20, 24, 29, 33, 51, 57, 63, 68, 88, 93, 97, 102, 114, 117, 122, 129, 145, 150, 158, 164, 182, 187, 192, 213, 219, 223, 237, 241, 255, 261, 272, 277, 283
  visual, 6, 11, 15, 21, 24, 29, 33, 51, 57, 63, 68, 88, 93, 97, 102, 114, 117, 122, 129, 145, 150, 158, 164, 182, 187, 192, 213, 219, 223, 237, 241, 255, 261, 272, 277, 283

Standard 1 (1989): mathematics as problem solving, activities related to, 2–7, 17–21, 22–26, 26–30, 31–34, 50–53, 53–58, 59–64, 64–70, 90–94, 95–98, 99–103, 112–115, 115–119, 120–124, 124–130, 141–146, 147–152, 153–159, 160–165, 178–183, 184–188, 189–193, 210–214, 215–220, 221–224, 234–238, 239–243, 250–256, 257–262, 268–273, 274–278, 279–284

Standard 1 (2000): number and operations, activities related to, **1–47,** 50–53, 53–58, 59–63, 64–69, 112–115, 115–119, 120–124, 124–130, 141–146, 147–152, 153–159, 160–165, 178–183, 184–188, 189–193, 210–214, 215–220, 221–224, 234–238, 239–242, 250–256, 257–262, 268–273, 274–278, 279–284

Standard 2 (1989): mathematics as communication, activities related to, 2–7, 8–12, 13–16, 17–21, 22–26, 26–30, 31–34, 50–53, 53–58, 59–64, 64–70, 86–89, 90–94, 95–98, 99–103, 112–115, 115–119, 120–124, 124–130, 141–146, 147–152, 153–159, 160–165, 178–183, 184–188, 189–193, 210–214, 215–220, 221–224, 234–238, 239–243, 250–256, 257–262, 268–273, 274–278, 279–284

Standard 2 (2000): algebra, activities related to, 2–7, 8–12, 13–16, 17–21, 22–25, 26–30, 31–34, **49–84,** 86–89, 90–94, 112–115, 115–119, 120–124, 124–130, 141–146, 147–152, 153–159, 160–165, 178–183, 184–188, 189–193, 210–214, 215–220, 221–224

Standard 3 (1989): mathematics as reasoning, activities related to, 2–7, 17–21, 22–26, 26–30, 31–34, 50–53, 53–58, 64–70, 95–98, 112–115, 115–119, 120–124, 124–130, 141–146, 147–152, 153–159, 160–165, 178–183, 184–188, 189–193, 215–220, 221–224, 234–238, 239–243, 250–256, 257–262, 268–273, 274–278, 279–284

Standard 3 (2000): geometry, activities related to, 50–53, 53–58, 59–63, 64–69, **85–109,** 112–115, 124–130, 141–146, 147–152, 153–159, 160–165, 184–188, 221–224, 250–256

Standard 4 (1989): mathematical connections, activities related to, 2–7, 8–12, 13–16, 17–21, 22–26, 26–30, 31–34, 50–53, 53–58, 59–64, 64–70, 95–98, 99–103, 112–115, 124–130, 141–146, 147–152, 153–159, 160–165, 178–183, 184–188, 189–193, 215–220, 221–224, 234–238, 239–243, 250–256, 257–262, 268–273, 274–278, 279–284

Standard 4 (2000): measurement, activities related to, 50–53, 59–63, 64–69, 95–98, **111–140**, 141–146, 147–152, 153–159, 160–165, 221–224, 234–238, 268–273, 274–278

Standard 5 (1989): estimation, activities related to, 53–58, 59–64, 64–70, 86–89, 95–98, 99–103, 141–146, 147–152, 153–160, 160–165, 178–183, 184–188, 210–214, 215–220, 268–273, 274–278

Standard 5 (2000): data analysis and probability, activities related to, 50–53, 115–119, 120–124, **141–176**, 178–183, 274–278, 279–284

Standard 6 (1989): number sense and numeration, activities related to, 2–7, 8–12, 13–16, 17–21, 22–26, 26–30, 31–34, 50–53, 53–58, 59–64, 64–70, 112–115, 124–130, 141–146, 147–152, 153–160, 160–165, 178–183, 184–188, 189–193, 215–220, 221–224, 239–243, 250–256, 257–262, 268–273, 274–278

Standard 6 (2000): problem solving, activities related to, 17–21, 22–25, 26–30, 31–34, 50–53, 53–58, 59–64, 64–69, 90–94, 95–98, 112–11, 215–2205, 115–119, 120–124, 124–130, 141–146, 147–152, 153–159, 160–165, **177–207,** 210–214, 221–224, 234–238, 239–242, 250–256, 257–262, 268–273, 274–278, 279–284

Standard 7 (1989): concepts of whole number operations, activities related to, 13–16, 17–21, 22–26, 26–30, 141–146, 147–152, 160–165, 178–183, 184–188, 189–193, 215–220, 221–224

Standard 7 (2000): reasoning and proof, activities related to, 17–21, 22–25, 26–30, 31–34, 86–89, 90–94, 95–98, 99–103, 112–115, 115–119, 120–124, 124–130, 178–183, 184–188, 189–193, **209–232**, 234–238,

239–242, 250–256, 257–262, 268–273, 274–278, 279–284

Standard 8 (1989): whole number computation, activities related to, 13–16, 26–30, 86–89, 90–94, 141–146, 147–152, 160–165, 189–193, 210–214, 221–224, 250–256, 268–273

Standard 8 (2000): communication, activities related to, 2–7, 8–12, 13–16, 17–21, 22–25, 26–30, 31–34, 50–53, 53–58, 59–64, 64–69, 99–103, 112–115, 115–119, 120–124, 124–130, 141–146, 147–152, 153–159, 160–165, 178–183, 184–188, 189–193, 210–214, , 215–220, 221–224, **233–248**, 250–256, 257–262, 268–273, 274–278, 279–284

Standard 9 (1989): geometry and spatial sense, activities related to, 50–53, 53–358, 59–64, 64–70, 141–146, 147–152, 153–160, 160–165, 221–224, 250–256, 274–278

Standard 9 (2000): connections, activities related to, 2–7, 8–12, 13–16, 17–21, 22–26, 26–30, 31–34, 50–53, 53–58, 59–64, 64–69, 86–89, 90–94, 95–98, 99–103, 112–115, 115–119, 120–124, 124–130, 141–146, 147–152, 153–159, 160–165, 178–183, 184–188, 189–193, 210–214, 215–220, 221–224, 234–238, 239–242, **249–266**, 268–273, 274–278, 279–284

Standard 10 (1989): measurement, activities related to, 50–53, 59–64, 64–70, 95–98, 112–115, 115–119, 120–124, 141–146, 147–152, 153–160, 160–165, 221–224, 234–238

Standard 10 (2000): representation, activities related to, 2–7, 8–12, 13–16, 17–21, 22–26, 26–30, 31–34, 50–53, 53–58, 59–64, 64–69, 86–89, 90–94, 95–98, 99–103, 112–115, 115–119, 120–124, 124–130, 141–146, 147–152, 153–159, 160–165, 178–183, 184–188, 189–193, 210–214, 215–220, 221–224, 234–238, 239–242, 250–256, 257–262, **267–296**

Standard 11 (1989): statistics and probability, activities related to, 279–284

Standard 12 (1989): fractions and decimals, activities related to, 26–30, 31–34, 115–119, 153–160, 239–243, 268–273

Standard 13 (1989): patterns and relationships, activities related to, 2–7, 8–12, 13–16, 17–21, 22–26, 26–30, 31–34, 86–89, 90–94, 99–103, 124–130, 141–146, 147–152, 153–160, 160–165, 178–183, 184–188, 189–193, 210–214, 215–220, 221–224, 239–243, 250–256, 257–262

Statistics and probability, activities related to, 279–284
Story problems, activities involving, 19–21, 272
Subitizing, 6
Subtraction, 17–22
Sum, 14

T-tables, activities involving, 14–15
Tangrams, activities involving, 89, 94
Three-dimensional shapes, activities involving, 99–103
Time, measuring, 115–119, 120–124
Timelines, activities involving, 274–278
Two-dimensional shapes, activities involving, 86–94

Visual disability, adaptations for, 6, 11, 15, 21, 24, 29, 33, 51, 57, 63, 68, 88, 93, 97, 102, 114, 117, 122, 129, 145, 150, 158, 164, 182, 187, 192, 213, 219, 223, 237, 241, 255, 261, 272, 277, 283

Weight, measuring, 115–119
Whole number computation, activities related to, 13–16, 26–30, 86–89, 90–94, 141–146, 147–152, 160–165, 189–193, 210–214, 221–224, 250–256, 268–273
Word problems, activities involving, 15

About the Authors

Photo by J. Davenport

Caroline W. Evans

Caroline received her Master's in Elementary Education from the University of Northern Colorado. She teaches first and second grade at Estes Park Elementary School. She has written for *Ranger Rick*, *CCIRA Journal*, *High Country Headlines*, *Chickadee,* and *Addison Wesley Explorations in Science 4th grade.* Caroline likes to travel, hike, sail, read, and spend time with her husband Joe, son Russell, daughter Libby, and cat Zang.

Anne J. Leija

Anne received her Master's in Elementary Education from the University of Northern Colorado. She lives in Estes Park, Colorado, with her husband Terry and her cat Poncho. She enjoys reading, hiking, camping, singing, and traveling. She teaches first and second grade and has a love for teaching children with special needs in the regular classroom. Anne is a member of the National Council of Teachers of Mathematics, PEO, a book club, and is a board member of PARTNERS.

Photo by J. Davenport

Trina R. Falkner

Trina received her Master's in Elementary Education from the University of Northern Colorado. She lives in Thornton, Colorado, with her husband Steve and a new daughter, Megan. She teaches first grade at Hudson Elementary School.

from *Teacher Ideas Press*

GLUES, BREWS, AND GOOS
Recipes and Formulas for Almost Any Classroom Project
Diana F. Marks

You've got to have it! This indispensable activity book pulls together hundreds of practical, easy recipes and formulas for classroom projects. From paints and salt map mixtures to volcanic action formulas, these kid-tested projects make learning authentic and enjoyable. All projects use ingredients that are easy to find and processes that are up-to-date. **Grades K–6.**
xvi, 179p. 8½x11 paper ISBN 1-56308-362-0

SCIENCE THROUGH CHILDREN'S LITERATURE, 2d Edition
Carol M. Butzow and John W. Butzow

The Butzows' groundbreaking, critically acclaimed, and best-selling resource has been thoroughly revised and updated with new titles and activities for today's classroom. More than 30 exciting instructional units integrate all areas of the curriculum and serve as models to educators at all levels. Adopted as a supplementary text in schools of education nationwide, this resource features outstanding children's fiction books that are rich in scientific concepts yet equally well known for their strong story lines and universal appeal. **Grades K–3.**
xix, 205p. 8½x11 paper ISBN 1-56308-651-4

MULTICULTURAL FOLKTALES
Readers Theatre for Elementary Students
Suzanne I. Barchers

Introduce your students to other countries and cultures through these engaging readers theatre scripts based upon traditional folk and fairy tales. Representing more than 30 countries and regions, the 40 reproducible scripts are accompanied by presentation suggestions and recommendations for props and delivery. **Grades 1–5.**
xxi, 188p. 8½x11 paper ISBN 1-56308-760-X

SUPER SIMPLE STORYTELLING
A Can-Do Guide for Every Classroom, Every Day
Kendall Haven

Aside from guides to more than 40 powerful storytelling exercises, you'll find the Golden List of what an audience really needs from storytelling, a proven, step-by-step system for successfully learning and remembering a story, and the Great-Amazing-Never-Fail Safety Net to prevent storytelling disasters. This system has been successfully used by more than 15,000 educators across the country. **All Levels.**
xxvii, 229p. 8½x11 paper ISBN 1-56308-681-6

MORE SOCIAL STUDIES THROUGH CHILDREN'S LITERATURE
An Integrated Approach
Anthony D. Fredericks

These dynamic literature-based activities will help you energize the social studies curriculum and implement national and state standards. Each of these 33 units offers book summaries, social studies topic areas, critical thinking questions, and dozens of easy-to-do activities for every grade level. The author also gives practical guidelines for integrating literature across the curriculum, lists of Web sites useful in social studies classes, and annotated bibliographies of related resources. **Grades K–5.**
xix, 225p. 8½x11 paper ISBN 1-56308-761-8

For a free catalog or to place an order, please contact:
Teacher Ideas Press • Dept. B050 • P.O. Box 6633 • Englewood, CO • 80155-6633
800-237-6124 • www.lu.com/tip • Fax: 303-220-8843